7 5 YEARS OF
EASTBOURNE
SPEEDWAY

ARLINGTON SPEEDWAY

President - - - - - - MAJOR P. C. BIRD

Programme

of the

OPENING DIRT TRACK
MOTOR CYCLE MEETING

*Organised by the Arlington Motor Sports Club, under the
General Competition Rules of the Auto Cycle Union.
A.C.U. Permit No. 023.*

Bank Holiday, Aug. 5th, 1929

(weather permitting)

at 3 p.m.

❖

Opening Ceremony by Mrs. P. C. BIRD.

OFFICIALS :

A.C.U. Steward - - - - - -	H. R. TAYLOR
Timekeeper - - - - - -	S. YEO
Starter - - - - - -	J. COLEMAN
Judge - - - - - -	W. PERHAM
Clerk of the Course - - -	G. W. WEDDLE
Secretary of the Meeting - -	T. T. HENLEY

"GAZETTE" AND "HERALD" PRESS," EASTBOURNE.

75 YEARS OF
EASTBOURNE
SPEEDWAY

NORMAN JACOBS
& KEN BURNETT

TEMPUS

This book is dedicated to the Dugard family.

Frontispiece: The programme cover for Arlington's first ever meeting, held on 5 August 1929.

First published 2006

Tempus Publishing Limited
The Mill, Brimscombe Port,
Stroud, Gloucestershire, GL5 2QG
www.tempus-publishing.com

© Norman Jacobs & Ken Burnett, 2006

The right of Norman Jacobs & Ken Burnett to be identified as the Authors of this work has been asserted in accordance with the Copyrights, Designs and Patents Act 1988.

British Library Cataloguing in Publication Data.
A catalogue record for this book is available from the British Library.

ISBN 0 7524 3751 8

Typesetting and origination by Tempus Publishing Limited
Printed in Great Britain

CONTENTS

INTRODUCTION AND ACKNOWLEDGEMENTS

In 1928, the year speedway started in Great Britain at High Beech, the Eastbourne Motor-Cycle Sports Club bought an open field at Arlington to build their own speedway track. The track was laid out with raw racing in mind and just the bare minimum by way of facilities for both riders and spectators. Sadly High Beech no longer reverberates to the sound of speedway bikes roaring round an oval track, but it is a very different picture at Arlington, where a modern stadium with some of the best facilities in the country now stands on that open field and plays host to one of Britain's top speedway teams, the Elite League Eastbourne Eagles.

The Arlington track celebrated its seventy-fifth anniversary in 2004 and this book is a celebration of those first seventy-five years of speedway, the growth of the stadium, the promoters and managers, the supporters, but most of all the story of the Eastbourne Eagles team itself, its ups and downs, its successes and failures and the riders who rode for it. We hope it brings back memories to the older supporters and will show the newer supporters the fine tradition behind Eastbourne speedway.

The authors would like to thank the following for their help and support in various ways: Colin Richardson, Reg Trott, Dave Lanning, Kevin Ling, Martin Dadswell. Alan Boniface, John Ling, Jackie Burnett, Mick Corby, Barry Stephenson, Derek Carruthers, Tony McDonald, Ken Taylor and hastingssaxons.doverathleticvideo.com/Hastings-Saxons.htm (the Hastings Saxons website)

Photographs not in the authors' own collections are reproduced by kind permission of John Somerville, Tony Sims, Mick Hinves, Simon P. Jones and Mike Patrick.

STATISTICS

Averages except where stated:
1938–1964 are actual match averages and do not include Bonus Points
1969–2004 are Calculated Match Averages (CMA) and include Bonus Points
Qualification for inclusion: 6 matches

THE 1920s AND 1930s

1928/29

On 5 October 1928 Eastbourne's local newspaper, the *Eastbourne Courier*, made the following announcement: 'The Eastbourne Motor-Cycle Sports Club have purchased a field at Arlington, with a view to building a dirt track.' It took up just two lines but was to lead to a seventy-eight-year association with speedway that is still going strong today. The field in question was on land originally owned by the Duke of Devonshire known as 'The Hyde', situated near Hailsham.

After much hard work, the track was ready to open its gates to the public the following year on Monday 5 August 1929. The sports lovers who turned up that day out of curiosity to see this new sport that was sweeping the country were welcomed by Mrs P.C. Bird, the wife of the club's president, Major P.C. Bird. In a short but interesting speech, she wished the riders every success and pointed out to the exceptionally large audience that all the preparatory work in connection with the track had been carried out on a voluntary basis. She also added that the venture was in a large measure due to the untiring enthusiasm and zeal of Mr T.T. Henley, the secretary of the Eastbourne Motor-Cycle Sports Club.

Considering it was the first time most of the riders had even seen a speedway track, they showed extraordinary skill and courage. There were a number of falls but those thrown from their machines mounted again without a moment's hesitation. The results of that first ever meeting were as follows:

Arlington Scratch Race:
Heat one: Winner: Jack Polley
Heat two: Winner: Not Known
Heat three: Winner: Bert Hele
Heat four: Winner: Les Ashdown
Heat five: Winner: Eddie Allchorn
First semi-final: Bert Hele
Second semi-final: Les Ashdown
Final: Les Ashdown (Time: 119.4 seconds)

Two match races were won by Jimmy Horton in times of 94.4 seconds and 92.6 seconds. A 'team' race was won by London with Eastbourne second and Arlington third. In a handicap event, Horton came out on top once more, winning the race in a time of 97.8 seconds. The ACU steward was Mr H.P. Taylor and other officials were Mr S. Yeo (timekeeper); Mr J. Coleman (starter) and Mr G. Weddle (clerk of the course).

A scene from the first ever meeting at Arlington held on 5 August 1929. Unfortunately it is not known who the rider is.

About 1,000 spectators turned up to watch the second meeting, which took place on 29 August. By this time speedway, like greyhound racing, had seized the public imagination, with tracks appearing all over the country. The only difference as far as Eastbourne was concerned was that the Arlington meetings were being run by volunteers and not a professional company. A dozen riders took part in this second meeting. Only a few of them had real dirt-track machines, but this in itself made for interesting racing. Jimmy Horton, Bert Hele and Rod Dutton were the most successful participants. Dutton shattered the four-lap track record, covering the full 1,200 yards in 87.8 seconds. In the Hailsham Handicap final it seemed as though he would break his new record but, unfortunately, he hit the safety fence on the last lap. A great gasp went up from the crowd as he was thrown from his machine and lay inert on the ground. Horton, who was not far behind, just managed to avoid him and went on to win the race. Meanwhile, Dutton had recovered sufficiently to tell the first-aid helpers that he was all right and did not need their assistance. Although there was no damage done to him, his gearbox was smashed and he was unable to ride again. Other winners that afternoon were Bert Spears, who won the Special 350cc class on his new Imperial, and Dutton, who won the Arlington Scratch Race. Two match races were held between Horton and Hele. with each winning one race.

The third and last meeting of that first season was held on 14 September. This meeting attracted a number of visiting riders including Sparks Burgess, Les Bourne and Bert Gerrish. Spears once again won the Special 350cc race while Horton won the Arlington Scratch Race in the fastest time of the afternoon, 91.8 seconds. Bourne won the Hailsham Handicap, but was beaten by Horton in a special match race held between the winners of the two main events. As the short season wound up, everyone agreed that the Arlington Motor Sports Club had done a great job, particularly the two promoters, Mr Henley and Major Bird.

Due to the success of speedway at Arlington, a grass track stadium was opened at Thornwell at nearby Wilmington and a meeting there on 22 September attracted over 1,000 spectators.

Charlie Dugard, founder of the Dugard dynasty that has been associated with Eastbourne from the early 1930s to the present day.

1930

The second season at Arlington began on Easter Monday 21 April. Once again the Eastbourne Motor Sports Club was congratulated on the wide interest and enthusiasm of the captivated spectators. The most exciting part of the day's events was the exhibition by Bryan Donkin. Donkin was a local lad and member of the Eastbourne Motor-Cycle Club who, before the advent of speedway, had been an expert trials rider in and around the Sussex area. When speedway arrived in London in 1928 he had gone off to try out the new sport and had progressed so well that by 1929 he had become a member of the Crystal Palace team then racing in the Southern League. This experience put him in a class of his own compared to the local amateurs and his method of taking corners was a revelation to them and the spectators alike as he proved the theory that the faster you take corners the safer you are. In his first ride he literally screamed round the four laps, flattening out at corners with the throttle full on. The crowd couldn't believe what they were seeing and when the time for the four laps was announced it was discovered that Donkin had broken the track record by almost ten seconds, lowering it to 78.4 seconds. Later in the meeting he went one better, knocking a further second off his own new track record.

It was the first time that Arlington had seen 'real' speedway and several of the riders tried to copy Donkin's method. The most successful was Jimmy Horton, who managed to win the President's Challenge Cup in 88.4 seconds. Other successful riders that afternoon were Rev Reynolds and Bert Hele. Two thousand five hundred turned up on Whit Monday to see some splendid racing from Bryn Lewis, E. Willis, Perry Gallivant and Tiny Lewis. There were many thrills and falls, due mainly to the fact that over 2,000 gallons of water had been poured on the track to keep the dust down.

A further meeting took place on 4 August when there were more thrills for the crowd to enjoy as the racing yielded some good performances. There was, however, a disappointing showing from Bryan Donkin, who did not show his usual reckless form and repeatedly fell at the same point on the track. Two new arrivals from Australia took part in the afternoon's racing, Steve Langton and Phil 'Tiger' Hart. Langton's style was described in, the *Eastbourne Courier* as 'unique': 'He stands on his right footrest and puts his left leg out stiff.' It sounds to the modern ear like a prototype foot-forward style. Langton beat Donkin in a special match race. Langton also won both the Arlington Scratch Race final and the Eastbourne Handicap final. As well as Donkin, Langton and Hart, the usual Arlington riders were out in force including Hele, Horton, Reynolds and Polley as well as Sparks Burgess. Admission to Arlington was one shilling and twopence for adults and sixpence for children. Buses left Hailsham Station every five minutes direct to the track. There were also special coaches from the Pier, Victoria Place and the Parade.

1931

No racing took place at Arlington in 1931. Both the local riders and the local supporters seem to have migrated to a new grass-track venue nearby at Horsebridge, also run under the auspices of the Eastbourne Motor Cycle Club by their secretary Stuart William 'Tiny' Lewis. Other 'Arlington' riders to appear during the year included Jack Polley, Rev Reynolds and D. Brock. A team event was held on 24 May, which saw Eastbourne defeat a team from Hastings by 16 points to 6.

Another match took place on 5 July when the Eastbourne team met a much more experienced team from Oxford called Layton's Motor Sports Club. Included in the Eastbourne team were Reynolds and Brock. Although the local team lost 15-9, they started off with a heat-one victory. According to the *Eastbourne Courier*, 'D. Brock scored a magnificent win, on the post, from F. French, racing up on the inside to win by inches, to the great surprise of French.' Four thousand people attended this match.

Scandal hit the Eastbourne Motor Cycle Club in August when the secretary, Tiny Lewis, was remanded on bail in the Magistrates' Court. He was charged with embezzlement and making a false entry in the ledger of his employers, Messrs F. Ray & Sons.

The last meeting of 1931 took place on 25 September. Lewis was conspicuous by his absence!

1932

Speedway returned to Arlington in 1932, the season starting on Good Friday, 25 March, and once again a good-sized crowd of around 3,000 turned up. Bryan Donkin lowered the track record to 75 seconds in winning the scratch race final from Bill Thompson, Jack Riddle and Harry Davidson. Three days later Davidson won the scratch race final when he beat Donkin. Donkin, however, gained quick revenge winning the handicap final. On 4 April history was made when the first proper team event was held at Arlington. The match between Arlington and Staines was run over nine heats and won by the visitors 31-23.

Speedway at Arlington now had strong opposition from grass-track racing being held just down the road at Stone Cross, with many of the cinder stars riding in both events. In one interesting incident over 20,000 spectators were expected at the Folkington grass speedway by the Black Horse public house. Special trains were laid on for the spectators as were many buses. So worried were the Folkington track promoters they had minders looking after the track all night for protection. The two meetings, though, were staged in pouring rain and the crowds of 3,000 and 6,000 were well below expectations.

Meanwhile, over at Arlington, Charlie Budden, riding a 1928 Douglas machine, set a new handicap track record. Other riders appearing up to the end of the season, which carried thirteen meetings, were Jack Stanselol, Pat Dixon, Lou Berger and Charlie Lumsden. In a

The start of a race at Eastbourne in 1932. From left to right: Leo Gregory, Harvey Swanson, Rube Wilson, Lou Berger.

pairs event won by Arlington, teams from Norwich, Cambridge, Wimbledon, Staines and Hammersmith took part.

1932 also saw the first staging of the Championship of Sussex, which was won by George Wilkie after Lou Berger had fallen when well in the lead. Other riders appearing in this history making Championship were Frank Chitty, who fell and broke his collarbone, Jack Williams, Fred Quinnell, Clem French, Percy Gullivant and Smoky Vielar. Jack Polley, the first ever winner of a race at Arlington, was considered too good for amateur riding and rode under the pseudonym Jack Thomas. This was a common practice throughout the pre-war years.

1933

The first two meetings of 1933 took place on Good Friday and Easter Monday in front of large crowds. Lou Berger won the Good Friday Scratch Race in a time of 79.6 seconds, while the honours on Easter Monday went to B. Linn in 84.8 seconds. Two weeks later George Wilkie beat Lou Berger in a match race for the two fastest riders, Wilkie's time being 80 seconds. The two main events of the day were the Golden Helmet Scratch Race, won by Wilkie and the now common Hailsham Handicap race, won by Lumsden. Lumsden also attempted to break the track record, which stood at 75 seconds, but unfortunately his time was five seconds outside.

However, on 25 June the track record was broken by a newcomer to Arlington calling himself Bill Bennett. By this time Eastbourne was being used by a number of the London clubs to try out their juniors and give them experience. One such to arrive was George Newton. The eighteen-year-old Newton had caused a sensation in 1932 when, in his first outing for Crystal Palace as reserve at West Ham, he had equalled Vic Huxley's track record. However, he was not able to live up to this promising start and, by 1933, he was struggling to hold on to the reserve spot. Freddie Mockford, the promoter of Crystal Palace, thought the young Newton would benefit from a few outings at Arlington. On his very first appearance, riding under the name of Bill Bennett, he lowered Donkin's track record to 73.8 seconds. At the same meeting, Freddie Douglas won the Friston Handicap while Lumsden won the Golden Helmet Scratch Race final. Several riders failed to arrive for the next meeting, but luckily the crowd did to see Stan Johns win the scratch race and handicap events in spite of being pushed all the way by Jock Elliott, Joe Brown, Cliff Ray and Rev Reynolds. On 9 September another visiting rider, Plymouth-based Jack Morrison, left all the locals behind. He stormed to victory in the Big Five scratch race event, though a spectacular fall let Bert Linn win the handicap event.

A 1935 line-up at Arlington. From left to right: Tidmarsh, Jack Polley, Charlie Page, Charlie Dugard, Salt, Rube Wilson, Bob Lovell, George Newton, Danny Lee, Cooper, Harvey Swanson, Jack Riddle, Lou Berger.

Using his real name, George Newton made a further attempt on the track record on 17 September, but he just failed, covering the course in 74 seconds, just 0.2 of a second outside. Stan Lemon won the second Championship of Sussex when he beat Jack Riddle, Harvey Swanson and Rube Wilson (who fell) in the grand final in a time of 81.2 seconds.

1934

1934 was a significant year in the club's history as it was in this year that Charlie Dugard, who had been riding at Arlington since 1932, together with Tiger Hart, bought a share in the club. The Dugard family have, of course, been associated with the club in one capacity or another ever since.

The season started once again on Good Friday and Newton continued to dominate proceedings for the next few meetings, though he was surprisingly beaten by Jack Riddle in the opening meeting's scratch race final. Riddle's previous best time around Arlington had been 96.0 seconds. In beating Newton, he scorched round in a spectacular 79.6 seconds.

Shortly after the start of the season, Newton was recalled to London by Mockford, who had by now moved the Crystal Palace team lock, stock and barrel to New Cross. Other riders now came to the fore including Riddle, Stan Lemon, a Wimbledon junior; Geo Saunders, Rube Wilson and Bill Roberts. In June and July, a serious drought threatened the running of meetings at Arlington, with the meetings during these months having to be stopped on regular occasions to allow copious amounts of water to be poured onto the track.

Riddle went from strength to strength, winning the Hailsham Handicap on 2 September, the same meeting in which Roberts managed to knock a whole second off Newton's track record. Unfortunately for him, Roberts was badly injured in the last meeting on 16 September, breaking his arm. This left Rube Wilson and Jack Riddle to mop up, Wilson winning both the Hailsham Cup and the Lewes Handicap and Riddle the Championship of Sussex. Others present at the final meeting of the season included Dugard, Berger and Swanson.

George Saunders leads George Newton, 1935.

1935

A very large crowd turned out for the opening meeting on 7 April to once again listen to the deafening roar of the speedway bikes after a winter's absence. Unfortunately the noise was accompanied by very heavy rain. The track had several new alterations, which included widening the corners and laying some twenty tons of cinders all over the course. But most important of all was the erection of the starting gate in a bid to ensure perfect starts. The combination of heavy rain and deep cinders made for plenty of thrills and spills and the crowd loved it. They also enjoyed seeing the success of Charlie Dugard turning in his best performances yet. But even he finished second best to Phil Phillips, who pipped him in the semi-final and final of the handicap event. Of the first five meetings only the fourth wasn't badly affected by rain. That was the Jubilee meeting, which was won by Jack Hawkins.

The meeting described as the best of the 1935 season took place on 16 June. There were no serious crashes but plenty of spills and thrilling finishes and, what was even better, good weather for a change. Once again the main event was the Hailsham Cup and the seventh round of this tournament was won by Rube Wilson. However, it was Joe Brown who really caught the eye with a time of 77.8 seconds in a heat of the handicap event. He then went on to win the final to crown a fine afternoon's entertainment. Wilson was presented with the Hailsham Cup after the eighth round despite the fact that on this occasion he did not win the final. However, he now had an unassailable lead with ten points to spare from previous rounds.

On 28 July the first evening meeting took place at Arlington, during which a collection was held for James Eden, who had been injured grass-tracking at Wilmington the previous week. This raised £20 19s 2d. Although Wilson was still winning meetings on a regular basis, Joe Brown, Harry Lewis and Jack Smythe improved enough to make sure he didn't have things all his own way through August. The wettest September for years played havoc with the end-of-season fixtures, though it didn't stop Jack Riddle from winning the Championship of Sussex.

The erection of the starting gate in 1935 led to quicker times from a standing start and, during the season, the record was brought down to 75.2 seconds by Rube Wilson. This was then equalled by George Newton and Joe Brown

Putt Mossman leads for the American team in the challenge match against Eastbourne, 1936.

1936

The 1936 season got under way on Good Friday, 10 April. There was a good crowd but a shortage of riders, which handicapped the meeting somewhat. George Newton, back to riding under the name of Bill Bennett, dominated the meeting, just failing to beat the clutch-start track record. On Easter Sunday however he managed to lower the flying-start record from 72.8 seconds to 71.6 seconds and the clutch-start record from 75.2 seconds to 74.8 seconds. Bennett's success continued as, on 26 April, a record crowd of 3,000, the largest for four years, witnessed his runaway victory in the Championship of Sussex. The track, with its new banking that assisted riders, was particularly fast and most winners were singled out long before the winning post was reached. Bennett twice broke the track record and, by the end of the day, it stood at 74.2 seconds. Following Bennett's runaway win, it was agreed that in future the Championship of Sussex would be confined to Second Division riders. Several top Second Division riders now began to appear every week at Arlington including Tiger Hart, Roy Virgo and Charlie White.

On 31 August a new addition was made at the track, a bell that was rung from the judges' box for the two-minute warning. On 20 September an exciting challenge match between Eastbourne and an All-American team led by the World Champion stunt rider Putt Mossman took place. The thrilling Americans beat the Eastbourne team 37-32. The teams for this encounter were: Eastbourne: Jack Riddle (captain), Charlie Dugard, Harry Lewis, Dan Lee, C. Anderson and Jack Tidbury. All-Americans: Putt Mossman (captain), Pee Wee Cullum, Pete Coleman, Dick Ince, Manuel Trujillo and Dick Lawton. So successful was this event that Mossman's circus was invited back the following week but heavy rain caused the meeting to be abandoned. To round off the season, Bennett returned to set new track records of 70.2 seconds flying start and 73.2 seconds clutch start.

1937

In many ways 1937 was the start of things to come. For the first time the season wasn't dominated by the Hailsham Cup, as team racing came to Arlington, although 4,000 watched the first round of the cup together with the Championship of Sussex, which was won by the 1935 champion Jack Riddle.

It was on 26 June that Arlington finally saw what many people thought speedway should be all about as Eastbourne got together its very own permanent team and called them the Eagles. That very first crop of Eagles was hatched and took flight with a stunning victory over the Dagenham 'Daggers', led by their skipper Frank Hodgson, by 57 points to 25. The team consisted of Jimmy James, Charlie Blythe, Stan Johnson, Charlie Sargeant, Jack Kirby, Jack Nash, C. Anderson and Harvey Swanson.

After the success against Dagenham, the next matches were home and away ties against Rye House. The Eagles went down 47-25 at Hoddesdon, where the racing was described as fast and exciting and a new track record of 90 seconds was set. The scorers were: Rye House: J. Boyd 12, T. Allott 11, R. Lovell 9, W. Lowther 8, F.L. Robinson 5, F. Curtis 2. Eastbourne: D. Lee 7, S. Johns 6, B. Desmond 3, J. Riddle 4, J. Tidbury 2, K. Tidbury 2, C Dugard 1. The return on 4 September proved to be an equally exciting match, with the Eagles putting in a great effort, winning 52-32 on the day but just going down on aggregate by two points, 79-77. To end the season Tiger Hart was presented with the Hailsham Cup after totalling most points throughout the season.

It was during this season that, for the first time, the 70-seconds barrier was smashed as George Newton recorded a time of 68.8 seconds, a track record that was to last until 1955, when the track was shortened by ten yards. Following the success of the season's challenge matches, it was hoped that the Eagles' followers would be able to enjoy league racing in 1938 as talks took place between the smaller non-league clubs such as High Beech, Dagenham, Eastbourne, Rye House and Smallford to see if they could form an amateur league.

1938

The talks proved successful and a new league competition was introduced in 1938, the Sunday Amateur Dirt Track League. Five teams entered the new league Eastbourne, Smallford, Rye House, Dagenham and Romford, the latter two both using the Dagenham track as their home base. High Beech chose not to take part but maintained a team for challenge matches.

Eastbourne were due to race their first-ever league fixture on 1 May. The team chosen for the match against Smallford was Phil 'Tiger' Hart (captain), Bob Lovell, Danny Lee, Charlie Dugard, Stan Johns, Charlie Page and Jack Collins with C. Anderson, Harold Saunders and Law as reserves. Unfortunately the match had to be postponed due to rain. With the home tie against Smallford being abandoned, Eastbourne began their campaign with an away match against Dagenham. The team saw a few changes from the one originally intended to start the season, comprising Tiger Hart (captain), Charlie Dugard, Bob Lovell, Stan Johns, Danny Lee and Charlie Page with Jack Collins and Harold Saunders as reserves. The Eagles got off to a great start as they took a 4-2 in the first heat with Hart defeating the nigh-on unbeatable Dagenham captain Frank Hodgson. Hart thus became the first rider ever to win a race for Eastbourne in an official league fixture. He went on to complete a superb maximum 12 points in the Eagles' fine 44-39 away win. Unfortunately, there was another first for Eastbourne in the second heat as Collins became the first Eagle to be excluded. His crime was to break the tapes.

Eastbourne followed up their fine win with another superlative performance seven days later to complete the double over Dagenham, beating them 57-27 at home. Once again Hart played a true captain's role by scoring a second maximum. The Eagles' triumphant start to the campaign received something of a setback the following week when they were heavily defeated at Smallford by 55 points to 27, but were back on track on 29 May with a home victory over Romford, 53-23. Surprisingly, Eastbourne lost their next match away at Romford by 46 points to 33. This was a very unexpected defeat as Romford had failed to win a single match before this, though it has to be said that Eastbourne were without the services of Hart, Dugard and Collins for the meeting.

Normal service was resumed on 28 June when the Eagles beat their closest rivals, Smallford, by 55 points to 28. This was the restaging of the match postponed from 1 May and was the one Eagles supporters had been looking forward to eagerly. However, it proved to be a bit of an anti-climax as Smallford arrived for the match with only five riders. The Eastbourne management demanded an explanation from Smallford, but never got one. This victory took

A programme from 1938, the year Eastbourne won the Sunday Amateur Dirt Track League.

the Eagles to the top of the league and they never looked back all season as they went through the rest of the card undefeated to win their first league championship.

During the season, Eastbourne also fitted in a number of challenge matches including one against Reading and one against 'The Internationals', captained by Putt Mossman, who put on one of his famous stunt shows before the match. The match itself was very one-sided as the Eagles ran out victors 53-12, with The Internationals failing to score any points at all in five of the heats!

1938 – Sunday Amateur Dirt Track League

Date	H/A	Against	W/L	Score
8 May	Away	Dagenham	Won	44-39
14 May	Home	Dagenham	Won	57-27
21 May	Away	Smallford	Lost	27-55
29 May	Home	Romford	Won	53-23
5 June	Away	Romford	Lost	33-46
28 June	Home	Smallford	Won	55-28
3 July	Away	Dagenham	Won	43-39
10 July	Home	Rye House	Won	56-27
17 July	Away	Rye House	Won	52-29
24 July	Home	Dagenham	Won	44-39
14 August	Away	Romford	Not held	–
21 August	Home	Romford	Not held	–
4 September	Home	Smallford	Won	51-32
18 September	Home	Rye House	Won	46-34

P12 W10 D0 L2 For 561 Against 418 Pts 10 Position 1st (out of 5)

Rider	Matches	Rides	Points	BP	Total	Average
Danny Lee	6	25	63	2	65	10.40
Phil 'Tiger' Hart	7	27	69	0	69	10.22
Charlie Page	7	29	63	11	74	10.21
Stan Johns	5	18	41	4	45	10.00
Charlie Dugard	6	22	41	7	48	8.73
Harry Saunders	6	21	27	8	35	6.67

(CMA inc. bonus points – home matches only. Qualification 5 matches)

Danny Lee leads a Wisbech rider in the Eastbourne v. Wisbech match held on 23 July 1939.

1939

The Sunday League was abandoned in 1939 and Arlington returned to its normal diet of challenge matches and individual events. The season opened on 9 April with a good crowd present to witness a fine meeting. Stan Johns won the Easter Scratch Race final, while Charlie Page took the Hailsham Handicap final. There was one unfortunate accident as Les Gore broke his collarbone following a fall.

A number of new riders began to make names for themselves at Arlington during the season, which made for better racing. The meeting on 11 June was described as the 'finest meeting for some time'. The main event was the Jempson Memorial Cup, presented by the Eastbourne chairman, Mr A.A. Jempson, in memory of his son Ken, who had been killed in a motorcycle accident in 1933. After some of the best racing seen at Eastbourne for a long time, the winner proved to be the Dagenham captain, Jim Baylais, who beat Tiger Hart into second place in the final.

On 23 July Eastbourne beat Wisbech 48-36 in a challenge match, while on August Bank Holiday a very large crowd turned out to see Dugard win the August Scratch Race final and Hart win the Summer Handicap final. The meeting finished with two match races. Tiger Hart beat Stan Johns in the first, while in the second Ken Tidbury beat Cyril Brine. Although no-one realised it at the time, this would be the last race held at Arlington for seven years. When war was declared on 3 September all speedway racing in this country came to a halt and, although some clubs managed to put on a few wartime events, notably Belle Vue, the Eastbourne track was taken over by the Canadian Army and speedway was completely abandoned for the duration.

THE 1940s

1946

Before speedway could resume at Arlington after the Second World War, the track didn't only have to be relaid – it had to be found! The stadium was under six feet of thistles, rubble and muck. The whole place was in a state of ruin. It was at this point that Charlie Dugard stepped in and bought the track outright. Eventually the racing track was found. It had sunk about two feet but it was still there. Finally, after weeks of hard solid graft, the place was cleaned up and the surface relaid.

On 14 July 1946, speedway resumed on the 368-yard circuit. Admission was 2s for adults and 10d for children. The car park was 1s. On a pleasant sunny day a very large crowd was treated to plenty of thrills. The track record of 68.5 seconds, still held by George Newton, was never threatened. The nearest anyone could get to it was Dick Harris with a time of 74.2 seconds in heat three of the scratch race. He went on to win the final in 76.0 seconds. Charlie Dugard won the handicap event after Reg Moore had bike trouble when well in front.

Meetings took place every two weeks until 6 October and, although they were all of the individual championship variety, there was surprisingly no Championship of Sussex. The track record was not broken all season, the fastest time being 72.2 seconds by Ron Clark in the final meeting. Riders appearing at Arlington in 1946 included Charlie Dugard, Cyril Brine, Reg Moore, Mike Erskine, Jimmy Coy, Basil Harris, Dick Harris, Dan Lee, Ron Lemon, Harry Saunders, Jock Grierson, Dennis Gray, Jack Tidbury and Ken Tidbury. Most were newcomers and were to form part of the Eagles' 1947 team, but a few were old stagers reappearing for the first time since the pre-war meetings at Arlington.

With speedway now entering its boom period many new tracks, or tracks that had lain dormant for many years, were opening up and so at a promoters' meeting held at the end of 1946 it was agreed to start a Third Division of the National League in 1947. Eastbourne applied to join and were accepted along with Hanley (Stoke), Southampton, Exeter, Wombwell, Plymouth, Tamworth and Cradley Heath.

1947

The new season promised to be of exceptional interest as Eastbourne began its new era as a semi-professional league team at 6 p.m. on Saturday 19 April 1947. The track was relaid for the opening meeting, an attractive challenge match against Hanley. Most of the favourite riders from 1946 represented the town in their new role. Ken Tidbury was made captain of the Eagles and the rest of the team was Ron Clark, Bob Sawyer, Dennis Gray, Jim Coy, Basil Harris, Dick Angell with Bob Griffiths and Les Tams the reserves. Supporters turned up in force to see

Ken Tidbury, the 1947 Eagles captain.

the Eagles win 49-29. The Eagles' scorers were Gray 11, Harris 10, Tidbury 9, Coy 9, Clark 4, Angell 3, Griffiths 2 and Tams 1. Top scorer for Hanley was Harry Saunders, who had been loaned to the Potters for the day. He scored 14. Eastbourne's next match was a challenge against Exeter and this time the score was a 63-20 win. Things were certainly looking good for the Sussex men, although they came down to earth at Exeter, losing 52-32 just two days later. The final challenge match before the league programme started was against local rivals Southampton. The Eagles again won, 49-32, with Gray and Harris recording maximums.

On 10 May, Peter Robinson of Southampton became the first post-war winner of the Championship of Sussex and shortly afterwards Tidbury, Harris, Gray and newcomer Jock Grierson were chosen to represent the Eagles in the first round of the Riders' Championship, the replacement for the World Championship. None of them progressed to the second round.

Despite their successful start to the season in challenge matches, Eastbourne were defeated in their very first home league match when, on 17 May, Southampton Aces played their trump cards and defeated the Eagles 46-35 at Arlington. The response from the embarrassed Eagles was instant, an away win at Tamworth 44-40. This was followed by a stunning away win by 43 points to 40 at Southampton's own Banister Court track, a win that brought back some of

Jimmy Coy (left) and Basil Harris lead for Eastbourne against Southampton's Jimmy Squibb, 1947.

Two of Eastbourne's leading
riders in 1947, Ken Tidbury
leads Jock Grierson.

the lost pride. Hanley came back for their league match and were trounced 55-29 with Eagles' new signing Wally Green scoring 9 points. He would have recorded a maximum but for a second-ride fall when well in front. The Eagles went back to Southampton, who were by now the league leaders and again won 44-39. Following this great victory Eastbourne moved up to third place in the table with a big win against Exeter, who were second. The Eagles then gained a massive away win at Plymouth 54-33 and won at Hanley 46-36. The Eagles were now flying high and attracting large crowds. One of the biggest of the season saw their next match against Southampton, which they won 48-34. Eastbourne then shocked the speedway world by beating Exeter on their home track by 51 points to 45 in The Midlands v. The South Cup. This was the first loss suffered by Exeter at home all season. Defeats at Cradley, Southampton, Exeter and surprisingly Plymouth followed in the league but home wins over these clubs evened things out. Back in the cup, the Eagles won 50-46 at Plymouth after a defeat at Southampton, which meant that they qualified for the final even before the home match against Exeter had been raced.

Although Southampton had led the league right from the start of the season, the situation entering October was that they had finished their fixtures and stood on 35 points. Behind them were Eastbourne and Cradley, both on 34. As luck would have it, the last two fixtures of the season were the home-and-away clashes between Eastbourne and Cradley, which meant that whatever happened Southampton could not win the league either Eastbourne or Cradley would. With Eastbourne holding a distinct race points advantage they looked odds-on favourites to take the title as they had to win just one of the encounters to become the inaugural National League Third Division champions.

Not only did the Eagles duly win the home encounter on 4 October, but they won it by the massive margin of 55 points to 28. The whole team contributed to the success with Wally Green scoring a maximum, Basil Harris 11, Jock Grierson 9, Harry Saunders 8, Ken Tidbury 6, Ron Clark 4, Jimmy Coy 3 and Eric Dunn 2. Five days later, on 9 October, the Eagles travelled to Cradley for the return leg and got hammered by 59 points to 25, their biggest defeat of the season. But by then it didn't matter – they were the champions.

Eastbourne had to wait almost a month before they knew whether they could add the cup to their league triumph as it wasn't until 5 November that they met Tamworth, a team they had already beaten four times in the League, in the final of The Midlands v. The South Cup. Unfortunately it was not to be as the Eagles went down by 55 points to 41. Nevertheless it had been a highly successful season for Eastbourne and it now meant that in the only two years they had entered a league, 1938 and 1947, they had won both times.

Wally Green, on loan from West Ham, was the top rider with an average of 9.68. On demob from the Army at the end of 1946 his ambition had been to ride for Wembley, but Wembley already had more juniors than they could handle and he was advised to try West Ham. After a trial at Rye House, Green was offered a contract. The West Ham management thought he ought to gain experience at a Third Division track before he would be ready for the big time, so he was packed off to Southampton. He was given a second-half ride but unfortunately his front tyre came off when he was leading. After the meeting Jimmy Baxter, the Southampton manager, told him he did not want him in the team as he had come last in his race. As he was leaving, the shrewd Charlie Dugard approached him. Dugard had been impressed by the youngster and asked him if he would like to ride for Eastbourne. The following week Green was riding at reserve. When Dennis Gray fell and severely damaged his hand shortly afterwards, Green was promoted to the team proper and never looked back.

Green was ably supported throughout the year by Basil Harris, who averaged 8.96, and Jock Grierson with 7.39. In the end-of-year rankings compiled by the authoritative Stenner's Annual, Green was placed fourth in the Third Division rankings with Harris fifth and Grierson tenth.

In spite of continuing his 100 per cent record in league competitions, Dugard had lost something like £2,000 during the year and decided not to run Eastbourne in the 1948 Third Division. Instead he transferred the team to Hastings. His reason for doing this was that Hastings had much better facilities than Arlington, which was still essentially just a track in an open field in the middle of nowhere with an old timber garage converted into dressing rooms and no running water. The Hastings track was also much nearer to a centre of population, being just on the outskirts of the town. Dugard hoped that all of this would lead to an increase in crowds.

An agreement was reached and completed between the Hastings town clerk, Mr N.P. Lester, and Hastings Speedway Ltd for the letting of the Pilot Field for the 1948 summer season for a term of seven years to enable them to establish a speedway team. Terms of the let were agreed between Hastings Speedway Ltd, Hastings Corporation and Hastings Football Club.

1947 – National League Third Division

Date	H/A	Against	W/L	Score
17 May	Home	Southampton	Lost	35-46
4 June	Away	Tamworth	Won	44-40
5 June	Away	Hanley	Lost	40-43
17 June	Away	Southampton	Won	44-39
21 June	Home	Hanley	Won	55-29
27 June	Away	Wombwell	Lost	37-46
28 June	Home	Wombwell	Won	51-33
5 July	Home	Plymouth	Won	56-27
12 July	Home	Tamworth	Won	54-27
14 July	Away	Exeter	Lost	32-50
17 July	Away	Plymouth	Won	54-30
26 July	Home	Exeter	Won	49-32
30 July	Away	Tamworth	Won	50-33
31 July	Away	Hanley	Won	46-36
9 August	Home	Hanley	Won	48-32
15 August	Away	Wombwell	Lost	40-43
16 August	Home	Wombwell	Won	52-30
23 August	Home	Southampton	Won	48-34
30 August	Away	Cradley Heath	Lost	34-50
6 September	Home	Plymouth	Won	52-29
9 September	Away	Southampton	Lost	33-51
13 September	Home	Cradley Heath	Won	58-24
15 September	Away	Exeter	Lost	37-47
20 September	Home	Tamworth	Won	44-39
25 September	Away	Plymouth	Lost	37-47
27 September	Home	Exeter	Won	50-33
4 October	Home	Cradley Heath	Won	55-28
9 October	Away	Cradley Heath	Lost	25-59

P28 W18 D0 L10 For 1,260 Against 1,057 Pts 36 Position 1st (out of 8)

Rider	Matches	Points	Average
Wally Green	25	242	9.68
Basil Harris	28	251	8.96
Jock Grierson	28	207	7.39
Jimmy Coy	28	181	6,46
Ken Tidbury	28	149	5.32
Harry Saunders	23	115	5.00
Ron Clark	15	70	4.67

The Midlands v. The South Cup

League

Date	H/A	Against	W/L	Score
19 July	Home	Plymouth	Won	60-34
18 August	Away	Exeter	Won	51-45
30 September	Away	Southampton	Lost	57.5-38.5
2 October	Away	Plymouth	Won	50-46
15 October	Away	Exeter	Lost	34-62

Final

Date	H/A	Against	W/L	Score
5 November	Away	Tamworth	Lost	41-55

1948

Although no longer in the league, Arlington did continue to operate as a training track as well as running a number of open meetings. The first of these was on 13 June 1948, when the Championship of Sussex was won by Wally Green. Sadly, however, the day will be more remembered as the day that Eric Dunn lost his life after a tragic crash on what is now the first turn. Dunn fell and was struck on the head as he lay on the track. He died two days later in hospital.

There was another open meeting a fortnight later, which was followed by a challenge match against Rye House on 12 July, won by the Eagles 42-30 to become the first team to beat the Roosters since before the Second World War.

There were no further meetings in 1948 and none at all in 1949, although car racing was staged at regular intervals and the Eagles did manage one away match, a challenge at Rye House that they lost 40-38. One of the Eastbourne team was Ken Middleditch, the father of Neil Middleditch, who was later to ride for Eastbourne in the 1970s.

The 1948 Hastings team. From left to right, back row: Dan English, Ron Clark, Eric Dunn, Ken Middleditch. Front row: Jock Grierson, Pete Mold, Wally Green, Ken Tidbury.

Above left: The Hastings mascot.

Above right: Ken Middleditch went from novice in 1948 to heat leader in 1949.

1948 – HASTINGS

Meanwhile Charlie Dugard's Eastbourne team had moved to Hastings to the Pilot Field Stadium. Speedway had been held in Hastings before the Second World War in 1933 at Marley Lane, Battle, organised by the Hastings Motor Cycle Club. Riders included Vic Pierce, Don Patterson, Jack Williams, Joe Linn, Vic Harrington and a contingent from Arlington, Stan Lemon, Tiny Lewis and Doug Buss. The meetings were run along the normal individual events lines common at that time. The track lasted a couple of years but was not successful and closed down in 1934. There were also a number of grass tracks in the area including one at a village called Three Oaks.

Dugard's new track, the Pilot Field, was a long-established sports stadium, originally opened in 1923 for Hastings Football Club. It was carved out of a hill to the north but built up on the south and east sides in order to form a level playing area. A large stand had been built in 1928 on the south side of the stadium and it was in front of this stand that the starting gate was established. The entrance was at the south-west corner. The hill and banking formed from carving out the playing surface made excellent natural terrace areas on the west and north sides of the stadium with a wooded area to the east and rising from the entrance on the west side of the stadium. The Pits were located in the north-east corner of the stadium with a track to the north giving access from Elphinstone Road. The 388-yard track, built by Rutherford's of Battle, was a cinder track and built tightly round the football field, making it a strange shape. It was almost rectangular with two very long straights and four very sharp corners, which made for two further short straights. Originally there was also a kink in the track opposite the pits that made a fifth bend, but Dugard straightened this out after complaints from riders. Nevertheless, the track was still a strange shape and described by a number of riders as 'dangerous'. The safety fence was constructed of thick steel panels.

Much discussion took place about the team's nickname, with three names, Hastings Warriors, Hastings Lions and Hastings Pirates, being proposed. In the end, none of these proposals were taken up and the team became known instead as Hastings Saxons. The colours were a white race jacket with a red 'H' on it. Being ever the showman, Dugard had the rakers led out each week by a Saxon warrior dressed in flowing robes with a King Harold-style bob haircut under a winged helmet.

The team continued Eastbourne's membership of the National League Third Division but with a weakened side as the three Wimbledon loanees, Jimmy Coy, Basil Harris and Harry Saunders, all left. 'Spud' Murphy, Wally Green, Jock Grierson, Ken Tidbury and Ron Clark remained as the backbone of the team. Shortly after the season started Bill Osborne arrived on loan from Bradford and the South African Buddy Fuller was signed up to give the team strong hopes of retaining the title in their new guise.

The new track was opened on 24 April by the mayor of Hastings, Alderman F.W. Chambers. The conditions were perfect and around 5,000 people packed in to watch Hastings Saxons beat Hanley by 44 points to 39. Among those watching this first meeting was Cllr George Steele, a director of Hastings Speedway Ltd, who had done so much towards the introduction of the sport to Hastings. For Hastings, both Green and Grierson scored maximums.

Nice wins at Hanley and Poole set the Saxons up for a title challenge and by the end of June Hastings' hopes were high. By mid-August they had disappeared. Wally Green broke his collarbone, Osborne was recalled permanently by parent club Bradford and Fuller had to return to South Africa following a bright start after being injured. Green made a comeback only to break the other collarbone, putting him out for the rest of the season. With skipper Ken Tidbury and Dan English also becoming casualties Hastings' hopes were dashed. However, it wasn't all doom and gloom for the team as other people's misfortunes gave Ken Middleditch, Pete Mold and Ken Smith a chance to make the grade. Middleditch in particular proved to be a real discovery.

All in all, it wasn't the best of seasons for the Saxons. At one time they had a team second to none but never once were they in a position to use all of their stars at the same time. In the end they finished in sixth place out of twelve teams, having won 18 home matches and lost 4 and having done the complete reverse away by winning 4 and losing 18. Green managed to appear in just half of the club's fixtures, recording not only the highest average of 10.61 but also the fastest time round Pilot Field, with 71.0 seconds. The other two heat leaders, Grierson and Osborne, turned in averages of 9.57 and 7.89 respectively.

The Speedway Control Board stated that, in their opinion, it was one of the finest speedway venues in the country but, despite this, the directors of Hastings Speedway said that they were still not satisfied with the facilities and that they were already looking at the acquisition of floodlights and proper terracing on the grass banks. Dugard also made some track improvements by easing the bends.

1948 (Hastings) – National League Third Division

Date	H/A	Against	W/L	Score
19 April	Away	Exeter	Lost	27-57
21 April	Home	Hanley	Won	44-39
24 April	Away	Cradley Heath	Lost	27-57
28 April	Home	Exeter	Lost	40-44
4 May	Away	Yarmouth	Lost	38-46
5 May	Home	Poole	Won	48-36
8 May	Away	Hull	Lost	39-45
12 May	Home	Cradley Heath	Won	57-27
17 May	Away	Coventry	Lost	41-43
26 May	Home	Poole	Won	51-33
2 June	Home	Southampton	Won	47-36
9 June	Away	Tamworth	Lost	36-48
11 June	Away	Wombwell	Won	43-41
16 June	Home	Wombwell	Won	59-25

17 June	Away	Hanley	Won	48-36
23 June	Home	Plymouth	Won	55-29
28 June	Away	Poole	Won	44-40
30 June	Home	Yarmouth	Won	58-26
5 July	Away	Exeter	Lost	28-56
6 July	Away	Southampton	Lost	27-57
7 July	Home	Coventry	Won	60-24
14 July	Home	Tamworth	Won	56-28
15 July	Away	Plymouth	Lost	34-49
21 July	Home	Wombwell	Won	52-31
28 July	Home	Cradley Heath	Won	56-28
2 August	Away	Poole	Lost	35-49
4 August	Home	Coventry	Won	48-33
11 August	Home	Exeter	Lost	41-43
18 August	Home	Hanley	Lost	39-44
25 August	Home	Hull	Won	43-40
1 September	Home	Plymouth	Won	44-40
8 September	Home	Hull	Won	45-37
11 September	Away	Coventry	Lost	18-65
15 September	Home	Southampton	Lost	31-53
22 September	Home	Yarmouth	Won	55-29
23 September	Away	Plymouth	Lost	26-57
28 September	Away	Southampton	Lost	23-61
29 September	Home	Tamworth	Won	45-38
1 October	Away	Wombwell	Won	42-41
5 October	Away	Tamworth	Lost	23-60
7 October	Away	Hanley	Lost	16-68
19 October	Away	Yarmouth	Lost	27-57
22 October	Away	Cradley Heath	Lost	22-62
23 October	Away	Hull	Lost	20-64

P44 W22 D0 L22 For 1,755 Against 1,924 Pts 44 Position 5th (out of 12)

Rider	Matches	Points	Average
Wally Green	23	244	10.61
Jock Grierson	42	402	9.57
Bill Osborne	18	142	7.89
Frank Bettis	12	67	5.58
Buddy Fuller	8	42	5.25
Ken Middleditch	38	166	4.37
Ken Tidbury	39	170	4.36
Ron Clark	44	188	4.20
Eric Dunn	12	67	3.25
Dan English	35	108	3.09
Ken Smith	22	67	3.05
Pete Mold	32	91	2.84

1949 – HASTINGS

When Hastings opened in 1949 it was without Wally Green, who had returned to his parent club West Ham. Fuller and Clark stayed with the team as did Grierson and Middleditch, both of whom had wintered out in South Africa with Fuller. Middleditch's sojourn out in South Africa had done him the world of good and he showed in the first few meetings at the Pilot Field that he had improved beyond all recognition and, for the rest of the season, he was vying with Grierson for the number one spot. Without Green, however, the team seemed to have little chance of improving on their sixth place in the league, let alone winning it. However they started off well, recording a number of massive victories at home, 50-28 against Leicester, 52-31 against Plymouth, 58-25 against Halifax and a stunning 65-16 against Rayleigh. But it was to prove to be a false dawn as they lost their next home match 44-40 to Hanley. By the end of the season they had won 18 matches at home but lost 5 and drawn 1, while away from home they had managed to win just 3, losing 21. The Saxons dropped two places to finish in eighth place. Part of the reason for the drop in form after the good start was an horrific injury to Fuller, who fractured his skull in a crash and had to return home to South Africa. As it was, Grierson and Middleditch were responsible for more than one-third of the team's points between them and it was this lack of support that did for Hastings. In the end, Grierson just topped Middleditch's average with 8.66 to 8.36, but it was Middleditch who took the track record with 70.4 seconds, a record that, of course, still stands to this day as there was to be no more speedway at Pilot Field after the end of the 1949 season.

Rumblings of discontent amongst the local community had been heard as far back as 1948 when thirteen local ratepayers, under the chairmanship of Mr Arthur Parsons, formed an organisation called 'Kill Hastings Speedway' and complained to the council about the noise. Eventually the residents took their objections to court, indicting Dugard on eleven charges. Ten of the charges were thrown out and the residents ordered to pay costs on them. However, the one remaining charge was upheld and this meant the end of speedway at Hastings. In other words, the Saxons lost the battle of Hastings.

The last meeting to take place at the Pilot Field was on 5 October 1949 when Hastings lost to Tamworth 44.5-39.5. One of Dugard's main reasons for moving the Eastbourne operation to Hastings was to be nearer to a centre of population. It was to prove a costly mistake.

1949 (Hastings) – National League Third Division

Date	H/A	Against	W/L	Score
31 March	Away	Plymouth	Lost	32-48
6 April	Home	Leicester	Won	56-28
13 April	Home	Plymouth	Won	52-31
15 April	Away	Tamworth	Lost	36.5-47.5
18 April	Home	Halifax	Won	58-25
20 April	Home	Rayleigh	Won	65-16
21 April	Away	Oxford	Won	47-37
4 May	Home	Hanley	Lost	40-44
11 May	Home	Oxford	Won	61-23
23 May	Away	Exeter	Lost	23-61
25 May	Home	Liverpool	Won	51-33
1 June	Home	Yarmouth	Lost	39-45
6 June	Away	Halifax	Lost	24-59
8 June	Home	Plymouth	Drew	42-42
11 June	Away	Hull	Lost	37-47

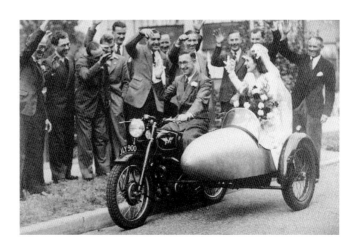

One of Hastings' leading riders Ron Clark off on his honeymoon, watched by his teammates.

13 June	Away	Liverpool	Lost	26-58
15 June	Home	Exeter	Won	48-36
17 June	Away	Leicester	Lost	32-52
22 June	Home	Hull	Won	45-39
27 June	Away	Poole	Lost	23-60
29 June	Home	Tamworth	Won	51-33
5 July	Away	Yarmouth	Lost	22-62
6 July	Home	Poole	Won	55-28
13 July	Home	Halifax	Won	43-40
20 July	Home	Rayleigh	Won	63-21
21 July	Away	Plymouth	Won	43-40
1 August	Away	Poole	Lost	38-46
3 August	Home	Liverpool	Won	55-28
8 August	Away	Exeter	Lost	31-52
10 August	Home	Hanley	Lost	40-44
17 August	Away	Tamworth	Lost	22-62
24 August	Home	Leicester	Won	53-31
25 August	Away	Oxford	Lost	37-47
26 August	Away	Leicester	Lost	38-46
27 August	Away	Hanley	Lost	24-60
31 August	Home	Exeter	Won	44-40
6 September	Away	Yarmouth	Lost	26-58
7 September	Home	Swindon	Won	54-30
10 September	Away	Rayleigh	Lost	25-59
14 September	Home	Oxford	Won	50-34
17 September	Away	Swindon	Won	43-41
19 September	Away	Liverpool	Lost	35-49
21 September	Home	Poole	Won	46-38
28 September	Home	Yarmouth	Lost	41-43
1 October	Away	Rayleigh	Lost	35-49
5 October	Home	Tamworth	Lost	39.5-44.5
12 October	Away	Halifax	Lost	17-67
22 October	Away	Hanley	Lost	28-56

P48 W21 D1 L26 For 1,936 Against 2,080 Pts 43 Position 8th (out of 13)

Rider	Matches	Points	Average
Jock Grierson	42	364	8.66
Ken Middleditch	47	393	8.36
Buddy Fuller	26	181	6.96
Ron Clark	18	107	5.94
Norman Street	43	188	4.37
Ken Smith	47	203	4.31
George Butler	31	126	4.06
Harold MacNaughton	26	98	3.76
Dan English	37	110	2.97
Harold Tapscott	31	92	2.96
Ken Tidbury	18	52	2.88
Pete Mold	7	17	2.42
B. Sivyer	7	3	0.42

National Trophy – Third Division Round One

Date	H/A	Against	W/L	Score
27 April	Home	Yarmouth	Lost	52-55
3 May	Away	Yarmouth	Lost	33-75

Hastings lost on aggregate 85-130

THE 1950s

1950

With the demise of Hastings, speedway returned to Arlington in the form of challenge matches. Although he was not yet prepared to risk another season in league racing, Charlie Dugard told the Eastbourne faithful that if the Eagles gained sufficient support there was a chance that he might consider re-entering the team into the Third Division. Unfortunately the crowds didn't turn out in as many numbers as at Hastings. Dugard himself felt that the main reason for this was because he was not able to race on what he considered to be the best day for drawing in the crowds, Sunday, because of the Lord's Day Observance laws. Being forced to race on a Saturday he felt was not in the best interests of the supporters or the club.

In all there were just six matches in 1950, the first of these being on 24 June when a team captained by Harold MacNaughton went down to Rye House 45.5-36.5. Although the track was coated with red shale and made thick by heavy rain, racing was as keen as ever between these two old rivals, even if the fastest time was a poor 79.4 seconds. Star of the match for the Eagles was MacNaughton, who dropped just one point to Rye House's maximum man Ron Barrett. The Eagles' scorers in this first match back at Arlington were: MacNaughton 11, R. Burnett 9, A. Hood 6, E. Steers 3.5, B. Sivyer 4, J. Hayles 2, B. Weston 1 and B. Grimes 0. Shortly after this match MacNaughton signed for Southampton for a fee of £50, though he still continued to turn out for the Eagles in their challenge matches.

The second match against High Beech saw a number of spills as Eastbourne's MacNaughton, Arthur Hood and Ian Hilton and Jon Fry of High Beech all bit the Arlington dust. Fry broke a leg, but the rest were all uninjured. Top scorers for the Eagles were MacNaughton, Hood and Sivyer with 8. On 23 July Ron Burnett became Champion of Sussex when he beat MacNaughton, John Hayles and Hood in the final, his time being 70.0 seconds.

For the first time in thirteen years it looked as if George Newton's track record might be broken when MacNaughton returned a time of 69.4 seconds, just 0.6 of a second outside the record.

With no meetings planned for a fortnight, the Eagles travelled to California (Berkshire) the following week and beat the home team 57-24. On 19 August the Eagles raced their last match of the season against the Rye House Roosters. It was an exciting end to the short season as the two teams drew 41-41 and McNaughton at last managed to equal Newton's track record.

1951-1953

Not only were the crowds not enough for Dugard to consider relaunching the league team at Arlington but they were so poor that he decided to pull the plug altogether on speedway for two years. Strangely enough, he applied to hold pony racing instead but the local authorities voted 'neigh' on the grounds that it would be a gambling sport. There was no racing of any sort therefore at Arlington in 1951 and 1952. Not happy with the lack of activity at his beloved Arlington, Dugard decided to try again and in 1953 he tested the water once again by staging the Championship of Sussex, which was won by Ron Barrett. With a reasonable crowd turning out, Dugard took the plunge and entered an Eagles team into a new league that was being inaugurated in 1954, the Southern Area League.

1954

And so, after a gap of seven years, league speedway racing returned to Arlington. The new league was intended to be a training league for junior riders and consisted of a number of training tracks then operating in the South, Eastbourne, Rye House, Brafield, California, Aldershot and Ringwood. All matches were to be with eight-man teams run over fourteen heats, with each team meeting every other team four times, twice at home and twice away.

The Eagles started the season away at Aldershot in a challenge match and were crushed 55-29. The first home match was against Rye House and, despite a brilliant 12-point maximum by Norman Street, Eagles went down by 49 to 34. The Eagles' other scorers were: Harry Willson 7, Wally Willson 5, Gordon Richards 4, Reeve Turrell 3, Bob Warner 2, Dave Yiannari 1 and Dave Freeborn 0.

Following this meeting, Eastbourne's leading rider and maximum man Norman Street was banned because he was too experienced. This proved to be a disaster for the Eagles. To say this wasn't a very successful season might be the greatest speedway understatement of all time. By 15 August the Eagles' record read won 0, drawn 0, lost 12 as defeat followed defeat, the worst being a 60-22 at California and a 59-25 at home to Ringwood. The best was a home defeat to Rye House 43-38. The best they had managed away was a 50-33 defeat at Brafield. Suddenly, out of the blue, came a 41-37 win over the team that had beaten them by the record score at home, Ringwood, who were back for their second fixture at Arlington. The Eagles gained a 5-0 in heat one and somehow managed to hold on throughout the next thirteen heats. The Eastbourne scorers in this historic victory were: Jim Preedy 9, Johnny Fry 8, Harry Willson 7, Steve Bole 5, John Grunow 4, Wally Willson 4, Bob Bunney 2 and Bob Gladwin 2. After the shock of winning their first match the Eagles soon returned to their old ways, crashing 49-34 the following week at home to California. Brafield came next, severely weakened by the loss of several riders, and Eagles duly recorded their second win, this time 47-31.

At the end of the season, after having a 100 per cent success record in all previous league competitions, Eastbourne found themselves rock bottom of the 1954 Southern Area League. After Street had gone, their top man was Harry Wilson, who averaged less than 7 points per match. The Eagles tried out no less than eighteen riders during the season and not one of them, apart from Street, measured up even to junior league status. On an individual level, Maurice McDermott became the new Champion of Sussex with Street winning the Silver Helmet Championship and Steve Bole taking the Supporters' Trophy.

1954 – Southern Area League

Date	H/A	Against	W/L	Score
17 April	Away	Aldershot	Lost	29-55*
25 April	Home	Rye House	Lost	34-49
2 May	Away	Brafield	Lost	33-50
9 May	Home	Aldershot	Lost	39-45*
16 May	Away	Ringwood	Lost	33-51
23 May	Home	Ringwood	Lost	25-59
13 June	Away	Rye House	Lost	22-60
20 June	Home	Brafield	Lost	27.5-54.5
4 July	Home	California	Lost	38-46

11 July	Away	Rye House	Lost	30-54
18 July	Home	Rye House	Lost	38-43
25 July	Away	Brafield	Lost	33-50
8 August	Away	Ringwood	Lost	29-50
15 August	Home	Ringwood	Won	41-37#
22 August	Home	California	Lost	34-49
29 August	Away	California	Lost	27-57
12 September	Home	Brafield	Won	47-31
19 September	Away	California	Lost	24-60

*Aldershot withdrew mid-season and their records were deleted from the final table
#Match played for double points

P16 W3 D0 L13 For 482.5 Against 750.5 Pts 6 Position 5th (out of 5)

Rider	Matches	Rides	Points	BP	Total	Average
Harry Willson	9	33	53	4	57	6.91
Steve Bole	12	47	66	4	70	5.96
Jim Preddy	10	36	46	5	51	5.67
Wally Willson	14	52	59	12	71	5.46
Johnny Fry	12	45	60	1	61	5.42
Dan English	7	23	28	3	31	5.39
Bob Gladwin	10	32	35.5	3	38.5	4.81
Bob Bunney	10	34	36	4	40	4.71
John Gronow	8	27	22	4	26	3.85

CMA includes bonus points
(inc. matches against Aldershot)

1955

On Sunday 17 April 1955 the Eagles started their second season in the Southern Area League. After finishing bottom the previous season with only 2 wins, it was felt that things could only get better. Unfortunately they got worse as Eastbourne managed just 1 league win.

Before the season started some track alterations were made and the track shortened by ten yards to 342 yards. The first match of the season was against California. Unfortunately for the Eagles those Berkshire Californians were as deadly as the Americans of today, notching up no less than nine 5-1 heat advantages to win 61-23, with only Wally Willson and Bert Little managing to win a heat for the home side. The Eagles' scorers were Willson 6, Little 6, B. Bunny 4, G. Smithson 2, D. Collett 2, R. Davies 1, R. Turrell 1 and A. Brett 1. The next home match was against Rye House and it was a much stronger-looking Eagles side that took to the shale, led by captain Harry Willson who scored 8 points. Although they put up a much better show it still wasn't good enough as they went down 47-33.

The Eagles had some success in the Championship of Sussex as it was won by the their own Bert Little – but then it wasn't surprising that an Eastbourne rider won as all sixteen entrants were theirs. Having an all-Eagles line-up though was to prove costly as Alan Brett, Ray Terry and Frank Bettis all sustained injuries. With these three now out and with Harry Willson deciding to retire, it was obvious that once again Eagles would have an uphill struggle. And so they did, as heavy defeats at Brafield, 61-23, and Rye House, 67-17, followed. When Ringwood closed during the season, Dugard bought Merv Hannam and Harold Carter from them for £300. In Hannam, Eastbourne at last had a decent rider but unfortunately he was destined not to stay very long. Because of the withdrawal of Ringwood, the scheduled league match against them was replaced by a challenge match against California. After ten successive defeats – four of them to California – the Eagles seemed to have little chance. Surprisingly Eastbourne trailed by just one point with one heat left. Even more surprising was the fact that in the last heat Hannam and Bob Bunney stormed to a match-winning 5-1 to give the Eagles their first win of the season.

Steve Bole, Eastbourne's second best rider in their disastrous 1954 campaign, seen here receiving the Supporters' Cup from Brian Anders and Johnnie Innis.

The fourth of September was a red-letter day for the Eastbourne Eagles, as it was on that day that they recorded their one and only league win of the campaign when they beat Brafield 49-33 at Arlington. The Eagles scorers were: T. Reader 10, Hannam 9, D. Collett 8, H. Carder 7, Bunney 6, J. Preedy 4, G. Bridson 4 and R. Terry 3. The Eagles' top scorer, Reader, had the chance of challenging Vic Hall for the Silver Sash Match Race title but met with defeat.

Individually, Tom Reader won the Southern Area League Riders Championship qualifying round. He went on to finish seventh with 8 points in the final. California's Bob Andrews took the Eagles' Silver Helmet Championship and in the final meeting of the term, Hannam beat a strong field to win the Supporters' Trophy. It was in this meeting that runner-up Mike Broadbank at last broke George Newton's eight-year-old track record, albeit on the new shorter track, with a time of 68.6 seconds.

Once again the Eagles finished bottom of the league, but this time with just 1 win to their credit. They had managed to use 23 riders in 12 matches. Wally Willson was top scorer with 45 points from 8 matches and only one, Bob Bunney, was ever present.

1955 – Southern Area League

Date	H/A	Against	W/L	Score
17 April	Home	California	Lost	23-61
24 April	Away	California	Lost	30-53
15 May	Home	Rye House	Lost	33-47
22 May	Away	Ringwood	Lost	27-55*
5 June	Away	Brafield	Lost	23-61
12 June	Home	Ringwood	Lost	39-43
19 June	Away	Rye House	Lost	17-67
26 June	Home	California	Lost	31-53
3 July	Away	California	Lost	27-56
10 July	Home	Rye House	Lost	36-47
28 August	Away	Rye House	Lost	23-61
4 September	Home	Brafield	Won	49-33

| 18 September | Home | Brafield | Lost | 36-48** |

*Ringwood withdrew mid-season and their records were deleted from the final table
** Match played for double points

P12 W1 D0 L11 For 327 Against 587 Pts 2 Position 4th (out of 4)

Rider	Matches	Points	Average
Merv Hannam	5	42	8.40
Wally Willson	8	45	5.63
Dave Collett	5	24	4.80
Gerry Bridson	5	21	4.20
Bob Bunney	13	44	3.38
Gerald Smithson	7	23	3.29
Bert Little	5	16	3.20
Jim Preddy	11	35	3.18
Dave Freeborn	5	12	2.40

(Inc. matches against Ringwood)

1956

After two consecutive wooden spoons for the Eagles, changes were made. Ringwood signing Harold Carter was appointed team manager and he managed to unearth some real talent for the 1956 campaign. His first signings were Ray Cresp, Jim Heard, Colin Gooddy, Frank Bettis and Cliff Greener, five top-class riders. Alan Brett also returned after a nine-month lay-off. The first meeting, the Easter Trophy, was won by ex-Hastings, West Ham and Rayleigh star Bettis, who went through the card unbeaten in front of a big crowd. But within a week there was trouble, with Gooddy and Bettis being refused permission to turn out for the Eagles by the control board because they had had First Division experience. For some strange reason, Gooddy was then allocated to the Eagles' first opponents, the Southern Rovers.

The Rovers, who as their name suggests, had no home base, came on 15 April and won 48-36 with Gooddy scoring 11 of their points. The Eagles scorers were: G. Bridson 10, J. Heard 7, B. Bunney 3, D. Collett 3, B. Little 3, A Brett 3 and D. Freeborn 0. Ray Cresp made his debut in the following match, an away fixture at California where he scored 11 points, helping the Eagles record their first away league win for nine years. Other scorers in that memorable meeting were: Heard 10, Reader 8, Bunney 5, Bridson 4, Collett 3, Brett 3 and Murrell 1. The Eagles completed the double a week later, winning 55-28 at Arlington.

With further scores of 11 and 12 in the next two matches it was obvious that Cresp was far too good for this level of speedway and he left to join the famous Wembley Lions. Dugard was not too happy about this and fumed, 'The Wembley Lions should be called the Wembley Eagles!' In 1962, Cresp went on to reach the World Championship final. Cresp's place was taken by Leo McAuliffe but he could not stop a home defeat at the hands of Rye House, 54-29.

Although now racing on Sundays again, Eastbourne hit further problems with the Lord's Day Observance Act as they found they were not allowed to charge admission to watch racing. They got round this by charging 2s 6d for a programme, although they also put on a few Saturday meetings as well. The first Saturday meeting was against the Southern Rovers and ended in a 41-41 draw with Rovers' Eric Hockaday setting a new track record of 66.0 seconds. Rye House came next and suffered their first defeat against the Eagles for many years on a very wet track, which accounted for two 5-0s, a 3-0 and two 3-2 heat results. The Eastbourne management were now getting very concerned about the crowd levels, which had dropped during the season, and put out a request for at least another 500 supporters to come through the turnstiles if they were to remain viable.

Following some good away victories, Sunday racing returned on 16 September with a 43-41 win over the Southern Rovers, a victory that sent the Eagles to the top of the league table.

In the end, the Eagles finished in second place behind Rye House, a far cry from their first two seasons in the Southern Area League. Top riders were Jim Heard, who scored 81 points from 12

Colin Gooddy, Eastbourne's leading rider in the 1959 Southern Area League.

Frank Bettis, the Eastbourne captain during the Southern Area League days.

matches, and Leo McAuliffe, who managed 65 from 9. McAuliffe and Heard also shone individually as they came first and second in the Southern Riders' Championship. Former Eagle Merv Hannam took the Championship of Sussex with a win over Ray Cresp, Frank Bettis and Colin Gooddy in the final while Tom Reader won the Supporters' Trophy in the last meeting of the season.

The Supporters' Club kiosk as it looked in the 1950s. Long-time Supporters' Club secretary Johnnie Innis is on the left.

1956 – Southern Area League

Date	H/A	Against	W/L	Score
15 April	Home	Southern Rovers	Lost	36-48
22 April	Away	California	Won	44-40
29 April	Home	California	Won	55-28
20 May	Away	Rye House	Lost	30-54
27 May	Home	Rye House	Lost	29-54
3 June	Away	Southern Rovers	Lost	36-47*
30 June	Home	Southern Rovers	Drew	41-41
14 July	Home	Rye House	Won	40-37
28 July	Home	California	Won	49-32
12 August	Away	California	Won	43-40
1 September	Away	Southern Rovers	Won	43-41#
14 October	Away	Rye House	Lost	28-56

*Raced at California
#Raced at Fastbourne

P12 W6 D1 L5 For 474 Against 518 Pts 13 Position 2nd (out of 4)

Rider	Matches	Points	Average
Leo McAuliffe	9	65	7.22
Jim Heard	12	81	6.75
Gerry Bridson	9	55	6.11
Tom Reader	10	55	5.55
Bob Bunney	9	38	4.22
Tom Preddy	7	29	4.14
Dave Collett	12	46	3.83
Michael Hard	6	15	2.50

1957

The new season opened on 21 April with everything looking good for a change. After finishing runners-up in the league in 1956 there was an air of optimism about, with talk of a possible championship-winning team. The season started with the Easter Trophy, which was won by Colin Gooddy, who went through the meeting unbeaten. Following a battle with the control board, Eastbourne had been given permission to sign up Frank Bettis, who took on the role of rider-cum-manager and seemed to be doing a fine job despite the restrictions due to petrol rationing.

The Eagles' first match at Arlington was a challenge against the Southern Rovers, which they duly won to the tune of 46-38. Eastbourne then went to Aldershot and came away with a 54-54 draw, only to lose at home to the same team a week later, 49-35. By now the Southern Rovers had found a permanent home at Rayleigh and it was therefore the Rayleigh Rovers who were Eastbourne's first league opponents of the season at Arlington. In spite of the optimism at the start of the season, the Eagles suffered a 48-35 reverse in this match. Rayleigh had put together a very strong team that included Brian Meredith, Colin Gooddy and Tommy Sweetman, who each scored 10 points. The Eagles scorers were: Frank Bettis 11, D. Collett 7, Leo McAuliffe 6, Reg Davies 6, John Dugard 3, Les Searle 2, Jim Preedy 0 and Bob Warner 0.

The gloom at Eastbourne continued as the Eagles were massacred at Rye House 66-17. However, just seven days later they won their first match of the season, beating the same Rye House 51-32. This was followed by a one-point defeat at Aldershot and a 52-31 victory back at Arlington. Part of the reason for the improvement in the team's performance was the signing of Colin Gooddy in place of McAuliffe. However, his help did not last for long as in the Eagles' 43-39 home defeat at the hands of Rayleigh, Gooddy was badly injured and was out for the rest of the season. He had lasted for just three matches. Dave Collett was also injured in the same match.

On 4 August, Arlington staged the Championship of Sussex. The meeting was won by former Eagle Ray Cresp. Making his debut at Eastbourne was a young New Zealander who went on to even greater heights than Cresp, later winning six World Titles and three Long Track World finals. It was none other than Kiwi superstar Ivan Mauger. In his first race Mauger could only manage third place behind McAuliffe and Cresp, but in heat nine he beat Ross Gilbertson, Les Searle and Bob Warner in 71.4 seconds. His final tally was 7 points from 5 rides. McAuliffe won the Southern Area League Riders' final on 15 September after a second run-off against the Eagles' own Maury Conway. The first had ended in a dead heat.

The final league match of the season, which the Eagles won 46-36, was against Rye House. With the match counting for four points as Rye House had no dates left for home meetings, it meant that Eastbourne finished the season with the same number of points as Rayleigh at the top of the league. Unfortunately for the Eagles, Rayleigh had more race points and were therefore declared champions. In the second half of the final meeting Jim Heard won the Supporters' Trophy in a thrilling finale.

Bettis had used his experience to good effect throughout the season and finished as Eastbourne's top scorer with 94 points from 10 matches. Jim Heard contributed 75 while third heat leader, Australian Maury Conway, also did well. In his three matches, Gooddy managed 28 points. Another generation of the Dugard family became involved with the Eagles this year as Charlie's son, John, showed considerable promise.

1957 – Southern Area League

Date	H/A	Against	W/L	Score
9 June	Home	Rayleigh Rovers	Lost	35-48
23 June	Home	Rye House	Won	51-32

29 June	Away	Aldershot	Lost	41-42
7 July	Home	Aldershot	Won	52-31
27 July	Away	Aldershot	Won	48-36
5 August	Away	Rayleigh Rovers	Lost	37-46
6 August	Away	Rye House	Lost	17-66
8 September	Home	Rayleigh Rovers	Lost	39-43*
15 September	Home	Aldershot	Won	52-31
6 October	Home	Rye House	Won	46-36*

*Raced for double points

P12 W6 D0 L6 For 418 Against 411 Pts 12 Position 2nd (out of 4)

Rider	Matches	Points	Average
Frank Bettis	10	94	9.40
Jim Heard	8	75	9.38
Maury Conway	8	54	6.75
Dave Collett	6	33	5.50
Noel Conway	7	34	4.86
John Dugard	9	38	4.22
Reg Davies	9	21	2.33
Les Searle	8	9	1.13

1958

With the withdrawal of Rayleigh from the Southern Area League at the beginning of 1958, leaving just three teams, it was felt that it would no longer be viable. The idea of a National League Second Division, made up of the three remaining teams, Eastbourne, Rye House and Aldershot, together with Exeter, Yarmouth and junior teams from First Division tracks Swindon and Norwich, was mooted to take its place. However it soon became apparent that the idea as originally conceived was a non-starter. Exeter and Yarmouth wanted ten-heat matches, Swindon and Norwich were only able to offer three home dates while Eastbourne, Rye House and Aldershot considered the proposed pay rates for the new league too high. The league eventually went ahead with Yarmouth plus Norwich, Swindon and Poole second teams but without Eastbourne.

As a result, Eastbourne reverted to a season of challenge matches and individual meetings. First up was the Easter Trophy, won by Leo McAuliffe after Colin Gooddy had dropped a chain in the final race. Two team matches against Rye House and Aldershot followed, both ending in victories for the Eagles. Frank Bettis won the Championship of Sussex in a meeting that saw Ivan Mauger come to Arlington on a more permanent basis. On 8 June he put on an Eagles race jacket for the first time and picked up 8 points as Eastbourne beat Chiswick Nomads 46-38. Against Coventry he did even better as, along with Colin Gooddy and Frank Bettis, he picked up 11 points in the Eagles' 61-23 success. On 20 July Mauger scorched to his first maximum as Eastbourne beat California 51-33. He then won the Silver Helmet Championship at Arlington by beating McAuliffe, Gooddy and Jim Gleed in the final.

On 31 August, Eastbourne was selected for its first Test match. Although only a junior Test it was still a major honour for a club who were not even staging league speedway. It was originally billed as Young England v. Young Australasia, but later changed to Young England v. Overseas. The match was notable for the fact that it heralded Ivan Mauger's first international team appearance. England were without Leo McAuliffe, who broke down on the way to the track, so Ross Gilbertson replaced him in the team and Bob Warner, who was attending the match as a spectator, borrowed novice Ken Vale's equipment to take over as reserve. It was to be an eventful meeting for Warner and the peak of his speedway career as, with Overseas holding a three-point lead after 11 races and with England robbed of the services of Bobby Croombs and Frank Bettis through injury, Warner was called on to ride in five of the last seven races and it was his 8 points that helped give Young England victory by 58 to 49.

The scorers were: Young England: C. Gooddy 16, T. Sweetman 9, R. Gilbertson 9, B. Warner 8, F. Bettis 7 and B. Croombs 3. Overseas: M. Conway 14, T. Blokdyk 14, I. Mauger 11, S. Schirmer 6, G. Bridgson 4, L. Spillsbury 0.

The last meeting of the season proved to be the Supporters' Trophy, which was won by Mauger, who also added his name to the track record at the same time. The last meeting of the season was scheduled to be a Best Pairs meeting but it was washed out by rain; a shame for the supporters as it meant there were none of the usual farewells from the riders and management. Although there had been no league this year, the season was nevertheless considered a 'Mauger' success!

1959

League racing returned to Arlington in 1959 when the Southern Area League was reintroduced, originally with four teams: Eastbourne, Rye House, Yarmouth and Rayleigh. Aldershot's application to join was originally turned down but they were later allowed in and then Rayleigh closed with the team moving to Ipswich. So the final line-up was Eastbourne, Rye House, Yarmouth, Aldershot and Ipswich.

The season opened (or almost did) with the Easter Trophy. Due to persistent rain supporters only saw two heats. The Eagles then lost 41-31 at Rye House in a challenge match but gained quick revenge, winning 43-29 the week after back at Arlington. Gooddy, broke the track record in heat one and again in heat eight and, but for an engine failure, would have had a maximum. The Eagles' scorers were: Gil Goldfinch 11, Frank Bettis 10, Colin Gooddy 9, Bob Warner 6, John Dugard 4, Ron Sharp 3 while reserve Reg Davies did not ride. Gooddy's first maximum came the following week as the Eagles beat the Kent Rovers 46-26 in another challenge match.

What was supposed to be the first league match was against Rayleigh. The Rockets took a 5-1 in the first heat after Gooddy fell and another in heat four, leaving the score at 12-12. The Eagles then hit five 5-1s and three 4-2s to win 49-23. Goldfinch scored a maximum and John Dugard a paid maximum to top the Eagles' scorecard. Eastbourne then won at Rye House 38-33 and subsequently beat Kent Rovers 38-34 in a challenge match thanks to a last-heat 5-1. The Championship of Sussex was next and was won for the first time by Colin Gooddy.

With Ipswich taking over from Rayleigh and the introduction of Aldershot to the league, the Speedway Control Board met to consider the position of the Southern Area League. On 15 July the board pronounced that the league would consist of one home and one away match. Up to this point it had been run on the understanding that each team would be meeting twice each home and away, so a number of matches that had already been run, including the Eastbourne v. Rayleigh encounter, were deleted from the records. In addition the board switched some riders around to try and even up team strengths and allowed the use of guest riders. As a result a number of riders found themselves appearing for different teams in successive weeks.

In the end, in spite of all the complications, it was Eastbourne who finished up as league champions, with 5 wins and just 1 loss out of 8 matches, their first success since 1947. This victory was based on Colin Gooddy, who averaged over 10 points per match and, amazingly, was never headed on an away track. Goldfinch scored well until he was transferred to Ipswich, while Dave Still provided strong backing. Ross Gilbertson returned for several matches and yet another Dugard, Bob, turned out several times for the team.

The Eastbourne Southern Area League team in 1959. From left to right, back row: Bob Dugard, John Dugard, Dave Still, Charlie Dugard (promoter), Bob Warner, Gil Goldfinch, Colin Gooddy. In front: Frank Bettis (captain) on bike.

1959 – Southern Area League

Date	H/A	Against	W/L	Score
17 May	Home	Ipswich	Won	49-23
24 May	Away	Rye House	Won	38-33
31 May	Home	Aldershot	Won	38-34
14 June	Home	Rye House	Won	38-33
28 June	Home	Yarmouth	Won	46-26
7 July	Away	Yarmouth	Drew	36-36
8 August	Away	Aldershot	Lost	32-39
17 September	Away	Ipswich	Lost	17-55

P8 W5 D1 L2 For 294 Against 279 Pts 11 Position 1st (out of 5)

Rider	Matches	Rides	Points	BP	Total	Average
Colin Gooddy	7	29	77	1	78	10.76
Gil Goldfinch	6	24	56	3	59	9.83
Dave Still	8	32	63	4	67	8.38
Frank Bettis	5	15	17	4	21	5.60
Ross Gilbertson	4	16	23	2	25	6.25
John Dugard	8	30	24	8	32	4.27
Bob Warner	8	24	18	2	20	3.33
Bob Dugard	5	12	3	1	4	1.33

(CMA inc. bonus points – qualification 4 matches)

Left: The next generation of Dugards: Bob in 1959.

Below: Bob Dugard's brother, John, another of the Dugard dynasty who rode for the Eagles.

THE 1960s

1960

For many years the number of speedway teams had been showing an alarming drop. Fewer riders were coming into the sport while more and more experienced men were retiring. Only the Southern Area League offered any real hope for newcomers, but the cost of learning the art of racing was spiralling and returns were very low. There were a few half-hearted attempts by the National League promoters to encourage novices, but many of them rapidly disappeared. However, during 1959 there was a sudden resurgence as a number of tracks reopened to stage open meetings, including New Cross, Plymouth and Bristol. These tracks operated under the auspices of the Speedway Control Board (SCB) but it was in the North of the country that the most significant developments were taking place as Mike Parker opened up Bradford, Liverpool and Cradley Heath to run unlicensed meetings. They were unlicensed because they only contained fifteen heats of racing instead of the minimum eighteen as laid down by the control board. Parker discovered that, in spite of the official ban, he had no shortage of youngsters on his hands wanting to take part. Parker followed up his success by opening Stoke with Reg Fearman and contacting the promoters of the Southern Area League and its secretary, John Wick, to see if they would be prepared to join together to form a new league. The SAL promoters agreed as long as it could be made official. The control board, for their part, realised that they could not allow the current situation to continue with so many unlicensed tracks running, so they called a meeting in November 1959 to which all interested parties were invited. At the end of the meeting, agreement was reached to form a new official league in 1960 to be called the Provincial League. All the Southern Area League tracks expressed an interest in joining and a number of former tracks including Rayleigh also applied to join.

With thirteen clubs involved, things looked bright and rosy, but out of the blue came a Speedway Control Board bombshell as Eastbourne and Rye House's applications were both refused on the grounds that their tracks were not up to standard and because they raced on Sundays. Dugard and Rye House promoter T. Lawrence both lodged appeals but both were turned down, though they were given permission to stage open meetings on Sundays. With Ipswich joining the National League and Yarmouth the Provincial League, the old Southern Area League was no longer viable, so Eastbourne were forced to revert to the old challenge and individual meetings routine.

Ross Gilbertson won the Easter Trophy on 17 April and then the Eagles lost two successive home meetings to Aldershot, 42-30, and Yarmouth, 35-34. They then drew 41-41 at Rye House before beating the Rye House Red Devils 36-35 at Arlington. Eric Hockaday became the new Champion of Sussex on 5 June. The next meeting was against the strong Rayleigh outfit, who were at the time one of the leading teams in the Provincial League. The Eagles, however, pulled off a shock win, defeating the Rockets 42-30. Rayleigh went on to win the

Provincial League title. Ipswich came and forced a draw and Cradley were sent packing 45-27. Aldershot returned and this time the Eagles won 44-27. The Eagles suffered a rare defeat at Rye House on 4 September but made up for it the following week by winning 41.5 to 31.5. Gilbertson won the Southern Riders' Championship and the season ended with Gil Goldfinch winning the Supporters' Trophy.

Although not in the league, Eastbourne had put on a successful season and with a team consisting of Colin Gooddy as captain, Jim Heard, Ross Gilbertson, John and Bob Dugard, Dave Still and Bob Warner, had taken on and beaten a number of Provincial League teams.

1961

The 1961 season began with the customary Easter Trophy, won by Colin Gooddy, who stayed unbeaten throughout the meeting despite the top-class line-up that included John and Bobby Dugard, Ross Gilbertson, Des Lukehurst and 'Speedy Pete' Jarman. Jim Heard and John Dugard then won a Best Pairs event before the first challenge match of the year against Rye House. Bill Osborne joined the team, which, his signature apart, stayed the same as the 1960 line-up. John Dugard top scored with 11 points as the Eagles beat Rye House 41-31. Gilbertson recorded three wins and a fall. Rye House won the return 38-34, with John Dugard again proving to be the Eagles' top scorer with 14 points. Gilbertson won the Championship of Sussex on 14 May.

Two more challenge matches against National League junior teams followed, the first against New Cross 'Colts', which Eastbourne won 41-31. The second was against Ipswich 'B', who included a young Len Silver. This proved to be an easy victory for the Eagles. There were several meetings run on the lines of the old Hailsham Cup before Gilbertson won the Silver Helmet Championship, equalling his own 63.8-second track record in the process. The Eagles lost 49-35 at Rye House, but a week later won by the same score after some controversy. Eastbourne actually won 50-34 but Jim Heard was adjudged to have broken the rules in the last race and the referee ordered it to be rerun. Rye House took a 5-1 to leave the aggregate 84-84. Poole Pirates made their first Arlington appearance in a challenge match on 3 September and, despite a brilliant 11 points by ex-Hastings and Eastbourne rider Ken Middleditch, lost to the Eagles. The final meeting of the season was, as usual, the Supporters' Trophy. Like pretty much everything else in 1961 the meeting was won by Ross Gilbertson.

During the year, on 1 July, Bill Osborne opened a training school at the track. This ran on alternate Sundays and on into the winter months. A machine was available for hire at a cost of £3 for twelve laps, although Osborne was not in favour of novices turning up without their own equipment. 'Any lad who expects to become a speedway rider must own his own bike,' he said. Among his first year discoveries was Johnny Guilfoyle.

1962

At the end of the 1961 season there was some talk of reviving the old Southern Area League with teams from Eastbourne, Rye House, Yarmouth and Weymouth taking part. Dugard himself had still not given up on the idea of entering the Provincial League and applied for membership once again. He agreed to switch Eastbourne's race day to Saturday but still had to satisfy the control board that the track was up to the standard required. In readiness for the move to the Provincial League, Dugard announced his team as John and Bob Dugard, Frank Bettis, Bill Osborne, Jimmy Gleed, Jim Heard and Bob Warner. He also originally proposed using Colin Gooddy as he claimed he was an Eastbourne-registered rider, even though he was now riding for Ipswich, but the board ruled that he had to stay at Ipswich.

On 18 March, two ACU inspectors passed the Arlington track fit for the Provincial League provided warning lights were erected and the safety fence was improved. Just under one month later, the control board made a further inspection and felt that neither of the two items referred to by the ACU inspectors had been sufficiently improved to allow for Provincial League racing to take place. The other Provincial League promoters offered their support to Eastbourne, saying they were prepared for their teams to race at Arlington and had no objection to Eastbourne taking its place in the league. The control board said they would announce their final decision in May. So it was a somewhat dubious start to the 1962 season as it still wasn't clear whether the Eagles would be operating in the SAL, the Provincial League or neither, and this was still the position when the first meeting, the Easter Trophy, won by Poole's Geoff Mudge, took place.

Until the SCB's final decision, Eastbourne were restricted to putting on challenge matches, the first of which was against local rivals Poole. The Pirates, who were a much stronger team on paper, were given a real fight with only a last-heat 5-1 robbing the Eagles of victory. The scorers for the Eagles were: Des Lukehurst 11, Dave Still 8, Jim Heard 8, Bob Dugard 6, Ron Swaine 2, John Dugard 2 and Frank Bettis 1. A very strong Plymouth team led by Jimmy Squibb came and put one over the Eagles to the tune of 52-26, this despite the fact the Eagles managed to get Colin Gooddy to help them out.

The final announcement from the Speedway Control Board came on 19 May. Eastbourne were refused permission to join the Provincial League. It was now too late to start the Southern Area League so once again it was back to challenge matches, which were strangely enough against Provincial League teams. It seemed distinctly odd to the Eastbourne management and to the many Eastbourne supporters that their track was safe for challenge matches against Provincial League sides but not for league matches against the same outfits.

The next home match was against Stoke, led by 'Speedy' Pete Jarman. Jarman top scored with 9 points but Eagles still won 46-32. Bob Dugard won the Championship of Sussex, beating a very strong field. The Eagles then beat Leicester, Poole, Wolverhampton and Exeter before finally drawing 39-39 against Rye House. The Eagles rode three matches away from home; at Exeter, where they went down 46-32, at Poole, where they lost 49-29 and at Rye House, again losing, this time by 43 to 34. Frank Bettis and Des Lukehurst won a Best Pairs event before the traditional final meeting, the Supporters' Trophy, won this year by Bob Dugard. Colin Gooddy, who had been allowed to ride for Eastbourne after all as they were now only riding challenge matches, finished top of the Eagles' averages for the year with 11.25, followed by Pete Jarman, who put in 3 appearances averaging 11.00. Frank Bettis was top of the 'regular' team with 7.70.

1963

The 1963 season started on 14 April when Colin Gooddy won the annual Easter Trophy. A high-class field was lined up for what should have been a first-class meeting but, unfortunately, heavy rain spoilt the proceedings. The second meeting, on 5 May, was a challenge against Rye House. The Eagles saw off their old rivals 47-29 with both John and Bob Dugard netting 12-point maximums on a dry and bumpy track. The Eastbourne scorers were: Bob Dugard 12, John Dugard 12, Dave Still 7, Bob Warner 6, Frank Bettis 5, Jim Heard 3 and Ken Vale 3. Eagles then rode away at Weymouth in a challenge match, losing 47-31, and away at Rye House, losing 40-38. The following week's home challenge with Weymouth was postponed and the prestigious Championship of Sussex was abandoned.

At this point, Eastbourne were told by the control board that they could no longer book top Provincial League or National League riders. Dugard was incensed and told the control board that without these riders the crowds would decrease and speedway at Arlington would no longer be viable. In June he defied the control board by putting on a composite meeting that included speedway and was fined £20 by the control board for using National League riders in the event. This was the final straw and Eastbourne shut down. The Speedway Riders' Association were horrified at this turn of events and protested to the control board about their ruling, which was eventually reversed, but the reversal came too late to rescue the 1963 season.

SPEDEWORTH LTD., DALE MARTIN PROMOTIONS, CHARLIE DUGARD PROMOTIONS

proudly present

CAVALCADE

Charlie Dugard Promotions

SPEEDWAY RACING

Spedeworth Limited

STOCK CAR RACING

of

Dave Hughes Promotions

'500' CAR RACING

Dale Martin Promotions

WRESTLING

★ **SPORT** ★

ARLINGTON STADIUM, EASTBOURNE

SUNDAY, 23rd JUNE, 1963

SOUVENIR PROGRAMME   -   ONE SHILLING

WEATHER PERMITTING   RIGHT OF ADMISSION RESERVED

Should it be necessary through any cause to abandon the meeting prior to the sixth race in the programme. Badges will be valid for the next meeting In no circumstances will any subscription be returned

BETTING STRICTLY PROHIBITED   Nº 1678

The programme cover for the meeting in 1963 that got Charlie Dugard into trouble with the Speedway Control Board and led to him shutting down operations at Arlington for the rest of the year.

1964

Before the 1964 season began, Dugard spent about £1,000 on improving the track as a precursor to another application to join the Provincial League. He rebanked the track and built a new stand for 1,000 spectators. In the end, however, they entered a revived Southern Area League, which was renamed the Metropolitan League. As well as Eastbourne the league comprised Ipswich, Rayleigh, Weymouth, Exeter 'B' and Newpool (a joint Newport/Poole junior team).

The season did not start until 24 May so there was no Easter Cup. Instead, the opening meeting was the Sussex Championship, which was won by Ross Gilbertson. The Eagles' first league fixture was an away match at Ipswich, which saw Ipswich run out victors by eight points. The first home league match was against Newpool, which the Eagles won 37-30, matches being staged over twelve heats. Ipswich came on 28 June and were dispatched 41-31.

It was at this point that the Metropolitan League ran into difficulties as Exeter 'B' pulled out and other teams failed to complete their fixtures. Not only that, but the riders seemed to swap teams with alarming regularity so that, for example, Geoff Penniket, as well as being Eastbourne's second-highest scorer, also rode for Newpool; Malcolm Brown rode for both Rayleigh and Weymouth, while Wal Morton rode for Ipswich and Weymouth and Vic Ridgeon rode for Eastbourne and Rayleigh. After one outing with Exeter 'B', Des Lukehurst became the Eagles' top scorer with 26 points. With Ipswich managing to complete more fixtures than any other team, six out of eight, they not surprisingly finished top of the league with Eastbourne, for what it was worth, in second place. One rider who rode in the second halves in 1964 was Eastbourne's current trackman, Roy Prodger. However, Roy's racing career came to an end when, in his own words, 'I crashed on the top bend and hit my nut.'

As a result of this farcical season, Dugard became very disillusioned with the state of lower-league speedway and decided to call it a day. He therefore closed Arlington to speedway and concentrated on stock car racing for the next four years, pulling in crowds of over 8,000. Every winter rumours circulated that speedway was about to return but it was not until the winter of 1968 that the rumours took on a more substantial air.

1964 – Metropolitan League

Date	H/A	Against	W/L	Score
7 June	Away	Ipswich	Lost	32-40
14 June	Home	Newpool	Won	37-30*
28 June	Home	Ipswich	Won	41-31

*Raced for double points

P4 W3 D0 L1 For 110 Against 101 Pts 6 Position 2nd (out of 5)

Rider	Matches	Rides	Points	Average
Geoff Penniket	2	8	21	10.50
Vic Ridgeon	2	8	21	10.50
John Dugard	2	8	17	8.50
Des Lukehurst	3	13	26	8.00
Dave Still	2	7	5	5.60
Ken Vale	1	4	5	5.00
Brian Davies	1	4	4	4.00
Charlie Benham	1	3	2	2.67
D. O'Flynn	3	11	7	2.55
Roy Prodger	1	2	1	2.00
John McAuliffe	1	1	1	1.00
D. Longhorn	1	2	0	0.00
P. Pittingale	1	1	0	0.00

(Only 3 matches ridden; all riders inc.)

A programme cover from 1964.

1969

After a break of four years, the smell of fumes and the roar of the JAP engines was to be heard once more in the Sussex countryside as it was announced that Eastbourne had entered the British League Second Division. A new promotion team calling itself Arlington Promotions, which was in effect former West Ham manager, journalist and ITV sports commentator Dave Lanning and Charlie Dugard's son Bob, with help from old Eagles' favourite Colin Gooddy, had taken over. The British League Second Division was in its second year of operation and included Belle Vue Colts, Canterbury, Rayleigh, Nelson, Middlesbrough, Berwick, Plymouth, Crayford and Reading as well as a new crop for 1969, Ipswich, Crewe, Romford, Long Eaton, King's Lynn II and Eastbourne.

Lanning made his intentions clear from the start: 'It is no good staging speedway at Eastbourne,' he said, 'with a mediocre team. We have to win all our home matches – and a good few away ones into the bargain. We are going to be the smartest team in the league and anyone who rides for us must have immaculate equipment... I'm mounting a publicity drive to make sure everyone in Sussex knows about Eastbourne speedway.' Over the winter, Arlington Promotions poured thousands of pounds into improving the stadium, probably spending more money on the place than had been spent in its entire history.

The new Eastbourne team was a combination of old and new with the biggest potential find being the sixteen-year-old Dave Jessup. To other youngsters Hughie Saunders, Derek Cook, Laurie

Sims and Tony Hall, Lanning added experience in the shape of former Wimbledon, Norwich and West Ham rider Reg Trott, who was appointed captain. But perhaps the biggest masterstroke was in wresting Barry Crowson away from Canterbury after a bitter close-season struggle as Crowson knocked up a string of double-figure scores in the early part of the season.

The new era for Eastbourne dawned on 6 April when the Eagles defeated the King's Lynn Starlets 39-37. As the scoreline shows, it was an exciting tussle with Eastbourne winning thanks to a last-heat decider. The large crowd was enthralled and vowed to return for more of this British League action. The fastest time of the day was 65.8 seconds, recorded by Crowson and Lynn's Graham Edmunds. The Eagles scorers in this, the first match of a new era, were: Crowson 11, Trott 8, Jessup 7, Saunders 5, Sims 4, Hall 2 and Cook 2.

The Eagles then drew at Canterbury in what turned out to be the first of many exciting local derbies. Unfortunately for Eastbourne the Crusaders, led by Graham Miles, Pete Murray and Martyn Piddock took full revenge by winning 40-35 at Arlington eight days later. After a few close results away from home in which the Eagles picked up three points, Ipswich came to Arlington for what can only be described as an amazing match. Following his early run of success, Crowson had been recalled by his parent club, West Ham, and was therefore only present at the stadium as a spectator. However his replacement, Brian Davies, failed to turn up so Crowson put on his leathers and rode for the Eagles. With one race to go, Eastbourne trailed 36-35. In the final race all four sped from the tapes and into the first bend. Unfortunately Ipswich rider Ernie Baker was rammed into the fence. He stayed down and the race was stopped. Baker was adjudged to be the cause of the stoppage and subsequently excluded. The Ipswich team and management were outraged by the decision as it was quite clear to them that Baker had been the victim of first-bend pushing and shoving. Consequently they pulled out of the match leaving the Eagles to take a match-winning 5-0. The Eagles then gained their only away win of the season, 40-38 at Plymouth. Canterbury's Martyn Piddock won the Championship of Sussex and then the Eagles beat Len Silver's Rayleigh 41-36. The experienced Alby Golden was signed as Crowson's replacement but he couldn't stop Eastbourne crashing 60-18 at Belle Vue and 57-21 at Crewe. On 21 September Eastbourne's new management were rewarded for all their hard work when Arlington was used as the venue for an England v. Australasia Test match, England winning 69-38 with Dave Jessup making a valuable contribution to England while another Eagle, Cec Platt, rode for the Aussies. Romford, led by Des Lukehurst, Brian Davies, Ross Gilbertson, Charlie Benham and Phil Woodcock, became the second team to take the league points from Sussex, but Eastbourne finished the season on a high note when they defeated eventual champions Belle Vue Colts 44-34.

The loss of Crowson and an injury to Saunders midway through the season, which kept him out for several matches, badly affected Eastbourne's chances of carrying out Lanning's wishes of winning all their home matches and 'a good few away ones.' Nevertheless it was a good return to league speedway as they finished mid-table, having won 14 and drawn 2 of their 30 matches. In Dave Jessup and Hughie Saunders they had unearthed some real talent, Jessup finishing the season with an average of 6.62 with Saunders going even better, recording 7.00. Lanning had also performed something of a masterstroke with his 'oldies' as well, as Trott finished the season with an 8.70 average and Golden with 7.88.

There is one final note from the season. On 25 May Crowson dead-heated with Crayford's Archie Wilkinson in a match at Arlington. This was the first dead heat ever recorded in the Second Division of the British League!

1969 – British League Second Division

Date	H/A	Against	W/L	Score
6 April	Home	King's Lynn II	Won	39-37
12 April	Away	Canterbury	Drew	39-39
13 April	Home	Berwick	Won	52-24

Above left: The programme cover for Eastbourne's first senior league match in the British League Division Two against King's Lynn on 6 April 1969.

Above right: Barry Crowson, Eastbourne's leading rider in 1969.

Left: Experience and youth. Reg Trott and Dave Jessup in 1969.

Opposite: Eastbourne take on Romford in 1969.

20 April	Home	Canterbury	Lost	35-40
27 April	Away	Doncaster	Lost	35-43
4 May	Home	Teeside	Won	43-35
11 May	Away	King's Lynn II	Drew	38-38
18 May	Home	Nelson	Won	41-37
22 May	Away	Ipswich	Lost	38-39
25 May	Home	Crayford	Won	49.5-28.5
31 May	Away	Rayleigh	Lost	36-42
1 June	Home	Doncaster	Won	47-30
14 June	Away	Nelson	Lost	33-45
18 June	Away	Long Eaton	Lost	30-48
22 June	Home	Ipswich	Won	40-36
30 June	Away	Reading	Lost	28-49
11 July	Away	Plymouth	Won	40-38
17 July	Away	Teeside	Lost	33-45
30 July	Away	Belle Vue II	Lost	18-60
3 August	Home	Rayleigh	Won	41-36
11 August	Away	Crewe	Lost	21-57
17 August	Home	Long Eaton	Won	47-31
23 August	Away	Berwick	Lost	36-41
27 August	Away	Crayford	Lost	26-51
31 August	Home	Crewe	Won	43-34
31 August	Home	Plymouth	Won	47-30
7 September	Home	Reading	Won	45-33
25 September	Away	Romford	Lost	33-45
5 October	Home	Romford	Lost	36-42
26 October	Home	Belle Vue II	Won	44-34

P30 W14 D2 L14 For 1,134.5 Against 1,185.5 Pts 30 Position 8th (out of 16)

Knock-Out Cup

Date	H/A	Against	W/L	Score
8 June	Home	Rayleigh	Lost	37-40

The Eagles' 1970 line-up: From left to right: Dave Jessup, Mac Woolford, Derek Cook, Reg Trott (captain, on bike), Dave Lanning (manager), Laurie Sims, Alby Golden, Hughie Saunders.

1969 – British League Second Division and Knock-Out Cup

Rider	Matches	Rides	Points	BP	Total	Average
Barry Crowson	15	59	145.5	1	146.5	9.93
Reg Trott	30	141	290	19	309	8.70
Alby Golden	14	68	126	8	134	7.88
Hugh Saunders	13	52	78	13	91	7.00
Dave Jessup	31	136	201	24	225	6.62
Derek Cook	28	103	113	24	137	5.32
Laurie Sims	26	101	102	24	126	4.99
Cec Platt	7	20	18	5	23	4.60
John Heddrick	8	26	23	4	27	4.15
Tony Hall	11	29	22	7	29	4.00
Joe Robson	7	17	12	4	16	3.77
Ray Boughtflower	7	15	9	1	10	2.67

THE 1970s

1970

Eastbourne's reasonable first year back in league speedway brought clear hopes of better things to come and the crowds returned to support the Eagles. So many attended the first meeting of the 1970 season that the 'house full' notices went up and hundreds had to be turned away. The Eagles started off the season with six very convincing league wins, although only one of them was away from home, a 41-37 victory at Crayford. The first of the home victories was against Canterbury, 45-33, on 29 March. This was followed by wins over Berwick and Ipswich, who both took heavy beatings. Canterbury came back again, this time in the Knock-Out Cup, with the Eagles clear favourites but, after thirteen heats of pure hard racing, the Crusaders came out on top, winning 44-34. The Eagles maintained their superb league form until 16 May when once again, the Canterbury Crusaders lowered their colours at Kingsmead 42-36.

After a brilliant 47-31 win at Rayleigh and more mammoth home wins, Eastbourne lost at Bradford 44-34. The very next day Eastbourne were thrashed at Ipswich 51-27 and for the first time that season lost the top-of-the-table spot to Canterbury. The Eagles hit back with fine wins at Workington, 45-33, and at third-place Romford 40-38, but defeats at Rochdale 53-25, Reading 45-33 and Doncaster 44-34 left them struggling to get on terms with the league leaders. The Crusaders were invited back, this time for the second leg of the South Coast Cup. The Eagles, who had lost 45-33 at Kingsmead the previous day, lost again at Arlington. However, Eastbourne bounced back, winning at Peterborough and Boston and then drawing at Long Eaton thanks to a last-heat 5-0. The Eagles hit 50-plus scores in all but one of their remaining home matches. Eastbourne finished the season with two away matches at Teeside and Crewe. Victory in either would have put them level on points with eventual league champions Canterbury. Victory in both would have given them the league title. Unfortunately it was not to be as they lost 45-32 at Teeside and 53-25 at Crewe. Although Eastbourne finished second in the league it had been a tremendous year for them and they had unearthed some spectacular junior talent, which augured well for the future. The seventeen-year-old Jessup continued on his record-breaking way, recording an average of 9.69 in just his second season, topping the Eagles' averages. For good measure he also won the Second Division Riders' Championship final. But this wasn't all for the Eastbourne production line as another sixteen-year-old, Gordon Kennett, was given his first run out on a speedway track on 29 March and by 12 April found himself in the team. So wild was Kennett when he started that he picked up the nicknames 'Bronco' and 'Cowboy'. One promoter even said he was so dangerous he should be banned. But by the end of his first season he had ridden in 29 matches for the Eagles and scored at a sensational average of 6.79. Nor were these the only two teenagers spotted by Lanning, as he also gave track debuts to Roger Johns and Gordon Kennett's brother David,

Above left: Former Southampton star Alby Golden added a bit of experience to the Eagles in 1969 and 1970.

Above right: Derek Cook was Eastbourne's second heat leader in 1970.

Reg Trott leads Canterbury's Barry Crowson in the 1970 Championship of Sussex.

Above left: Mac Woolford rode for Eastbourne in 1970 and 1971.

Above right: After the Dugard family, the name most associated with Eastbourne is that of Gordon Kennett, seen here in action. He first rode for the club as a sixteen-year-old junior in 1970. His last season with the Eagles was in 1991. In all he rode 477 times for the club, scoring 5,339 points.

both of whom would turn out to be top riders. One of the reasons Eastbourne was able to unearth such precocious talent was its training school, which ran regularly through the winter months. The cost was £2 plus £4 10s for the hire of a bike for twenty laps.

Of the rest of the team, Cook was second-highest scorer with an average of 8.44, while Trott scored at 7.52 and Golden, Phil Pratt (signed from Poole in mid-season) and Mac Woolford all contributed over 6 points per match. Sims recorded the lowest average and that was only fractionally below 6 at 5.98. No wonder the Eagles had had such a good season.

1970 – British League Second Division

Date	H/A	Against	W/L	Score
29 March	Home	Canterbury	Won	45-33
5 April	Home	Ipswich	Won	53-25
8 April	Away	Crayford	Won	41-37
12 April	Home	Berwick	Won	55-23
10 May	Home	Peterborough	Won	44-33
10 May	Home	Workington	Won	44-34
16 May	Away	Canterbury	Lost	36-42
24 May	Home	Crewe	Won	58-20
30 May	Away	Rayleigh	Won	47-31
31 May	Home	King's Lynn II (Boston)	Won	44-34*
14 June	Home	Rayleigh	Won	56-22
24 June	Away	Bradford	Lost	34-44
25 June	Away	Ipswich	Lost	27-51
28 June	Home	Teeside	Won	47-31

3 July	Away	Workington	Won	45-33
4 July	Away	Berwick	Lost	34-42
9 July	Away	Romford	Won	40-38
12 July	Home	Reading	Won	41-37
18 July	Home	Long Eaton	Won	56-22
19 July	Away	Rochdale	Lost	25-53
20 July	Away	Reading	Lost	33-45
1 August	Home	Doncaster	Won	50-28
16 August	Away	Doncaster	Lost	34-44
29 August	Home	Crayford	Won	51-27
30 August	Home	Romford	Won	50-28
6 September	Home	Bradford	Won	52-26
11 September	Away	Peterborough	Won	45-33
16 September	Away	Boston	Won	40-38
17 September	Away	Long Eaton	Drew	38.5-38.5
24 September	Away	Teeside	Lost	32-45
28 September	Away	Crewe	Lost	25-53
18 October	Home	Rochdale	Won	42-35

*King's Lynn II moved to Boston during the season

P32 W22 D1 L9 For 1,364.5 Against 1,125.5 Pts 45 Position 2nd (out of 17)

Knock-Out Cup

Date	H/A	Against	W/L	Score
26 April	Home	Canterbury	Lost	34-44

1970 – British League Second Division and Knock-Out Cup

Rider	Matches	Rides	Points	BP	Total	Average
Dave Jessup	30	123	285	12	297	9.66
Derek Cook	23	90	169	21	190	8.44
Reg Trott	33	142	242	25	267	7.52
Alby Golden	18	73	112	18	130	7.12
Phil Pratt	13	48	73	12	85	7.08
Gordon Kennett	29	116	166	31	197	6.79
Mac Woolford	29	103	140.5	22	162.5	6.31
Laurie Sims	32	111	147	19	166	5.98
David Kennett	8	25	17	4	21	3.36

1971

With their ever-improving youngsters, it looked as though 1971 would be Eastbourne's year and that they would go one better and become league champions. However, the season started badly when Jessup moved up a division, transferring to Wembley, and Golden decided it was time to retire following a serious injury the season before. Pratt refused to ride for Eastbourne and Cook was whisked back to his parent track Poole after four matches for the Eagles in which he had averaged 10.25. However, none of this seemed to faze the Eastbourne youngsters, who rattled off 11 wins and 1 draw in their first 12 fixtures, starting with a win over reigning champions Canterbury 58-20 followed by Sunderland 59-19, Peterborough 53-25, Workington 45-32, Crewe 54-24, Rochdale complete with a young Peter Collins on his first visit to Arlington 44-34, Romford 50-28 and Boston 49-28 all at home, and 39-39 at Rayleigh, 41-36 at Canterbury, 41-37 at Workington and 40-37 at Romford. Eastbourne's first defeat came in a controversial meeting at Boston where, after several dubious refereeing decisions, the Eagles finally lost 33-45.

In the cup the Eagles again drew Canterbury but there was to be no repeat of the previous year as Eastbourne won the first leg 47-31 at Arlington. With Laurie Sims injured, the Eagles drafted in Bob Dugard for the second leg at Kingsmead. Eastbourne hit three quick 5-1s to lead 18-6 after heat four. In heat nine, Dugard went in hard on the Crusaders' Ted Hubbard, who fell. Much to the amazement of most spectators it was the Canterbury rider who was excluded. This was a signal for pandemonium to break loose. Protesting home supporters climbed on to the track and just about everywhere else with a few even trying to get into the referee's box. When the match was restarted some twenty-five minutes later the Eagles, who had already done enough to ensure the aggregate victory, took it steady, with a 39-39 draw the result. Dugard himself took no further part in the meeting or indeed the season.

Unbeaten after twelve matches and through to the next round of the cup, Eastbourne had a lot to thank their production line of youngsters for. The Kennett brothers were improving all the time and were now both heat leaders and Roger Johns came into the team as a more-than-useful second string but it was yet another junior, Malcolm Ballard, who proved to be this year's sensational find. In his first four matches in league speedway, he scored paid 9 from three rides, paid 10, paid 11 and paid 14. Just fifty days after making his debut, he became an international when he rode for Young England against Young Sweden at Ipswich on 17 June. Three days later he turned out for Young England again, this time at Arlington. He was top scorer with 14 paid 16. On 27 June he became the new Champion of Sussex, beating a top-class field that included Peter Collins, Dave Jessup and John Louis. He was to finish the season with an incredible average of 8.74 and was Eastbourne's top scorer. Lanning had done it again!

In spite of the rise of the juniors, the Eagles received a big blow to their championship hopes on 4 July as Rayleigh came to Arlington, superbly led by ex-Eagles rider Hugh Saunders, and won 40-36. Rocked by this result, Eastbourne followed this with disastrous results away at Crewe, losing 54-24, and two days later at Hull, 41-37, despite a 15-point maximum by guest Arthur Price. The Eagles fought back, however, and responded by thumping Teesside 58-20. Unfortunately, at Workington in the cup, the Eagles hit all sorts of problems and lost 51-27. In the return two days later it looked as though Eastbourne would pull back the deficit but, tragically, Mac Woolford, in trying to avoid a fallen opponent, hit the safety fence in an alarming crash and broke his neck. Although the Eagles won 45-31 they were out of the cup. Yet another product of the Eastbourne training school was brought in to replace Woolford, a young man who had spent most of his boyhood as a track raker, Trevor Geer.

After their cup setback, Eastbourne continued their winning ways in the league, beating Ipswich 46-31. The return was an astonishing demonstration of the strength in depth the Eagles were now showing as, in spite of Ipswich's John Louis, Tony Davey and Pete Bailey all scoring maximums, Eastbourne managed to come away with a 39-39 draw. Big home wins followed at Arlington. A crushing 52-26 defeat at fast-rising Bradford was the only blemish on what was now turning out to be the Eagles' most exciting season for many years. Wins at Teesside 43-35 and Sunderland 46-31 left the Eagles needing just two points from their remaining three matches to take the league title. These were easily secured with a magnificent 39-38 victory at Peterborough on the same day that close rivals Bradford were crashing at Rochdale. Eastbourne then drew at Birmingham and beat Hull to lift the championship by a margin of four points. They had lost just 7 matches out of a total of 32 ridden. The team completed the season by winning the South Coast Cup against Canterbury and the KEN-EX Four-Team Championship.

The previous year, when finishing second, Eastbourne had seven riders who had scored at an average of 6 points per match or more. This year, not counting Derek Cook, who left after just four matches, they had eight, with the lowest being Woolford at 6.67. This would have been enough to make the Eagles' eighth-best rider a heat leader in the Sunderland team!

The Eagles were rewarded for their successful season with a civic reception at which Eastbourne's mayor, Councillor John Robinson, congratulated the Eagles on their achievement. Dave Lanning commented that this was 'an unprecedented gesture in speedway history'.

Left: Laurie Sims rode for Eastbourne from 1969 to 1971.

Below: One of Eastbourne's many young discoveries, Malcolm Ballard avoids his fallen teammate Bobby McNeil in a match against Workington in 1972. Malcolm McKay and Lou Sansom are bringing up the rear.

1971 – British League Second Division

Date	H/A	Against	W/L	Score
4 April	Home	Canterbury	Won	58-20
11 April	Home	Sunderland	Won	59-19
12 April	Away	Rayleigh	Drew	39-39
18 April	Home	Peterborough	Won	53-25
24 April	Away	Canterbury	Won	41-36
25 April	Home	Workington	Won	43-32
7 May	Away	Workington	Won	41-37
9 May	Home	Crewe	Won	54-23
13 May	Away	Romford	Won	40-37
16 May	Home	Rochdale	Won	44-34

Malcolm Ballard was an instant success. He is seen here riding for Young England against Young Sweden just fifty-three days after his league debut.

23 May	Home	Romford	Won	50-28
30 May	Home	Boston	Won	49-28
31 May	Away	Boston	Lost	33-45
24 June	Away	Long Eaton	Won	41-36
4 July	Home	Rayleigh	Lost	36-40
12 July	Away	Crewe	Lost	24-54
14 July	Away	Hull	Lost	37-41
18 July	Home	Teesside	Won	58-20
1 August	Home	Ipswich	Won	46-31
5 August	Away	Ipswich	Drew	39-39
8 August	Home	Birmingham	Won	57-21
25 August	Away	Bradford	Lost	26-52
29 August	Home	Bradford	Won	42-33
9 September	Away	Teesside	Won	43-35
10 September	Away	Rochdale	Lost	37-41
12 September	Home	Berwick	Won	49-29
18 September	Away	Berwick	Lost	29-49
19 September	Away	Sunderland	Won	46-31
26 September	Home	Long Eaton	Won	54-23
1 October	Away	Peterborough	Won	39-38
3 October	Home	Hull	Won	46-32
4 October	Away	Birmingham	Drew	39-39

P32 W22 D3 L7 For 1,394 Against 1,087 Pts 47 Position 1st (out of 17)

Knock-Out Cup

First Round
Bye

Second Round

Date	H/A	Against	W/L	Score
6 June	Home	Canterbury	Won	47-31
12 June	Away	Canterbury	Drew	39-39

Won 86-70 on aggregate

Third Round

Date	H/A	Against	W/L	Score
23 July	Away	Workington	Lost	27-51
25 July	Home	Workington	Won	45-31

Lost 72-82 on aggregate

1971 British League Second Division and Knock-Out Cup

Rider	Matches	Rides	Points	BP	Total	Average
Malcolm Ballard	28	113	235	12	247	8.74
Gordon Kennett	35	148	294	28	322	8.70
David Kennett	36	141	234	30	264	7.49
Laurie Sims	28	93	148	17	165	7.10
Reg Trott	36	135	184	52	236	6.99
Roger Johns	34	126	183	34	217	6.89
Bobby McNeil	21	78	114	19	133	6.82
Mac Woolford	18	57	78	17	95	6.67

1972

Following their success Eastbourne felt that they should be automatically promoted to the First Division but this was refused, so they applied in the normal manner for membership, which was also refused because they were not prepared to pay the £3,500 licence fee. Bob Dugard said he felt Eastbourne were 'entitled to promotion as the new Second Division champions, but if we do well again in 1972 we will go for the top grade even if it means buying a place'.

There were a number of enforced changes to the line-up for 1972. Dave Kennett was transferred to Hackney for £350 and Laurie Sims also moved on. Sadly, Mac Woolford was forced to retire due to the injuries suffered in the cup tie against Workington. Lanning kept faith with his juniors and, instead of splashing out in the transfer market, tried out a number of them including Paul Gachet, Tim Ballard, Simon Bruce and yet another of Charlie's sons, Eric Dugard, to slot in behind Gordon Kennett, Malcolm Ballard, Reg Trott, Derek Cook (who returned to the team), Bobby McNeil, Roger Johns and Trevor Geer. Crowds were around the 3,000 mark and it was considered surprising if three or four coaches full of travelling supporters did not go to the away matches to cheer on their heroes. Unfortunately the Eagles did not live up to expectations, often throwing away silly points on their travels. In fact they only managed away wins at Sunderland 42-36, Ellesmere Port 42-36 and Bradford 40-38 and a 39-39 draw at Rayleigh. Six matches were lost by just two points, though there were also two teams who managed 50 against the Eagles, those being Peterborough and Crewe within three days of each other.

At home the Eagles dropped just one point at home to Rayleigh, while most teams were beaten before they arrived. Scunthorpe, Ellesmere Port, Workington, Berwick, Hull, Bradford and Sunderland were all hit for 50-plus. It was Crewe who were to take Eastbourne's place as the star team of the Second Division as they took the League title, the Knock-Out Cup and provided the Second Division Riders' champion in super Aussie Phil Crump. Crump proved his brilliance wherever and whenever he rode, including at Arlington where it was due to him that Crewe put Eastbourne out of the cup in the semi-finals by just six points after Eastbourne had beaten Long Eaton and Boston on their way there.

Eastbourne dropped down the league to finish in fifth position but did have some success, beating Rayleigh for the Manser Trophy and thrashing Canterbury in the South Coast Cup. During the year they were invited to ride in West Germany against a local side, Olching, and despite a gallant effort lost 49-29. On the plus side for Eastbourne, Ballard continued his meteoric rise, topping the averages with 9.94, setting a new track record of 62.4 seconds and representing the Eagles in the Second Division Riders' final scoring 8 points from his final 3 outings. Kennett also showed great improvement, especially in technique, as in came a more polished style to replace a lot of the wildness. The biggest improvement of all came from Bobby McNeil, who rose from reserve to heat leader during the season. Towards the end of the season, with the youngsters doing so well, Reg Trott decided to call it a day. This left Malcolm Ballard, at the grand old age of twenty-two, as the oldest member of the team. Rayleigh's Allen Emmett won the Championship of Sussex and, along with sixteen-year-old Paul Gachet, won the Southern Best Pairs. Emmett also won the British Junior Championship, forcing Eastbourne's Gordon Kennett into the runner-up position.

1972 – British League Second Division

Date	H/A	Against	W/L	Score
2 April	Home	Boston	Won	47-31
3 April	Away	Boston	Lost	35-43
9 April	Home	Canterbury	Won	46-32
16 April	Home	West Ham	Won	46-32
18 April	Away	West Ham	Lost	32-45
24 April	Away	Birmingham	Lost	30-48
30 April	Home	Long Eaton	Won	42-36
30 April	Home	Scunthorpe	Won	55-22
6 May	Away	Berwick	Lost	37-40
7 May	Away	Sunderland	Won	42-36
13 May	Away	Canterbury	Lost	38-40
14 May	Home	Ellesmere Port	Won	56-21
15 May	Away	Rayleigh	Drew	39-39
21 May	Home	Workington	Won	51-26
28 May	Home	Teesside	Won	43-34
11 June	Home	Peterborough	Won	48-30

Above left: Roger Johns, later to become a Wimbledon stalwart, rode for Eastbourne from 1971 to 1973.

Above right: Trevor Geer had two spells at Arlington as a rider from 1972 to 1974 and 1979 to 1981. He later returned as manager.

16 June	Away	Peterborough	Lost	25-52
19 June	Away	Crewe	Lost	19-59
20 June	Away	Ellesmere Port	Won	42-36
12 July	Away	Bradford	Won	40-38
13 July	Away	Teesside	Lost	32-46
16 July	Home	Berwick	Won	51-26
11 August	Away	Workington	Lost	31-47
13 August	Home	Rayleigh	Drew	39-39
3 September	Home	Hull	Won	53-24
4 September	Away	Scunthorpe	Lost	37.5-39.5
10 September	Home	Birmingham	Won	40-36
20 September	Away	Hull	Lost	38-40
21 September	Away	Long Eaton	Lost	35-43
24 September	Home	Bradford	Won	58-20
1 October	Home	Crewe	Won	41-37
8 October	Home	Sunderland	Won	55-23

P32 W18 D2 L12 For 1,323.5 Against 1,160.5 Pts 38 Position 5th (out of 17)

Yet another of Eastbourne's young sensations, Bobby McNeill, seen here shortly after winning the Silver Helmet from Lou Sansom of Workington in 1973.

Knock-Out Cup

First Round
Bye

Second Round

Date	H/A	Against	W/L	Score
8 June	Away	Long Eaton	Won	40-38
25 June	Home	Long Eaton	Won	50-28

Won 90-66 on aggregate

Third Round

Date	H/A	Against	W/L	Score
2 July	Away	Boston	Lost	38-40
9 July	Home	Boston	Won	45-33

Won 83-73 on aggregate

Semi-Final

Date	H/A	Against	W/L	Score
30 July	Home	Crewe	Won	44-34
31 July	Away	Crewe	Lost	31-47

Lost 75-81 on aggregate

1972 – British League Second Division and Knock-Out Cup

Rider	Matches	Rides	Points	BP	Total	Average
Malcolm Ballard	32	134	322	11	333	9.94
Gordon Kennett	38	164	324	32	356	8.68
Bobby McNeil	37	154	268	34	302	7.88
Roger Johns	37	148	236	32	268	7.24
Reg Trott	21	75	88	17	105	5.60
Trevor Geer	36	118	131.5	31	162.5	5.51
Derek Cook	22	73	86	13	99	5.43
Paul Gachet	19	63	67	14	81	5.14
Simon Bruce	16	43	34	8	42	3.90

1973

With Eastbourne only finishing fifth in 1972, Dugard did not pursue his plan to seek promotion to the First Division. The main consequence of this was that both Malcolm Ballard and Gordon Kennett left for higher-grade racing with Oxford. Derek Cook also left for Canterbury. This left Bobby McNeil and Roger Johns to take over the two major positions in the Eagles side at the start of the 1973 season. To replace the experience of Trott, Lanning brought in the even older fifty-year-old Jimmy Squibb. Squibb had first ridden at Arlington as far back as 1947 when he was a member of the visiting Southampton team. Mike Vernam was signed from Reading and, after a long wrangle, Ross Gilbertson from Canterbury, who took Eric Dugard's place after the latter was injured later in the season.

The season started badly with two successive home defeats in challenge matches to Canterbury and Peterborough as well as two away defeats, none of them league matches. When the league did get under way the first match at home to Boston was abandoned with the score 7-5 to the visitors. The Eagles then suffered a double blow, a home Knock-Out Cup reverse to Canterbury followed by a 54-24 defeat at Barrow. On 11 May the tide began to turn as Eastbourne snatched a 39-39 draw at Sunderland and then a 41-37 win at Berwick the next day. After just fourteen matches with Eastbourne, Vernam left to go to Hull. His place was taken by yet another sixteen-year-old training school sensation, Neil Middleditch, the son of the former Hastings star Ken. It was an event surrounding Middleditch that was to cause great controversy later in the season. In the ninth heat of the match at Long Eaton, with the scores 26-22 in Long Eaton's favour, Middleditch was excluded for ducking under the tapes at the start of heat eight. Eastbourne argued that Strachan had rolled forward and it was this that had caused Middleditch to get a flyer and that therefore the referee, Mr E.W. Roe, should have ruled an unsatisfactory start with all four riders back. Mr Roe, however, refused to change his decision, so the whole Eastbourne team walked out, handing Long Eaton five 5-os and the match 51-22.

After the somewhat shaky start to the season, the Eagles were proving invincible at home and won every home league match for the first time since 1970. Only Workington and Barrow, along with eventual champions Boston, came close. In the match with Boston on 18 August, Eastbourne were trailing 37-35 with one heat left and took a gamble by giving Neil Middleditch a reserve ride. In third place throughout the race, Middleditch just did not give up, finally catching Boston's Arthur Price on the line to give his team a 5-1 and victory in the match, 40-38. Beating the eventual champions was a great achievement in itself, but it was made all the more remarkable by the fact that the oldest rider in the team that day was just twenty years fifty-five days old. The age of many of the Eastbourne team created an unexpected problem as Dave Lanning pointed out that they had difficulties in transporting their riders to meetings as 'half of them aren't old enough to drive'. Lanning's help in getting them to the track each week didn't stop them throwing him into the Arlington well, which was situated in the middle of the centre green, at the end of each season! In the end, in spite of managing only two away wins all season, Eastbourne finished third in the league. McNeill was top of the Eagles' averages with 9.34, followed by Gilbertson on 8.88 and Johns on 8.59.

Individually it was a successful year for McNeil as he took the Silver Helmet from Workington's Lou Sansom in July and came second in the Second Division Riders' Championship after losing to Arthur Price in a run-off for first place. Along with Geer, he also rode for England against Poland and Sweden. Johns won the Championship of Sussex.

Eastbourne made a little bit of history in the final meeting of the season as they lost away at Rayleigh 48-47. It was to prove to be the last ever meeting at the Rayleigh Weir stadium.

1973 – British League Second Division

Date	H/A	Against	W/L	Score
17 April	Away	Barrow	Lost	24-54
23 April	Away	Boston	Lost	30-48
11 May	Away	Sunderland	Drew	39-39
12 May	Away	Berwick	Won	41-37
20 May	Home	Crewe	Won	48-29
27 May	Home	Berwick	Won	55-23
3 June	Home	Ellesmere Port	Won	51-27
10 June	Home	Peterborough	Won	50-28
15 June	Away	Peterborough	Lost	29-49
19 June	Away	Ellesmere Port	Lost	29-49
23 June	Away	Rayleigh	Won	44-34
24 June	Home	Sunderland	Won	53-25
1 July	Home	Barrow	Won	40-37
9 July	Away	Crewe	Lost	30-48
11 July	Away	Bradford	Lost	35-43
15 July	Home	Scunthorpe	Won	47-31
22 July	Home	Chesterton	Won	43-35
23 July	Away	Birmingham	Lost	37-41
29 July	Home	Workington	Won	40-38
2 August	Away	Chesterton	Lost	31-47
12 August	Home	Rayleigh	Won	42-36
18 August	Home	Boston	Won	40-38

23 August	Away	Teesside	Lost	27-51
26 August	Home	Teesside	Won	45-33
2 September	Home	Hull	Won	52-26
6 September	Away	Long Eaton	Lost	22-51
9 September	Home	Birmingham	Won	42-35
10 September	Away	Scunthorpe	Lost	34-44
16 September	Home	Canterbury	Won	43-35
19 September	Away	Hull	Drew	39-39
23 September	Home	Bradford	Won	49-29
23 September	Home	Long Eaton	Won	51-27
5 October	Away	Workington	Lost	32-46
13 October	Away	Canterbury	Lost	35-42

P34 W19 D2 L13 For 1,349 Against 1,294 Position 3rd (out of 18)

Knock-Out Cup

First Round

Date	H/A	Against	W/L	Score
13 May	Home	Canterbury	Lost	37-41
19 May	Away	Canterbury	Lost	34-44

Lost 71-85 on aggregate

Above left: Jimmy Squibb in 1973. He had first ridden at Arlington in 1947 as a member of the Southampton team.

Above right: The third of Charlie Dugard's sons, Eric, rode for the Eagles for nine seasons from 1973 to 1981.

1973 – British League Second Division and Knock-Out Cup

Rider	Matches	Rides	Points	BP	Total	Average
Bobby McNeil	34	140	311	16	327	9.34
Ross Gilbertson	11	41	81	10	91	8.88
Roger Johns	32	135	274	16	290	8.59
Paul Gachet	36	141	239	19	258	7.32
Trevor Geer	36	131	169	36	205	6.26
Mike Vernam	14	47	59	7	66	5.62
Neil Middleditch	22	83	89	11	100	4.82
Eric Dugard	26	81	75	17	92	4.54
Jimmy Squibb	28	92	79	17	96	4.17

1974

There were more changes to the team in 1974 as Dave Lanning and Bob Dugard were determined to get back to the top of the league so that they could apply for that First Division place again. Gilbertson, who had only been a temporary replacement, retired and Johns left to try his luck with First Division Wimbledon. In their places came Pete Sampson from Barrow, the veteran former Eagles rider Pete Jarman from Stoke and, incredibly, yet another sixteen-year-old prodigy in Steve Weatherley.

The season started well for the Eagles. Not since 1971 had Eastbourne produced such a magnificent run of scores home and away. Week in, week out opponents were defeated as the team took off in sensational style. Out of 18 home matches the Eagles notched up 50 points in 12 of them. And yet incredibly they managed to lose one match, 39-38, to Canterbury, who could only finish tenth in the league and who Eastbourne had already knocked out of the cup, beating them 47-31 at Arlington. Away from home, they won 7 and drew 3. Significantly however, they lost a further 5 away matches by the tantalising score of 40-38. In the end, Eastbourne could only manage second place in the league to Birmingham, finishing four points behind them. Having drawn 3 away matches and lost 5 40-38, it meant that just 14 more race points would have netted the Eagles 15 match points and a runaway victory in the league by 11 points. A real case of so near and yet so far. What was even worse for Eastbourne was that Birmingham also won the cup after the Eagles had established what looked like a winning 16-point first-leg lead. Just to rub the salt in, Birmingham's Second Division individual champion, Phil Herne, took the Championship of Sussex with a 15-point maximum, as well as winning the Eastbourne round of the World Championship. During the season there proved to be some needle between the Birmingham and Eastbourne supporters as, following a great 39-39 draw at Birmingham, the windows on the Eagles Supporters' Club coach were smashed in. It was a long cold journey home for the Eastbourne faithful but the league point had made it worthwhile.

McNeil, Geer and Gachet proved to be a formidable heat-leader trio in 1974, with all three of them averaging over 8 points per match. They were given able backing by Sampson, Middleditch, Jarman and newcomer Steve Weatherley, who scored a paid 9-point three-ride maximum on his very first outing. He finished his first-ever season with an average of 6.41. With so many brilliant youngsters now in the team, the British Junior Championship looked almost like an Eastbourne home meeting although, in the end, only Middleditch finished in the top three.

1974 – British League Second Division

Date	H/A	Against	W/L	Score
7 April	Home	Ellesmere Port	Won	49-29
28 April	Home	Weymouth	Won	52-26
29 April	Away	Scunthorpe	Won	46-32
6 May	Away	Crewe	Lost	23-55
7 May	Away	Weymouth	Won	48-30

12 May	Home	Teesside	Won	44-34
14 May	Away	Ellesmere Port	Drew	39-39
19 May	Home	Sunderland	Won	55-23
26 May	Home	Peterborough	Won	57-21
27 May	Away	Rye House	Won	49-29
2 June	Home	Barrow	Won	47-31
7 June	Away	Peterborough	Lost	35-43
23 June	Home	Bradford	Won	58-20
28 June	Away	Workington	Drew	39-39
30 June	Home	Canterbury	Lost	38-39
7 July	Home	Crewe	Won	54-24
12 July	Away	Sunderland	Lost	38-40
13 July	Away	Berwick	Lost	38-40
14 July	Home	Coatbridge	Won	51-27
23 July	Away	Barrow	Won	39-38
24 July	Away	Bradford	Lost	38-40
27 July	Away	Canterbury	Won	44-34
4 August	Home	Scunthorpe	Won	54-23
5 August	Away	Birmingham	Drew	39-39
11 August	Home	Stoke	Won	51-27
22 August	Away	Stoke	Won	42-36
25 August	Home	Boston	Won	41.5-36.5
26 August	Away	Boston	Lost	38-40
1 September	Home	Long Eaton	Won	55-23
15 September	Home	Berwick	Won	58-20
19 September	Away	Teesside	Won	40-37
20 September	Away	Coatbridge	Lost	36-42
22 September	Home	Rye House	Won	59-19
26 September	Away	Long Eaton	Lost	38-40
29 September	Home	Workington	Won	57-21
20 October	Home	Birmingham	Won	47-31

P36 W24 D3 L9 For 1,636.5 Against 1,166.5 Pts 51 Position 2nd (out of 19)

Knock-Out Cup

First Round
Bye

Second Round

Date	H/A	Against	W/L	Score
4 May	Away	Canterbury	Lost	34-44
5 May	Home	Canterbury	Won	47-31

Won 81-75 on aggregate

Third Round

Date	H/A	Against	W/L	Score
14 July	Home	Workington	Won	50-28
26 July	Away	Workington	Lost	35-43

Won 85-71 on aggregate

Semi-Final

Date	H/A	Against	W/L	Score
23 August	Away	Coatbridge	Lost	29-48
1 September	Home	Coatbridge	Won	56-21

Won 85-69 on aggregate

Final

Date	H/A	Against	W/L	Score
20 October	Home	Birmingham	Won	47-31
21 October	Away	Birmingham	Lost	27-50

Lost 74-81 on aggregate

1974 – British League Second Division and Knock-Out Cup

Rider	Matches	Rides	Points	BP	Total	Average
Bobby McNeil	33	124	254	18	272	8.77
Trevor Geer	43	174	346	22	368	8.46
Paul Gachet	43	176	317	48	365	8.30
Mike Sampson	35	134	242	19	261	7.79
Neil Middleditch	43	169	280	46	326	7.72
Pete Jarman	41	139	200	43	243	6.99
Steve Weatherley	20	59	78.5	16	94.5	6.41
Martin Yeates	34	122	170	21	191	6.26
Eric Dugard	9	25	27	6	33	5.28

1975

In 1975, the British League Second Division changed its name to the New National League. Eastbourne's record in the Second Division since 1970 looked like this: second, first, fifth, third, second. The most impressive aspect of this was that this run of success was nearly all down to the never-ending stream of teenage talent coming out of its own training school. This incredible run continued as Gachet, Middleditch and Weatherley became the three heat leaders for 1975 following the departures of McNeil and Geer.

Having finished runners-up in both the league and cup the previous year, the Eagles' management were determined to go one better in at least one of the trophies. Things started well as Eastbourne thumped Boston 52-26 in the league on 30 March in Arlington's opening meeting of the season. This was followed by further league victories against Weymouth and Crayford and a cup success over close rivals Canterbury. Away from home the Eagles were not quite so successful, having to wait until 20 May for their first away victory, over Weymouth, 45-33. This was followed by another away victory over Rye House, but a shock defeat at home at the hands of Newcastle, 40-37, dented the Eagles' title aspirations. There were further away defeats at Stoke and Scunthorpe, but Eastbourne got back into their stride with a 60-18 massacre of Paisley and an away win at Crayford.

In the cup, Eastbourne put one over on their previous year's rivals Birmingham, beating them 82-74 in the quarter-finals. More league success followed with some further high scores, 53-25 against Teeside and 61-17 against Mildenhall. Results were also going well away from home as the Eagles beat Mildenhall 41-37 and recorded a fine win at Crewe 46-31; this at a venue where Eastbourne's highest previous score had been 31. Having already won two matches by scores of 60-18 and 61-17, incredibly they were to do even better with a 63-15 annihilation of Bradford. Only Eric Dugard's fall prevented the Eagles from scoring a perfect 65.

Back in the cup semi-final, Eastbourne were once again to hit the 60-point mark as they dispatched Weymouth 60-18 at home to win 96-60 on aggregate and march into the final against Workington. After losing the first leg away 47-41 in a match in which only Middleditch rode to his true potential, the Eagles were determined not to be runners-up again and pulled out all the stops to record a magnificent 52-25 victory back at Arlington to take the 1975 Knock-Out Cup 83-72 on aggregate.

Although in the end Eastbourne managed 7 away victories in the league it wasn't good enough and they found themselves slipping down the table to fourth place. Nevertheless it had been another good year for the Eastbourne youngsters. Both Gachet and Middleditch upped their averages to 9.87 and 9.62 respectively, while Weatherley, in only his second season, turned in an incredible 8.06. On 3 August, he became the first rider to get round the Arlington circuit in under sixty seconds when he set a new track record of 59.8 seconds. Middleditch scored a superb victory in the British Junior Championship at Canterbury in which Steve Weatherley was runner-up. Gachet represented Eastbourne in the New National League Riders' Championship and scored 6 points from his first 2 rides. His chances of a win, however, were dashed after a nasty pile-up in his third ride.

It goes without saying, of course, that yet another Eastbourne Training school junior joined the ranks of the first team this year. His name was Colin Richardson, coming in with a first-year average of 5.24.

1975 – New National League

Date	H/A	Against	W/L	Score
3 March	Home	Boston	Won	52-26
31 March	Away	Boston	Lost	30-48
9 April	Lost	Bradford	Lost	36-42
28 April	Away	Birmingham	Lost	33-45
3 May	Away	Paisley	Lost	32-45
4 May	Home	Weymouth	Won	43-34
20 May	Away	Weymouth	Won	45-33
25 May	Home	Rye House	Won	52-26
26 May	Away	Rye House	Won	45-31
1 June	Home	Coatbridge	Won	55-23
8 June	Home	Crayford	Won	41-37
15 June	Home	Newcastle	Lost	37-40
19 June	Away	Stoke	Lost	24-54
23 June	Away	Scunthorpe	Lost	38-40
29 June	Home	Paisley	Home	60-18
1 July	Away	Crayford	Won	40-38
13 July	Home	Mildenhall	Won	61-17
13 July	Home	Teesside	Won	53-25

'Speedy' Pete Jarman had ridden for Eastbourne in the 1960s. He returned to lead them to their first Knock-Out Cup win in 1975.

16 July	Away	Mildenhall	Won	41-37
20 July	Home	Scunthorpe	Won	57-21
27 July	Home	Workington	Won	46-32
1 August	Away	Peterborough	Lost	34-44
3 August	Home	Stoke	Won	52-26
4 August	Away	Newcastle	Lost	34-44
10 August	Home	Crewe	Won	55-23
10 August	Home	Peterborough	Won	59-19
11 August	Away	Crewe	Won	46-31
17 August	Home	Ellesmere Port	Won	53-24
24 August	Home	Birmingham	Won	45-33
28 August	Away	Teesside	Won	40-38
29 August	Away	Workington	Lost	38-40
31 August	Home	Bradford	Won	63-15
16 September	Away	Ellesmere Port	Lost	30-48
28 September	Home	Berwick	Won	50-28
28 September	Home	Canterbury	Won	48-30
3 October	Away	Coatbridge	Won	40-38
4 October	Away	Berwick	Lost	31-47
25 October	Away	Canterbury	Lost	37-40

P38 W25 D0 L13 For 1,676 Against 1,280 Pts 50 Position 4th (out of 20)

Knock-Out Cup

First Round
Bye

Second Round

Date	H/A	Against	W/L	Score
10 May	Away	Canterbury	Lost	37-40
11 May	Home	Canterbury	Won	49-29

Won 86-69 on aggregate

Third Round

Date	H/A	Against	W/L	Score
6 July	Home	Birmingham	Won	45-33
14 July	Away	Birmingham	Lost	37-41

Won 82-74 on aggregate

Semi-Final

Date	H/A	Against	W/L	Score
21 September	Home	Weymouth	Won	60-18
23 September	Away	Weymouth	Lost	36-42

Won 96-60 on aggregate

Final

Date	H/A	Against	W/L	Score
17 October	Away	Workington	Lost	31-47
19 October	Home	Workington	Won	52-25

Won 83-72 on aggregate

1975 – New National League and Knock-Out Cup

Rider	Matches	Rides	Points	BP	Total	Average
Paul Gachet	44	184	431	23	454	9.87
Neil Middleditch	44	185	422	23	445	9.62

Steve Weatherley	42	173	294	55	349	8.07
Pete Jarman	45	177	286	38	324	7.32
Mike Sampson	42	166	261	41	302	7.28
Eric Dugard	46	148	163	40	203	5.49
Colin Richardson	40	123	133	28	161	5.24
Terry Barclay	6	18	13	4	17	3.78

1976

Once again, Eastbourne lost their two top riders to the British League as Gachet left for White City while Middleditch went to Poole. At first Eastbourne were not too worried. They were hoping for big things from Weatherley and Richardson and had found their winter discoveries in Steve Naylor and Roger Abel. But things did not turn out quite as hoped. The Eagles started the season well enough at home, but away from home they suffered several heavy defeats, including a 51-27 loss at Workington. Abel did not start like the usual Eastbourne discovery and was dropped from the team while, although Naylor did get off to a good start and looked like being well on his way to becoming the next teenage star, he broke his ankle in a motorcycle accident and was out for the rest of the season. Another youngster was drafted in, though unusually not an Arlington discovery, as Ian Gledhill was loaned from Reading.

Eastbourne lost their undefeated home record on 23 May, going down 40-38 to Newcastle, but it was to be the only home match they lost all season and for a four-week run in August and September they looked invincible at home, rattling off scores of 57-21 against Crayford, 50-28 against Ellesmere Port, 50-26 against Berwick, 55-23 against Weymouth and 53-24

Above left: Two more of Eastbourne's discoveries, Steve Weatherley (left) and Neil Middleditch. Middleditch is holding the 1975 Junior Championship trophy, Weatherley the runner-up cup.

Above right: Colin Richardson, another highly successful junior from the Eastbourne production line.

against Canterbury. Unfortunately it was their away form that let them down as they could only manage to win one away match all season and that was not until 7 September, when they defeated Crayford 42-36. In the end they finished in their worst league position since 1969, coming eighth. It was a similar story in the cup as they were bundled out in the first round, 84-72 on aggregate by Oxford.

Towards the end of the season, Eastbourne took part in an Inter-League Four-Team event at Arlington, where they met White City, Wimbledon and Belle Vue, who included the new World Champion Peter Collins. A very large crowd saw White City, led by a former Eagle, the brilliant Gordon Kennett, win the event. Individually, Steve Weatherley lived up to his reputation, finishing the season with an unbelievable 10.27 average and once again finishing runner-up in the British Junior Championship. This time he had the great misfortune to come up against another precocious youngster just starting out in speedway, future World Champion Michael Lee. Weatherley also won the Championship of Sussex with great ease and represented the Eagles in the National (the 'New' had been dropped) League Riders' final, where he scored 10 points.

Behind Weatherley, Richardson, although still showing promise, had not quite lived up to the expectations of many who had been somewhat spoiled by the immediate success of riders like Jessup, Kennett, Ballard, McNeil and Weatherley, although he did manage third place in the British Junior Championship behind Lee and teammate Weatherley. In fact it was the third of the Dugard brothers, Eric, who proved to be second-highest scorer with an average of 7.03, while the veteran Jarman was the third heat leader with 6.74. After his initial lack of success, Abel fought his way back into the team and began to show real promise towards the end of the season. In spite of what by their own high standards was a poor season, the Eastbourne management, now back in the sole hands of the Dugard family (Charlie, Bob and John), had ambitious plans for the stadium and launched a development fund aimed at improving facilities so that they could bring First Division speedway to Arlington. The plans included a new covered grandstand with a restaurant, bar and glass enclosure overlooking the track.

1976 – National League

Date	H/A	Against	W/L	Score
11 April	Home	Stoke	Won	52-26
18 April	Home	Rye House	Won	45-33
19 April	Away	Rye House	Lost	33-44
24 April	Away	Berwick	Lost	33-45
2 May	Home	Paisley	Won	54-24
7 May	Away	Coatbridge	Lost	32-45
9 May	Home	Scunthorpe	Won	59-19
23 May	Home	Newcastle	Lost	40-38
4 June	Away	Peterborough	Lost	29-49
6 June	Home	Peterborough	Won	41-36
10 June	Away	Teesside	Lost	37-41
19 June	Away	Paisley	Lost	31-47
20 June	Away	Workington	Lost	21-57
25 June	Away	Boston	Lost	24-54
27 June	Home	Boston	Won	42-36
4 July	Home	Coatbridge	Won	59-19
8 July	Away	Stoke	Lost	35-43
18 July	Home	Mildenhall	Won	45-33
21 July	Away	Mildenhall	Lost	28-50
25 July	Home	Workington	Won	41-35
26 July	Away	Scunthorpe	Lost	30-48
5 August	Away	Oxford	Lost	25-53
8 August	Home	Teesside	Won	46-32
15 August	Home	Crayford	Won	57-21
17 August	Away	Weymouth	Lost	29-49

22 August	Home	Ellesmere Port	Won	50-28
29 August	Home	Berwick	Won	50-26
29 August	Home	Weymouth	Won	55-23
5 September	Home	Canterbury	Won	53-24
7 September	Away	Crayford	Won	42-36
13 September	Away	Newcastle	Lost	23-55
14 September	Away	Ellesmere Port	Lost	35-42
3 October	Home	Oxford	Won	49-29
16 October	Away	Canterbury	Lost	32-45

P34 W17 D0 L17 For 1,361 Against 1,281 Pts 34 Position 8th (out of 18)

Knock-Out Cup

First Round
Bye

Second Round

Date	H/A	Against	W/L	Score
13 May	Away	Oxford	Lost	31-47
16 May	Home	Oxford	Won	41-37

Lost 72-84 on aggregate

1976 – National League and Knock-Out Cup

Rider	Matches	Rides	Points	BP	Total	Average
Steve Weatherley	32	143	362	8	370	10.35
Eric Dugard	36	149	231	31	262	7.03
Pete Jarman	35	122	185	21	206	6.75
Colin Richardson	36	152	214	33	247	6.50
Mike Sampson	24	101	150	14	164	6.50
Ian Gledhill	15	46	65	9	74	6.44
Steve Naylor	13	47	53	11	64	5.48
Roger Abel	26	88	98	18	116	5.27
Ian Fletcher	20	62	57	10	67	4.32

1977

There is no doubt that 1977 will go down in history as the most successful season the Eagles have ever had both as a team and individually. Steve Weatherley left at the end of 1976 to move up a division and was replaced by former Eagle Dave Kennett. With that one change, which on the face of it looked as though it would weaken the team, Eastbourne's poor showing in 1976 turned into a total triumph in 1977. Success followed success, win followed win, thrashing followed thrashing as the rest of the league found it impossible to live with the Eagles. At Arlington the only visitors to perform well were British League sides Wolverhampton, in the Inter-League Cup, and Belle Vue in a challenge match.

In the National League it was records all the way, particularly at home, where the 60-point barrier was broken against Berwick 62-16, Workington 63-15, Mildenhall 61-17, Glasgow 60-18 and Berwick again in the National League Knock-Out Cup final 61-16, still the record score for a cup final leg. Only Canterbury, Edinburgh and Ellesmere Port were able to stop Eastbourne hitting the 50-point mark and they were all 49-point scores.

Away from home there were league wins at Rye House 47-31, Coatbridge 46-32, Berwick 47-31, Workington 41-37, Stoke 54-24, Scunthorpe 45-33, Crayford 49-29, Mildenhall 40-38, Edinburgh 48-30, Weymouth 41-37, Newport 43-35 and Newcastle 43-34, as well as four-team victories at Canterbury, Rye House and Crayford and a challenge at Crayford 52-25. The team steamrollered its way through the opposition. In one two-month period from 12 June to 12

August, they won fourteen straight league matches as well as performing a Knock-Out Cup double over reigning league champions and cup holders Newcastle. At the end of the season they won the league by seven clear points, going on to complete the double by annihilating Berwick in the cup final 98-57. As if this wasn't enough, the crowning glory came on 4 September when the Eagles stunned the speedway world by beating three British league clubs, Poole, Wimbledon and eventual British League champions White City, in a four-team event.

Much of this came about because of the staggering improvement in form of all four of Eastbourne's leading riders. Richardson upped his average to 10.63, the highest yet recorded by an Eastbourne rider. In all, he recorded twenty league maximums. Kennett averaged 8.37 and Dugard 8.25. But the real revelation was Mike Sampson. Sampson had plodded along with the Eagles since 1974, averaging 6 or 7 points per season. This year his average shot up to double figures as he turned in a score of 10.09. Unsurprisingly, Richardson took the National League Riders' Championship at Wimbledon with a 15-point maximum, the first time this had been achieved, and this in spite of suffering from flu. He also took the Silver Helmet from Brian Clark on 31 May and defended it successfully against Tom Owen, Ted Hubbard and Steve Koppe before losing it to Martin Yeates on 3 October. He also equalled the Arlington track record. At the end of the season, skipper Pete Jarman retired, still on an average of 7.25.

During the season, Eastbourne held a special challenge match against Ipswich, the 1976 British League champions. The Eagles' team was not the current team but a special team made up of their training school discoveries who had moved on. The line-up was Gordon Kennett, Steve Weatherley, Trevor Geer, Bobby McNeil, Dave Jessup, Roger Johns and Neil Middleditch. They defeated the British League champions by 42 points to 36. It was a very proud moment for all those involved with Eastbourne's winter training school.

1977 – National League

Date	H/A	Against	W/L	Score
27 March	Home	Ellesmere Port	Won	49-29
9 April	Away	Boston	Lost	36-42
10 April	Home	Rye House	Won	51-27
11 April	Away	Rye House	Won	47-31
17 April	Home	Newport	Won	59-19
24 April	Home	Edinburgh	Won	49-29
1 May	Home	Berwick	Won	62-16
10 May	Away	Ellesmere Port	Lost	35-43
19 May	Away	Oxford	Lost	34-44
22 May	Home	Oxford	Won	53-25
29 May	Home	Newcastle	Won	52-26
30 May	Away	Newcastle	Lost	37-39
12 June	Home	Canterbury	Won	49-29
17 June	Away	Coatbridge	Won	46-32*
18 June	Away	Berwick	Won	47-31
19 June	Home	Scunthorpe	Won	57-21
26 June	Home	Crayford	Won	51-26
3 July	Home	Teesside	Won	59-19
8 July	Away	Workington	Won	41-37
9 July	Away	Stoke	Won	54-24
18 July	Away	Scunthorpe	Won	45-33
24 July	Home	Workington	Won	63-15
26 July	Away	Crayford	Won	49-29
31 July	Home	Weymouth	Won	54-24
3 August	Away	Mildenhall	Won	40-38
5 August	Home	Boston	Won	57-20
13 August	Away	Canterbury	Lost	37-41
14 August	Home	Mildenhall	Won	61-17
18 August	Away	Teesside	Lost	38-40

19 August	Away	Edinburgh	Won	48-30
30 August	Away	Weymouth	Won	41-37
11 September	Home	Glasgow	Won	60-18*
11 September	Home	Peterborough	Won	54-24
16 September	Away	Peterborough	Lost	36-42
18 September	Home	Stoke	Won	59-19
7 October	Away	Newport	Won	42-36

*Coatbridge moved to Glasgow mid-season

P36 W29 D0 L7 For 1,752 Against 1,052 Pts 58 Position 1st (out of 19)

Knock-Out Cup

First Round

Date	H/A	Against	W/L	Score
3 April	Home	Canterbury	Won	55-23
23 April	Away	Canterbury	Won	52-26

Won 107-49 on aggregate

Second Round

Date	H/A	Against	W/L	Score
3 May	Away	Crayford	Won	43-35
15 May	Home	Crayford	Won	54-23

Won 97-58 on aggregate

Third Round

Date	H/A	Against	W/L	Score
10 July	Home	Newcastle	Won	54-24
8 August	Away	Newcastle	Won	43-34

Won 97-58 on aggregate

The 1977 team, Eastbourne's most successful ever. From left to right, back row: Eric Dugard, Pete Jarman, Colin Richardson, Mike Sampson. Front row: Steve Naylor, Roger Abel, David Kennett.

A spectacular action shot of Gordon Kennett's brother David.

Semi-final

Date	H/A	Against	W/L	Score
2 September	Away	Ellesmere Port	Lost	28-50
25 September	Home	Ellesmere Port	Won	57-21

Won 85-71 on aggregate

Final

Date	H/A	Against	W/L	Score
8 October	Away	Berwick	Lost	37-41
23 October	Home	Berwick	Won	61-16

Won 98-57 on aggregate

1977 – National League and Knock-Out Cup

Rider	Matches	Rides	Points	BP	Total	Average
Colin Richardson	45	187	475	22	497	10.63
Mike Sampson	46	184	441	23	464	10.09
David Kennett	46	182	332	49	381	8.37
Eric Dugard	45	179	321	48	369	8.25
Pete Jarman	19	64	96	24	120	7.50
Roger Abel	46	164	256	44	300	7.32
Paul Woods	30	94	127	34	161	6.85
Steve Naylor	42	131	178	39	217	6.63

1978

With the inevitable happening and Richardson moving off to Wimbledon, Bob Dugard took the decision not to replace him as the Dugards were concerned that the 1977 team had been too strong! In his piece in the opening-night programme, he said, 'We got caught up on the success treadmill last year. Never was there a more successful NL team tracked than the 1977 Eagles, but it had dreadful drawbacks. No NL team reached the

30-point scoreline. Here and there were very few cases of genuine effort on the track to provide value-for-money entertainment, but in the main the majority failed miserably in their responsibility, which caused us to make a policy decision that goes completely against the grain. We have purposely weakened our team in the hope that you the fans may once again see some competitive racing.' He went on to explain that there had been a dramatic fall in attendances the previous season, 'purely due to the fact that our overall strength made it impossible for any team to provide reasonable entertainment, and a lot of fans justifiably stayed away'. Nevertheless, Eastbourne still made a good start to the season. The first success was the South Coast Cup against Canterbury, in which the Eagles won both legs.

When the league got underway, Oxford, Peterborough and Scunthorpe were all well beaten at Arlington before Eastbourne crashed to a heavy 48-30 defeat at Ellesmere Port. Two more home victories against Weymouth and Milton Keynes followed as the Eagles moved to the top of the table. The Eagles' first away success came at Edinburgh on 19 May as they recorded a 46-32 victory and then just four days later there was another away win, this time by the mammoth score of 50-28 at Weymouth. Newcastle, placed second in the table, arrived at Arlington next and in a cracking match the Eagles edged home 42-35. The next day at Brough Park the score was even closer as Newcastle won 40-38. After crushing Berwick 61-17 at home, Eastbourne began to lose their way in the league, losing five matches in a row away from home.

Although they were beginning to slip up in the league, things were still going well in the Knock-Out Cup. A 104-49 thrashing of Scunthorpe in the second round was followed by an 83-69 victory over Peterborough in the quarter-finals. Two away wins in the league, against Mildenhall 40-38 and Teeside 45-33, revived hopes of a double double, but defeats at Rye House, Oxford, Canterbury, Stoke and Milton Keynes meant that Eastbourne could only eventually finish fourth in the league, nine points behind the champions Canterbury.

Things were going better in the cup, however, as the Eagles disposed of Oxford in the semi-finals, winning 56-22 and 45-32, setting up a fascinating final against their old rivals from the Southern Area League days, Rye House. With the Eagles winning the first leg at Arlington by fourteen points, 46-32, it looked as though a fascinating second leg was in prospect and so it proved as a solid team performance, led appropriately by Eric Dugard, saw the Eagles lose by just four points, 41-37, to win the Knock-Out Cup for the second year by an overall margin of ten points, 83-73.

Once again, Sampson had been superb all season, picking up 482 points from 46 meetings for an average of 9.74. He represented Eastbourne in the National League Riders' final and might well have won the meeting but for a Teeside supporter who had a red flashing light on his hat, which he put on in the middle of a race, causing Sampson to pull up, thinking the race had been stopped. He also challenged Tom Owen for the Silver Helmet without success.

Sampson was the only non-Eastbourne-trained member of the 1978 team that, even in its weakened state, had still managed to finish fourth in the league and win the Knock-Out Cup. This completed ten seasons in the Second Division (under its various names), during which time Eastbourne had won two championships, two Knock-Out Cups, finished runners-up in the league twice and third once. This was easily the most impressive record of any Second Division team and in many ways the 1978 season summed up the reasons for this success as six of the seven regular team members were products of the Arlington training school. Dave Kennett and Eric Dugard averaged over 8 points per match, Roger Abel (who recorded 62 bonus points), and Steve Naylor over 7 and Paul Woods 6.64. This year's new find, John Barker, who came in as reserve, scored 5.79.

During the season several Friday meetings were held to see if the crowd numbers would hold up should the Eagles decide to apply for First Division status the following season. Although the crowds were never really outstanding, they were healthy enough to convince the Dugard family that it was now time to take the plunge and move up to the top echelon.

With Bob Dugard's other promotion at White City in obvious difficulties, he applied to have the licence transferred and so, for the first time in its history, Eastbourne entered speedway's elite and became a member of the British League. The man that had been involved with Eastbourne speedway since the early 1930s, Charlie Dugard, became the promoter.

1978 – National League

Date	H/A	Against	W/L	Score
2 April	Home	Oxford	Won	51-27
9 April	Home	Peterborough	Won	46-32
16 April	Home	Scunthorpe	Won	56-22
21 April	Away	Ellesmere Port	Lost	30-48
23 April	Home	Weymouth	Won	49-26
30 April	Home	Milton Keynes	Won	61-17
7 May	Away	Boston	Lost	38-40
14 May	Home	Workington	Won	54-23
19 May	Away	Edinburgh	Won	46-32
21 May	Home	Barrow	Won	54-24
23 May	Away	Weymouth	Won	50-28
4 June	Home	Newcastle	Won	42-35
5 June	Away	Newcastle	Lost	38-40
6 June	Away	Barrow	Drew	39-39
18 June	Home	Berwick	Won	61-17
25 June	Home	Stoke	Won	56-20
30 June	Away	Peterborough	Lost	31-47
7 July	Home	Edinburgh	Won	46-31
16 July	Home	Glasgow	Won	57-21
23 July	Home	Boston	Won	42-35
28 July	Away	Workington	Lost	35-43
29 July	Away	Berwick	Lost	32-46
4 August	Away	Glasgow	Lost	33-45
13 August	Home	Mildenhall	Won	54-24
16 August	Away	Mildenhall	Won	40-38
20 August	Home	Ellesmere Port	Won	46-32
24 August	Away	Teesside	Won	45-33
27 August	Home	Rye House	Won	54-24
28 August	Away	Rye House	Lost	36-42
29 August	Away	Crayford	Won	44-34
10 September	Home	Crayford	Won	58-20
10 September	Home	Teesside	Won	57-20
1 October	Home	Canterbury	Won	48-29
5 October	Away	Oxford	Lost	36-42
7 October	Away	Canterbury	Lost	33-45
14 October	Away	Stoke	Lost	30-48
16 October	Away	Scunthorpe	Won	41-37
17 October	Away	Milton Keynes	Lost	35-42

P38 W25 D1 L12 For 1,704 Against 1,248 Pts 51 Position 4th (out of 20)

Knock-Out Cup

First Round
Bye

Second Round

Date	H/A	Against	W/L	Score
11 June	Home	Scunthorpe	Won	57-21
12 June	Away	Scunthorpe	Won	47-28

Won 104-49 on aggregate

Third Round

Date	H/A	Against	W/L	Score
6 August	Home	Peterborough	Won	45-30
11 August	Away	Peterborough	Lost	38-39

Won 83-69 on aggregate

Semi-final

Date	H/A	Against	W/L	Score
27 August	Home	Oxford	Won	56-22
7 September	Away	Oxford	Won	45-32

Won 101-54 on aggregate

Final

Date	H/A	Against	W/L	Score
22 October	Home	Rye House	Won	46-32
29 October	Away	Rye House	Lost	37-41

Won on aggregate 83-73

1978 – National League and Knock-Out Cup

Rider	Matches	Rides	Points	BP	Total	Average
Mike Sampson	46	198	455	27	482	9.74
David Kennett	41	167	350	23	373	8.93
Eric Dugard	45	177	351	42	393	8.88
Roger Abel	45	166	245	62	307	7.40
Steve Naylor	43	169	276	33	309	7.31

Above left:
Mike Sampson rode for Eastbourne from 1974 to 1978. His average of 10.09 in 1977 is still the sixth-best in Eastbourne's history.

Above right:
Paul Woods rode for Eastbourne throughout their first spell in the First Division from 1979 to 1984.

Colin Ackroyd	12	33	42	7	49	5.94
John Barker	40	121	140	35	175	5.76

1979

Along with the transfer of the licence came a number of former Eagles who had moved to White City, including the World number two Gordon Kennett, Trevor Geer and Steve Weatherley as well as the flying Finn Kai Niemi. Dave Kennett, Eric Dugard, Roger Abel, Steve Naylor, Paul Woods and John Barker all retained their places in the squad. The track was altered with the bends being widened and the total distance being shortened to 302 metres.

The Eagles' season opened at Wimbledon with a 44-33 defeat in the Gauntlet Gold Cup. But it was on Friday 30 March that a new era of speedway began at Arlington. Wimbledon were the visitors, led by Roger Johns and Colin Richardson. Dave Kennett won the first heat from Larry Ross and Stefan Solomonsson after brother Gordon had suffered an engine failure while way out in front. The Dons went ahead in heat two with a 5-0 and the Eagles were never able to pull back the deficit. Needing a 5-1 to win in the last heat, their hopes of an opening victory were dashed when Larry Ross led home Weatherley and Niemi. The Eagles' first win came in the second home match against Poole, again in the Gauntlet Gold Cup, with Gordon Kennett scorching to a maximum. But even he couldn't match Belle Vue's Peter Collins, who beat him for the Golden Helmet Match Race title. On 12 April the Eagles completed the double over Poole, winning 43-35 at Wimborne Road.

Eastbourne's first British League match was at home to Hull on 13 April and resulted in an easy victory for the Eagles 50-27, with Gordon Kennett and Kai Niemi both scoring 10 paid 11. In the Hull team that day was a young American who managed just 4 points. His name was Kelly Moran. On Sunday 15 April, Cradley came in search of league points. They also had two Americans in their team, Bobby Schwartz and Bruce Penhall. Schwartz scored 8 paid 11 while Penhall managed 8 paid 10, as the Midlanders won a stormy match 41-36. Eastbourne's consolation was that Gordon Kennett set a new track record of 59.92 seconds in heat one.

Things began to improve for the Eagles as they beat Ipswich in the Knock-Out Cup, winning 65-43 at home and 54-53 away. This was followed by an away win at Newcastle, 46-32, in the Inter-League Cup. But, on 8 June, Eastbourne's season was to come crashing down in tragedy. Entering the third lap of the last heat of the semi-final of a new four-team tournament between Hackney, Eastbourne, Wimbledon and Canterbury at Hackney's Waterden Road track, Weatherley and Hackney rider Vic Harding collided and were both thrown across the track, crashing into a lamp standard. A dreadful hush descended on the crowd as it was obvious this was a very serious accident and so it proved. Harding died from the injuries received while Weatherley was paralysed for life. The tragedy knocked the stuffing out of the Eastbourne team. 'All we wanted to do was get the season over. It affected some members of the team very badly,' was Bob Dugard's comment. It wasn't just that Weatherley was a very promising star of the future, but he was also a very popular member of the side with many friends both among the riders and officials as well as the supporters. Trevor Geer in particular was very badly affected by the accident, although he managed to soldier on to the end of the season. The incident overshadowed the whole of the rest of the season at Arlington and the fact that they finished sixteenth out of eighteen teams was largely irrelevant.

1979 – British League

Date	H/A	Against	W/L	Score
13 April	Home	Hull	Won	50-27
15 April	Home	Cradley Heath	Lost	36-41
16 April	Away	King's Lynn	Lost	25-53
12 May	Away	Coventry	Lost	24-54
13 May	Home	Hackney	Won	51-27

18 May	Home	Leicester	Won	48-30
19 May	Away	Cradley Heath	Lost	27-51
25 May	Away	Wolverhampton	Lost	34-44
27 May	Home	Poole	Drew	39-39
31 May	Away	Wimbledon	Lost	36-42
1 June	Home	Halifax	Won	44-34
10 June	Home	Wolverhampton	Lost	32-46
16 June	Away	Belle Vue	Lost	32-46
18 June	Away	Exeter	Lost	28-50
22 June	Home	Birmingham	Lost	36-42
23 June	Away	Swindon	Lost	30-48
29 June	Home	Swindon	Lost	31-47
11 July	Away	Hull	Lost	28-50
13 July	Home	Wimbledon	Won	42-36
20 July	Home	Exeter	Won	49-28
27 July	Away	Hackney	Won	40-38
1 August	Away	Poole	Lost	34-44
3 August	Home	Sheffield	Won	50-28
24 August	Home	Ipswich	Drew	39-39
26 August	Home	Coventry	Won	43-35
29 August	Away	Birmingham	Won	40-38
31 August	Home	Reading	Lost	37-41
3 September	Away	Reading	Lost	29-49
11 September	Away	Leicester	Lost	33-44
14 September	Home	King's Lynn	Lost	35-43
15 September	Away	Halifax	Lost	36-42
27 September	Away	Ipswich	Lost	37-41
7 October	Home	Belle Vue	Lost	38-40
11 October	Away	Sheffield	Lost	29-49

P34 W10 D2 L22 For 1,242 Against 1,406 Pts 22 Position 16th (out of 18)

Knock-Out Cup

Preliminary Round

Date	H/A	Against	W/L	Score
19 April	Away	Ipswich	Won	54-53
20 April	Home	Ipswich	Won	65-43

Won 119-96 on aggregate

First Round

Date	H/A	Against	W/L	Score
11 June	Away	Reading	Lost	31-77
6 July	Home	Reading	Won	65-43

Lost 96-120 on aggregate

1979 – British League and Knock-Out Cup

Rider	Matches	Rides	Points	BP	Total	Average
Gordon Kennett	34	172	416	10	426	9.91
Kai Niemi	34	164	348	11	359	8.76
Steve Weatherley	13	59	97	6	103	6.98
David Kennett	15	58	67	14	81	5.59
Trevor Geer	34	150	172	19	191	5.09
Eric Dugard	35	119	109	18	127	4.27
Roger Abel	28	91	73	16	89	3.91
Steve Naylor	18	48	40	5	45	3.75
Paul Woods	12	41	28	7	35	3.42
John Barker	7	22	15	2	17	3.09
Veijo Tuoriniemi	14	50	32	5	37	2.96

THE 1980s

1980

At the start of the 1980 season consideration was given to the race day. For many years, Eastbourne had been a Sunday track; now, with their elevation to the First Division, they had changed to a Friday evening but, in spite of the presence of the sport's top stars, attendances had not risen. On just a few occasions during 1979 they had reverted to Sunday afternoon. On those occasions the gate showed a significant increase. In 1980, therefore, the Dugards decided to run more Sunday meetings, with twenty-one of the thirty-one fixtures being run on that day. The long-awaited grandstand-restaurant complex was at last opened in time for the start of the season, which didn't start too well as the American Steve Columbo, who had been signed up as the third heat leader behind Gordon Kennett and Niemi, flew in to the country and then promptly flew out again before riding in one league match, causing Bob Dugard to complain about his lack of professionalism. From that shaky start things did not get much better. In Eastbourne's first match, away to Hull, Niemi was involved in a bad crash that resulted in a serious arm injury, which kept him out for several weeks. Eastbourne were now down to one heat leader and six riders in total and they were forced to operate rider replacement. They tried signing a number of foreign riders to plug the gap, but this did not prove very successful. The Swede Borje Klingberg lasted three weeks before becoming homesick and leaving; the Pole Jozef Kafel raced in 5 matches, averaging a pathetic 0.92 while fellow-countryman Jan Puk somehow managed to be even worse, riding in two matches and failing to score at all. Then, just as Niemi returned, Gordon Kennett was taken into hospital suffering from diabetes and told he needed a long rest.

The second and third heat-leader spots were effectively being filled by Dave Kennett and Paul Woods, who had been recalled from Crayford at the beginning of the season. Until July when perhaps the only good thing to happen at Arlington that season occured with the arrival of Finn Veijo Tuorieniemi. Tuorieniemi had ridden for the Eagles in 1979 but had spent the first three months of 1980 trying to obtain a work permit from the Department of Employment. He had not had a very good time of it in 1979, but the Eastbourne management decided to persevere with him and it was just as well they did, as he blossomed into a heat leader, along with Niemi and Woods. By the time Kennett returned in September, Eastbourne had already lost 19 of their 25 matches, including 6 at home. His return heralded a small revival as he put in scores of 12, 11, 9, 14, 12, 12 and 9 in the Eagles' last seven matches. However, the last match of the season just about summed up Eastbourne's year as they were hammered 52-26 at home by Reading. Once again the Eagles finished in sixteenth place in the league and were bundled out of the cup in the first round by Swindon, 117.5-98.5 on aggregate. The only real individual success of the season was Niemi's World final appearance, where he finished seventh with 8 points.

1980 – British League

Date	H/A	Against	W/L	Score
16 April	Away	Hull	Lost	32-46
19 April	Away	King's Lynn	Lost	15-63
20 April	Home	Sheffield	Won	46-32
28 April	Away	Birmingham	Won	45-33
3 May	Away	Belle Vue	Lost	25-53
4 May	Home	Wimbledon	Drew	39-39
10 May	Away	Coventry	Lost	31-47
11 May	Home	Halifax	Won	41-37
16 May	Away	Wolverhampton	Lost	34-43
29 May	Away	Sheffield	Lost	32-46
31 May	Away	Leicester	Lost	29-49
5 June	Away	Ipswich	Lost	30-48
20 June	Home	Leicester	Lost	31-47
28 June	Away	Cradley Heath	Lost	21-57
18 July	Home	Birmingham	Lost	37-41
24 July	Away	Wimbledon	Lost	31-47
10 August	Home	Hull	Lost	37-41
16 August	Away	Swindon	Lost	35-43
17 August	Home	Ipswich	Won	40-38
22 August	Away	Hackney	Lost	34-44
24 August	Home	Hackney	Lost	34-43
25 August	Away	Poole	Lost	32-46
31 August	Home	Coventry	Won	47-31
6 September	Away	Halifax	Lost	26-56
7 September	Home	Swindon	Lost	30-48
14 September	Home	Poole	Lost	34-44
21 September	Home	Wolverhampton	Won	41-37
22 September	Away	Reading	Lost	26-52
28 September	Home	Cradley Heath	Won	45-31
5 October	Home	Belle Vue	Won	45-33
12 October	Home	King's Lynn	Won	42-36
12 October	Home	Reading	Lost	26-52

P32 W9 D1 L22 For 1,093 Against 1,454 Pts 19 Position 16th (out of 17)

Knock-Out Cup

First Round

Date	H/A	Against	W/L	Score
31 May	Away	Swindon	Lost	46-62
6 June	Home	Swindon	Lost	52.5-55.5

Lost 98.5-117.5 on aggregate

1980 – British League and Knock-Out Cup

Rider	Matches	Rides	Points	BP	Total	Average
Gordon Kennett	24	116	281.5	0	281.5	9.71
Kai Niemi	23	113	228	8	236	8.35
Paul Woods	22	107	151	17	168	6.28
Veijo Tuoriniemi	13	49	64	11	75	6.12
David Kennett	33	125	151	23	174	5.57
Trevor Geer	16	60	64	9	73	4.87
Eric Dugard	23	87	83	18	101	4.64
Richard Greer	9	33	27	8	35	4.24
Steve Naylor	9	30	24	5	29	3.87
Jan Davidsson	24	72	47	18	65	3.61
Sigvart Pedersen	12	42	15	4	19	1.18

The Flying Finn Kai Niemi rode for Eastbourne in 1979 and 1980.

1981

Over the close season, Bob Dugard took over the promotion from his father and brought in his old colleague from his Oxford and White City days, Danny Dunton, as co-promoter. Both of them realised that much needed to be done to bring Eastbourne up to strength and there was a great deal of activity in the transfer market. Both Gordon Kennett, at his own request, and Niemi were placed on the transfer list. Agreement was reached with Birmingham to swap Niemi for their American star Kelly Moran, but Dugard shrewdly refused to allow Niemi to leave the club until Moran actually arrived back in Britain. With no sign of Moran arriving, Niemi lined up for the Eagles in their first match of the season, a League Cup tie away at Hackney on 3 April. Having been assured that Moran would be available for the following Sunday's meeting at home to King's Lynn, Dugard agreed to let Niemi go. As the tapes went up for the first heat of the League Cup match on 5 April, Moran was still en route to the track straight from the airport following his transatlantic flight. He eventually arrived halfway through the match just in time to take his last two rides. Not surprisingly he came last in both of them. However, those two point-less rides were to be the last time all season that Moran disappointed the Eastbourne management and the fans. His combination of showmanship, spectacular style and sheer class brought him instant popularity and was one of the major reasons why Eastbourne was one of the few tracks in the British League in 1981 to report an increased attendance.

Gordon Kennett, meanwhile, had dropped his transfer request following discussions with Charlie Dugard, who agreed to give him a generous sponsorship deal from his own machine tool business. Other new signings for the 1981 season included the Pole Robert Slabon and another Finn, Olli Tyrvainen, who took the place of fellow countryman Tuorieniemi. Eastbourne entered the season with two class heat leaders in Moran and Kennett but lacked that third heat leader that would have enabled them to climb their way up the table. In terms of scoring, Woods took the role of third heat leader but, in reality, he should have been the number four that would have given the Eagles the edge over many of their opponents. The league season started with a heavy defeat, 58-20, away at Cradley Heath, followed by another defeat at Hull, 46-32. At home, things looked a little brighter as they started off with two good victories over Wimbledon, 48-30, and Halifax, 50-28, Kennett scoring a maximum in both.

Eastbourne's first point away from home came at Reading as they drew 39-39, but this was followed almost immediately by a draw at home as Belle Vue took a point away from Arlington. In general the season followed a fairly predictable pattern with wins at home and losses away until 23 August, when the Eagles lost their first home match by the narrowest of margins to Swindon, 39-38. This was following an injury to Slabon on 9 August in a match against Hull that put him out for the rest of the season. His place was taken by Eric Dugard, who returned to his home track following an early season spell with Wimbledon. Unfortunately Dugard failed to come up with the goods, finishing the season with an average of just 2.80. Towards the end of the season, Eastbourne suffered a number of home reverses, including the very last home match against Coventry, which they lost 40-38. In all it left Eastbourne very little better off than the previous two seasons, though they did manage to climb just three places in the table to finish in thirteenth place.

Gordon Kennett and Moran both finished the season with 9-plus averages, Kennett 9.68 and Moran 9.29. Behind them were Woods with 6.96, Trevor Geer 4.24, Dave Kennett on 3.92 and Tyrvainen with 3.75. In Gordon Kennett and Moran, Eastbourne had two of the best heat leaders in the British League but it was obvious that they had to strengthen that tail if they were to stand any chance of success. Consequently, Dugard announced that he was putting aside £25,000 for a team-building project and that they were to return to the policy that had done so well for them in their Second Division days of unearthing their own talent through the winter training school. He felt that since joining the British League this aspect of their former success had been neglected; foreigners were costing a lot of money and their commitments did not always coincide with the needs of Eastbourne. A new 135-yard training track was prepared in the corner of the car park and Alan Johns put in charge of the project. The first two juniors to emerge from this new training school proved to be yet another generation of Dugards, as Paul and Martin emerged as the picks of the bunch.

1981 – British League

Date	H/A	Against	W/L	Score
2 May	Away	Cradley Heath	Lost	20-58
20 May	Away	Hull	Lost	32-46
31 May	Home	Wimbledon	Won	48-30
16 June	Away	Leicester	Lost	35-43
21 June	Home	Halifax	Won	50-28
25 June	Away	Swindon	Lost	27-51
5 July	Home	Birmingham	Won	40-38
13 July	Away	Reading	Drew	39-39
17 July	Away	Hackney	Lost	36-42
19 July	Home	Belle Vue	Drew	39-39
25 July	Away	Coventry	Lost	33-45
2 August	Home	Sheffield	Won	46-32
9 August	Home	Hull	Won	48-30
15 August	Away	Halifax	Lost	30-47
16 August	Home	Ipswich	Drew	39-39
23 August	Home	Swindon	Lost	38-39
30 August	Home	Hackney	Won	43-35
31 August	Away	Poole	Lost	34-44
3 September	Away	Sheffield	Lost	22-56
6 September	Home	Poole	Won	41-37
12 September	Away	Belle Vue	Lost	26-52
17 September	Away	Ipswich	Lost	24-54
20 September	Home	King's Lynn	Lost	38-40
26 September	Away	King's Lynn	Won	42-36
27 September	Home	Reading	Won	44-34
2 October	Away	Birmingham	Lost	34-44
4 October	Home	Cradley Heath	Lost	35-43
8 October	Away	Wimbledon	Lost	33-45

| 11 October | Home | Leicester | Won | 40-38 |
| 25 October | Home | Coventry | Lost | 38-40 |

P30 W10 D3 L17 For 1,094 Against 1,244 Position 13th (16)

Knock-Out Cup

Preliminary Round

Date	H/A	Against	W/L	Score
4 June	Away	Middlesbrough	Won	53-43

First Round

Date	H/A	Against	W/L	Score
7 June	Home	Cradley Heath	Won	49-47
20 June	Away	Cradley Heath	Lost	36-60

Lost 107-85 on aggregate

1981 – British League and Knock-Out Cup

Rider	Matches	Rides	Points	BP	Total	Average
Gordon Kennett	42	203	483	8	491	9.68
Kelly Moran	41	193	438	10	448	9.29
Paul Woods	47	226	358	35	393	6.96
Richard Greer	6	18	16	4	20	4.44
Trevor Geer	47	180	171	20	191	4.24
David Kennett	45	147	117	27	144	3.92
Olli Tyrvainen	37	146	114	23	137	3.75
Robert Slabon	26	76	45	10	55	2.90
Eric Dugard	15	50	28	7	35	2.80

Eastbourne's charismatic American star Kelly Moran.

1982

Dugard spent £10,500 of his £25,000 fund on another American, Ron Preston, so that now, at last, Eastbourne had three recognised heat leaders and a solid number four. But it was still that tail that worried the Eastbourne management, who signed up Borje Ring to replace Tyrvainen as well as another Swede, Lars Hammarberg. The opening tournament of the season was the League Cup, in which Eastbourne made a good start with away wins at Hackney 42-36, King's Lynn 40-38, and Reading 41-37, plus a 39-39 draw at Swindon. At home the Eagles were also doing well. A magnificent League Cup match at home to Wimbledon saw the lead change hands several times before the Dons snatched a draw with a last-race 5-1 from ex-Eagles Kai Niemi and Dave Jessup over Preston and Moran. With just one loss at home, a 45-33 defeat at the hands of Ipswich, Eastbourne finished runners-up in the Southern Section. The main talking point in this early season success was the form of Preston, who had taken to Arlington like a duck to water.

Eastbourne started well in the Knock-Out Cup as well, defeating Swindon in the first round, 86-70 on aggregate. Then the first home league match saw Halifax, led by top English rider Kenny Carter, beaten 43-35. The previous year's pattern of wins at home and losses away followed in the league as the Eagles beat Leicester 50-28, Wimbledon 51-27 and Reading 48-30 at home while losing 48-30 at Leicester, 41-37 at Birmingham and 48-30 at Belle Vue. The Eagles' first home setback came in a cracker of a match against Ipswich that resulted in a 39-39 draw and then, even worse, eventual champions Belle Vue came to Arlington and took both points with a big 48-30 victory. In the end there was not much change for Eastbourne as far as the league position went, as they finished in twelfth place.

Eastbourne's promising start to the season had been undermined somewhat by their charismatic American star Kelly Moran. In June he was fined £1,000 for failing to arrive for a match against Ipswich. In August he was in trouble again when the track doctor ruled him unfit to ride in the match at Belle Vue. This match was twenty-four hours after Moran had qualified for his second World Championship final. The Eastbourne management were not impressed with the doctor's ruling. They issued a statement that said, 'the rider had been celebrating reaching the World final the previous night in Sweden, and had not slept for more than twenty-four hours and was obviously in no fit condition to ride.' Moran was fined £10 by the referee and reported to the control board. Moran said that the whole thing had been a mix-up and although he agreed he had been celebrating and was a little hungover, which he felt was only natural, he said the real reason why he had not slept was because, 'there was a lot of confusion about the homecoming arrangements' and that he had seemed to be driving around Sweden for half the night. Moran's World final appearance resulted in his scoring 11 points and finishing in fourth place.

Moran finished the season with an average of 9.61 but rode in only thirty-five out of a possible forty-eight matches for Eastbourne. Gordon Kennett and Ron Preston also finished the season with 9-plus averages. Backing up the three star heat leaders was the ever-reliable and solid Paul Woods on 6.62. But behind them, the next highest scorer was mid-season signing Lillebror Johannson, with an average of just 3.55. The Eagles still had far too long a tail.

Although without doubt it is the Dugard family who are synonymous with Eastbourne, it is interesting to note that in 1982 the three Kennett brothers, Gordon, Dave and Barney, all rode for the Eagles. The leading Kennett brother and Eastbourne's top scorer for the past four seasons since their promotion to the British League, Gordon, had a shock in store for him at the end-of-season supporters' club meeting when he heard that he had been transfer listed by Bob Dugard. 'I was surprised. I thought I would be the last one to go. I am one of the only two English riders at the club and I have been with Bob for twelve years – my entire speedway career,' he said afterwards. Dugard put Kennett's fee at £15,000, saying he needed the money to go towards covering a £20,000-plus operating loss for the 1982 season. If he was unable to raise £15,000 for Kennett, Dugard said that Eastbourne was in danger of closing. Fortunately for the future of the club, King's Lynn agreed to the fee and Kennett was transferred.

1982 – British League

Date	H/A	Against	W/L	Score
3 May	Away	Poole	Drew	39-39
23 May	Home	Halifax	Won	43-35
25 May	Away	Leicester	Lost	30-48
31 May	Away	Birmingham	Lost	37-41
5 June	Away	Halifax	Lost	24-54
13 June	Home	Leicester	Won	50-28
20 June	Home	Ipswich	Drew	39-39
24 June	Away	Wimbledon	Lost	37-41
27 June	Home	Wimbledon	Won	51-27
3 July	Home	Reading	Won	45-33
18 July	Home	Swindon	Won	44-34
24 July	Away	Belle Vue	Lost	30-48
25 July	Home	Belle Vue	Lost	35-43
31 July	Away	King's Lynn	Lost	36-42
8 August	Home	Birmingham	Won	46-32
14 August	Home	Hackney	Lost	38-40
16 August	Away	Reading	Lost	37-41
21 August	Away	Cradley Heath	Lost	29-49
22 August	Home	Sheffield	Drew	39-39
27 August	Away	Hackney	Lost	34-43
4 September	Home	Poole	Won	54-24
9 September	Away	Ipswich	Lost	38-40
11 September	Away	Swindon	Won	48-30
12 September	Home	King's Lynn	Won	45-33
18 September	Away	Coventry	Lost	32-46
19 September	Home	Cradley Heath	Won	39-38
7 October	Away	Sheffield	Lost	31-46
10 October	Home	Coventry	Won	49-29

P28 W11 D3 L14 For 1,099 Against 1,082 Pts 25 Position 12th (out of 15)

Knock-Out Cup

First Round

Date	H/A	Against	W/L	Score
22 May	Away	Swindon	Lost	38-40
6 June	Home	Swindon	Won	46-32

Won 84-72 on aggregate

Second Round

Date	H/A	Against	W/L	Score
1 August	Home	Wimbledon	Won	43-35
19 August	Away	Wimbledon	Lost	38-40

Won 81-75 on aggregate

Semi-Final

Date	H/A	Against	W/L	Score
18 September	Away	Cradley Heath	Lost	30-48
19 September	Home	Cradley Heath	Won	41-36

Lost 71-84 on aggregate

1982 – British League and Knock-Out Cup

Rider	Matches	Rides	Points	BP	Total	Average
Gordon Kennett	48	212	493	22	515	9.72
Kelly Moran	35	146	322	29	351	9.62
Ron Preston	38	162	354	18	372	9.19

Another leading American, Ron Preston.

Paul Woods	45	194	289	32	321	6.62
David Kennett	29	89	71	8	79	3.55
Lillebror Johansson	18	71	55	8	63	3.55
Lars Hammarberg	44	134	90	23	113	3.37
Borje Ring	39	125	91	14	105	3.36
Keith Pritchard	9	22	14	4	18	3.27

1983

This wasn't the last big surprise in store for the Eastbourne faithful as, over the close season, Kelly Moran dropped a bombshell by saying that he would not return to England for the 1983 season. With no money to replace him, Dugard felt that without Kennett and Moran he did not have a team capable of competing in the British League and had little option but to ask the British Speedway Promoters' Association (BSPA) to put Eastbourne's racing licence on ice for a year while he built up the club's finances. The BSPA refused to agree and instead offered to help the Eagles assemble a competitive side. Three names were put forward to replace Kennett and Moran, those being another American, John Cook, and Poles Edward Jancarz and Roman Jankowski. In the end Eastbourne had to settle for John Eskildsen and Mike Lanham, two good solid team men, but neither of whom could be called top-class replacements.

Just when Dugard thought his troubles couldn't get any worse he received a message from his one remaining heat leader, Preston, to say that he would not be returning to Arlington until May. Management assistant and programme editor Tony Millard said he was prepared to fly to America to try and convince both Moran and Preston to change their minds and return to Eastbourne in time for the start of the season. At the end of March a crisis meeting was called at the club and supporters told by Dugard that his initial reaction to all the goings on over the winter was to 'pack it in'. He went on, 'We could wind up the club quite easily. But our second thought was if the supporters want us to carry on, we will do so. Quite frankly, we will have a terrible team. You supporters are going to be humiliated by some of the results.' A show of hands among the supporters present showed there was overwhelming support for the club to continue and they all agreed to do all they could to help raise funds. Jim Langford, already one of the club's individual sponsors, was put in charge of co-ordinating fundraising efforts. Another positive outcome of the meeting was the reactivation of the dormant supporters' club as well as the setting up of a new branch in Brighton to join the highly successful Hastings Supporters' Club.

Dugard made one last attempt to persuade Moran to return. In a phone call, Moran intimated that he was prepared to come to Britain for the England-USA Test series and that he might stay on for two weeks to take part in a few matches for Eastbourne. Dugard was not impressed. 'This proposal is completely useless,' he fumed. 'It would do more damage than good to Eastbourne Speedway and make us look ridiculous.' Moran was immediately transfer listed for £20,000. Dugard also called for the American star to be banned from international and World Championship racing in Britain. As far as Preston was concerned it became obvious by April that he had no intention of returning to Arlington in May. He had gone to Mexico and, in spite of Dugard leaving messages with friends and relatives, he had not contacted the Eastbourne management to let them know what he was doing.

And so Eastbourne prepared for the new season with a team consisting of Paul Woods, Lillebror Johansson, Barney Kennett, Trevor Geer, John Eskildsen, Mike Lanham and new signing Peter Schroek. Before a wheel was turned, Johansson broke a foot while guesting for a Dutch team at Canterbury and, in heat one of the first match of the season, Schroek collided with the safety fence and broke his collarbone. Barney Kennett lasted just under one lap of Eastbourne's second match on Easter Sunday before falling and splitting his forehead open. Three races later, Eskildsen fell in front of Geer with both riders receiving collarbone injuries, putting them out for two months. When Geer returned he broke his toe and chose to retire. Already the weakest team in the league, it had, by the end of its second match, lost five of its riders, leaving just captain Paul Woods and Mike Lanham. A crowd of 1,500 attended the Easter Sunday fixture. Four years previously the corresponding fixture had attracted 8,000 paying customers. Could anything else go wrong for Eastbourne? The answer to that was 'yes', as Eastbourne signed up Zimbabwean Denzil Kent to help overcome the rider shortage. He was then promptly arrested and served with a deportation order for overstaying his permitted time in Britain. In the end he escaped deportation but had to pay a £250 fine.

It was no real surprise that the Eagles lost their first match of the season, a League Cup match at Wimbledon. What was perhaps a little surprising was that it was by the narrow score of 40-38. The first home match was a challenge against a Swedish touring team, but rain put paid to that so it was Good Friday before any racing actually took place. Swindon were the visitors in a League Cup match. Eastbourne won 43-35. Two days later, however, on Easter Sunday, Poole were the visitors and they took the two points, beating the Eagles 46-32.

Swede Anders Eriksson was signed up but he couldn't stop Hackney winning 41-37 at Arlington or the 54-24 defeat at King's Lynn. Next, Reading came, saw and hammered the Eagles 46-32, this defeat following four successive away defeats at Reading, Poole, Hackney and Birmingham. Two more home defeats, 47-31 at the hands of Wimbledon and 42-36 by Coventry, came next. Unsurprisingly, Eastbourne were bundled out of the Knock-Out Cup, 90-65, in the first round by King's Lynn. Meanwhile on the road the team were still suffering heavy defeats and for the Eagles to make a final score of 30 points in a match was a bonus. More team changes were made. In came Pole Piotr Pyszny as well as a Danish rider called Rene Christiansen. Both were to make little impact. The match against Leicester, in which the Eagles pulled off a fine 43-35 win, saw another new face in twenty-two-year-old Dane Finn Jensen. In keeping with Eastbourne's luck that season, Jensen scored no points in two matches and then went home, never to return. Ipswich and Hackney were the next visitors, both completing easy league doubles. A good 41-36 win over Birmingham was followed by two heavy away losses, 50-28 at Leicester and 51-27 at Halifax. However, home matches were close, with a 40-38 win over King's Lynn before a massive 58-20 slaughter at Coventry. Amazingly, in the very next away match, Eastbourne recorded their only away win of the season, beating Poole 40-38. This was followed by a visit to Arlington by the powerful Cradley outfit, who murdered the Eagles 56-22 in front of a packed Arlington crowd. Paul Woods scored 13 of the Eagles' 22 points.

The final home match finished off the season in the manner to which Eastbourne had become accustomed, as they went down 46-32 to Reading. In spite of this, the Eagles' seven were applauded by the fans who reserved the biggest cheer for captain Paul Woods, who through a disastrous season for the Eagles had managed to improve his average to 8.94. He told the crowd that he wanted to remain an Eagle and hoped for better things from the 1984 season. Not including guests, Eastbourne used a total of twenty-three riders through the season. Following Woods, Eskildsen had an average of 6.53. The third heat leader, Mike Lanham, recorded just 4.18. To put that in some sort of perspective, league champions Cradley Heath's number eight had an average of 6.00. And yet, astonishingly, in spite of the nightmare year the Arlington faithful had endured, Eastbourne did not finish bottom of the league; that honour was reserved for Swindon, who finished with the same number of points as Eastbourne but lost out on race points.

At a meeting held in the Arlington clubhouse on a cold winter's evening at the end of November, a long discussion was held between the management and the supporters on the future of the club or, indeed, if it had one. The outcome of this was to give the British League one more 'make or break' season. A new team manager, Russell Lanning, son of former promoter Dave Lanning, was signed up and a new team sponsor, SSL Travel of Tunbridge Wells, was found.

1983 – British League

Date	H/A	Against	W/L	Score
16 May	Away	Birmingham	Lost	23-55
28 May	Away	Belle Vue	Lost	35-45
29 May	Home	Coventry	Lost	36-42

John Eskildsen rode for Eastbourne in 1983 and 1984 and was second-highest scorer both years.

12 June	Home	Halifax	Won	42-36
16 June	Away	Wimbledon	Lost	33-45
18 June	Away	Cradley Heath	Lost	22-56
23 June	Away	Sheffield	Lost	24-54
3 July	Home	Poole	Lost	38-40
5 July	Away	Hackney	Lost	33-45
7 July	Away	Ipswich	Lost	33-45
10 July	Home	Swindon	Won	40-38
16 July	Away	Swindon	Lost	32-46
24 July	Home	Leicester	Won	43-35
31 July	Home	Ipswich	Lost	35-43
6 August	Home	Hackney	Lost	31-47
13 August	Away	Halifax	Lost	27-51
14 August	Home	Birmingham	Lost	_*
21 August	Home	Sheffield	Won	45-33
28 August	Home	Wimbledon	Draw	39-39
29 August	Away	Coventry	Lost	20-58
7 September	Away	Poole	Won	40-38
11 September	Home	Reading	Lost	32-46
13 September	Away	Leicester	Lost	28-50
18 September	Home	King's Lynn	Won	40-38
19 September	Away	Reading	Lost	34-43
24 September	Away	King's Lynn	Lost	27-51
25 September	Home	Cradley Heath	Lost	22-56
2 October	Home	Belle Vue	Won	40-38

*The result of the match against Birmingham was 41-36 to Eastbourne but the match was awarded to Birmingham after Eastbourne were found to have illegally used a guest rider.

P28 W7 D1 L20 For 933 Against 1,249 Pts 15 Position 14th (out of 15)

Knock-Out Cup

First Round

Date	H/A	Against	W/L	Score
11 June	Away	King's Lynn	Lost	31-47
19 June	Home	King's Lynn	Lost	34-43

Lost on aggregate 65-90

1983 – British League and Knock-Out Cup

Rider	Matches	Rides	Points	BP	Total	Average
Paul Woods	44	204	429	20	449	8.80
John Eskildsen	37	161	242	21	263	6.53
Ashley Pullen	6	18	20	0	20	4.44
Mike Lanham	23	89	80	13	93	4.18
David Kennett	11	32	24	7	31	3.88
Lillebror Johansson	22	78	63	11	74	3.80
Anders Eriksson	25	95	78	12	90	3.80
Piotr Pyszny	13	48	38	7	45	3.75
Denzil Kent	9	34	28	3	31	3.65
Trevor Geer	14	36	24	8	32	3.56
Ottaviano Righetto	20	58	31	6	37	2.55
Rene Christiansen	10	29	10	4	14	1.93
Peter Schroeck	7	15	1	0	1	0.27

1984

Having given up entirely on Moran and Preston, Dugard now turned his attention to signing up another American in time for the 1984 season. His target was another flamboyant showman,

Reading's Bobby Schwartz. The only drawback to Dugard's plan was that Reading were asking a transfer fee of £25,000. Fortunately a mystery sponsor came up with the money just in time for Eastbourne to beat Exeter to Schwartz's signature. Unlike Moran's point-less debut, Schwartz began as he meant to go on with a 12-point maximum in Eastbourne's first match against King's Lynn. He was well supported by Woods, who scored 11. The rest of the Eagles team comprised Eskildsen, Kent, Paul Bosley, another American, Steve Lucero and Eastbourne discovery Colin Richardson, who was making his return to the Eagles for the first time since 1977. The Eastbourne management also wanted to re-sign Tyrvainen, but they encountered a number of problems and were unable to start the season with him, signing the Dane Eric Knudsen instead. A season ticket to see this team do battle in the British League would have set you back £70.

In the next match Exeter were thumped 52-36 with a second Schwartz maximum, before a ground-breaking meeting held at 11 a.m. on Sunday 15 April, a three-team tournament with Reading and Poole. The match was televised live on the local TVS channel and was a big success. In the Poole side that day was former World Champion Michael Lee, ex-Eagle Neil Middleditch and the American Sam Ermolenko, making his first visit to Arlington. The Eagles won a superb meeting with 44 points to Poole's 33 and Reading's 31. Schwartz was yet again unbeaten, as was Eskildsen.

Easter was a busy time for the Eagles with matches away to Wimbledon on Maundy Thursday, which they lost 46-32, home to Wimbledon on Good Friday, which they won 45-33, home again on Sunday to Poole, won 51.5-26.5, away on Easter Monday morning at Exeter, drawn 39-39 and then back to Poole on Easter Monday evening, won 41-37. With 3 wins and 1 draw out of 5 matches it provided an excellent start to the season. Shortly afterwards, a superb match at home to Swindon saw the Eagles gain a narrow victory 40-38.

Eastbourne eventually got their man and Tyrvainen made his return in time for the match against Ipswich, with Erik Knudsen being the man he replaced. Tyrvainen's 4 paid 6 from the reserve berth helped the Eagles to a 42-36 win. With Eastbourne defeating a Hans Nielsen-inspired Oxford 42-36, it was the best start to a season that the Eagles had experienced since their elevation to the First Division. But just as things seemed to be going so well they suffered two heavy defeats, 49-29 at Ipswich and, even worse, a 64-14 humiliation at Belle Vue. Top scorers for Eastbourne in this match were Schwarz and Richardson with 4 points each. It was only a second place by Richardson that stopped a complete whitewash. One reason for the poor showing was the fact that Paul Woods was out of the team as, earlier in the season, a crash had left him with fractured ribs. On his return to the team he seemed to be suffering some reaction to having to shoulder much of the burden for keeping the team going in 1983. At one time he even retired saying, 'I am sick and tired of speedway. It is ruining me mentally.' He was eventually to return to the team completely revitalised, scoring paid 12 in his first match but, for now, Eastbourne were having to manage without his services. Two more away defeats at Coventry, 48-30, and Wolverhampton, 41-36, followed and then, even worse, on 3 June, King's Lynn came to Arlington and left with a 42-36 victory. In mitigation, Eastbourne could argue that not only were they without Woods for this match but also Schwartz, who was back in the USA. Amazingly the team came back from these defeats with wins at Poole, 41-37, in the cup, at Oxford, 41-37, in the League Cup and against Exeter, 49-28, in the league. It was in the latter match that Woods made his paid maximum return with 10 paid 12. A 44-34 defeat at Cradley was followed by a 48-30 win over Sheffield, with Woods gaining another maximum, while Kent contributed 10 paid 11. Eastbourne kept up the momentum in the next few matches and the poor results earlier in the season were forgotten as the blue and gold flag flew proudly once more. Poole were bundled out of the Knock-Out Cup as Eastbourne won the second leg 41-36 and then defeated King's Lynn in the first leg of the second round 57-21. The return leg looked a mere formality as a place in the semi-finals beckoned, but things didn't go quite according to plan as the visit to Norfolk resulted in a 57-21 defeat, levelling the scores at 78 each. This meant a replay, with the Eagles winning the home leg 42-34 but, unfortunately, the away leg was an exact repeat of the first meeting with the 51-27 loss giving King's Lynn the tie by 85 points to 69 on aggregate. Following this exit from the cup, Belle Vue visited Arlington and won 42-36. Some pride was restored as the Eagles

Yet another charismatic American, Bobby Schwartz, had just one year with Eastbourne in 1984.

defeated Coventry Bees 42-36 seven days later and then thumped Halifax 52-36, with Woods and the recently signed Antonin Kasper both riding to maximums. In line with the rest of the season further good wins and poor losses followed, leaving Eastbourne in eleventh place in the final table. It wasn't a great season by any means but it was a world away from the year before.

Sadly, although there had been a big improvement in the team itself, Eastbourne's financial troubles were far from over. In November, Bob Dugard announced that the club's losses for the season had been in the region of £40,000, £10,000 worse than the 1983 figure. A fractional increase in support, up 3.5 per cent on the previous year to an average attendance of 1,260, had been heavily outweighed by substantially higher running costs. Having unsuccessfully put forward plans to the BSPA for a new pay policy and been equally unsuccessful in trying to obtain a new sponsorship deal, the Dugards decided there was no alternative but to drop back into the National League. In some ways the decision came as a relief to both the Eastbourne management and its supporters. As a Second Division team it had been the most successful side in the country, while as a First Division team it had done nothing but struggle. In addition, as a Second Division team, there had been the satisfaction of being able to develop its own raw talent, whereas as a First Division side it had had to get the chequebook out to sign up foreign riders in an attempt to keep pace with the rest of the league. Eastbourne were not the only team to feel the pressure as both London clubs, Hackney and Wimbledon, also dropped down a division.

1984 – British League

Date	H/A	Against	W/L	Score
19 May	Away	Belle Vue	Lost	14-64

26 May	Away	Coventry	Lost	30-48
28 May	Away	Wolverhampton	Lost	36-41
3 June	Home	King's Lynn	Lost	36-42
10 June	Home	Exeter	Won	49-28
16 June	Away	Cradley Heath	Lost	34-44
17 June	Home	Sheffield	Won	48-30
1 July	Home	Newcastle	Won	54-24
2 July	Away	Newcastle	Won	40-37
8 July	Home	Cradley Heath	Won	42-35
19 July	Away	Sheffield	Lost	31-47
22 July	Home	Ipswich	Lost	38-40
29 July	Home	Reading	Lost	35.5-42.5
1 August	Away	Poole	Lost	37-41
3 August	Away	Oxford	Lost	37.5-40.5
12 August	Home	Oxford	Won	45-33
18 August	Away	Halifax	Lost	37-41
26 August	Home	Wolverhampton	Won	47-31
30 August	Away	Wimbledon	Lost	36-42
7 September	Away	Exeter	Lost	37-41
15 September	Away	Swindon	Drew	39-39
23 September	Home	Belle Vue	Lost	36-42
30 September	Home	Coventry	Won	43-35
7 October	Home	Halifax	Won	52-26
13 October	Away	King's Lynn	Lost	34-44
14 October	Home	Swindon	Won	40-38
18 October	Away	Ipswich	Lost	27-51
21 October	Home	Poole	Won	40-38
28 October	Home	Wimbledon	Won	47-30
29 October	Away	Reading	Lost	35-43

P30 W12 D1 L17 For 1,157 Against 1,178 Pts 25 Position 11th (out of 16)

Knock-Out Cup

First Round

Date	H/A	Against	W/L	Score
6 June	Away	Poole	Won	41-37
15 July	Home	Poole	Won	41-36

Won on aggregate 82-73

Second Round

Date	H/A	Against	W/L	Score
5 August	Home	King's Lynn	Won	57-21
25 August	Away	King's Lynn	Lost	21-57

Drew 78-78 on aggregate

Second Round Replay

Date	H/A	Against	W/L	Score
5 September	Away	King's Lynn	Lost	27-51
16 September	Home	King's Lynn	Won	42-34

Lost 69-85 on aggregate

1984 – British League and Knock-Out Cup

Rider	Matches	Rides	Points	BP	Total	Average
Bobby Schwartz	40	179	412.5	9	421.5	9.42
John Eskildsen	45	193	354.5	35	389.5	8.07
Paul Woods	38	159	294	26	320	8.05
Antonin Kasper (jnr)	22	81	124	13	137	6.77
Colin Richardson	41	155	198	35	233	6.01

Olli Tyrvainen	44	156	171.5	20	191.5	4.91
Denzil Kent	52	173	160	29	189	4.37
Steve Lucero	31	110	97	18	115	4.18
Martin Goodwin	10	33	26	7	33	4.00
Paul Bosley	8	21	16	4	20	3.81

1985

With the drop down, it meant having to say goodbye to Paul Woods, who had stayed with the Eagles throughout their British League campaign from 1979 to 1984, but his place as captain was taken by the returing former Eastbourne stalwart, Gordon Kennett. Colin Richardson remained with the club and these two were joined by Paul Clarke, a teenager signed from King's Lynn, the experienced Mick Hines, Derek Harrison, Keith Pritchard and Chris Mulvihill. The first match of the new campaign was a challenge match away at Wimbledon's Plough Lane circuit. It was not an auspicious start as the Eagles were well and truly beaten, 49-29. The one bright spot was the form of Kennett, who won two races and finished as top scorer with 12. The first home meeting was on 24 March, a four-team event, won by Arena-Essex with 27 points from Hackney on 26 with Eastbourne third on 25. Canterbury were last with 18.

After a couple of challenge matches and an abandoned Championship of Sussex due to rain, the opening league match took place on 14 April with the Stoke Potters providing the opposition. Kennett with 11 and Richardson (9) helped the home side to a narrow 41-37 win. Barrow were the next visitors and the Eagles won the battle of the birds as they hammered the Blackhawks by 51-27. However. a short trip up the A2 to Hackney saw a 50-28 defeat just five days later. Another defeat followed at Canterbury, this time by 45 points to 33. Kennett (13) and Richardson (11) totalled 24 out of the Eagles' 33 which told its own story, and it was time for some team changes, as in came Bob Kinning and Mike Summerfield. With Poole Pirates closing during the winter, the Weymouth Wildcats had moved into Poole's Wimborne Road stadium to become the Poole Wildcats. The Eagles met the wildcats in a brilliant but stormy match on 5 May. Although Poole's Stan Bear scored a maximum for the visitors it was not enough to prevent a 42-35 win for the Eagles. It was a much better all-round performance for the Eagles with Paul Clarke (7 paid 9) and Keith Pritchard (9 paid 10) catching the eye. Another terrific match followed when Ellesmere Port came seven days later. At various stages of the match, the Eagles led by 22-14, 27-21 and 36-30 but Joe Owen, Dave Morton and Louis Carr saw the Gunners snatch a 39-39 draw. The Eagles then pulled off a superb 42-35 Knock-Out Cup win at Milton Keynes with Colin Richardson the top man. Gordon Kennett missed the 41-37 win over Peterborough but Richardson's 15-point maximum ensured a home win.

With the return to the Second Division, the training school once again played a big part in Eastbourne's planning for the future. Several discoveries, including Garry Tagg, Dean Standing, Ray Morton, Kevin Pitts and Martin Dugard were now taking part in second-half junior races at Arlington. The return Knock-Out Cup match against Milton Keynes saw the expected win, 50-28, putting Eastbourne through to the quarter-finals 92-63 on aggregate. This match saw the signing of lanky Andy Buck from Scunthorpe. His 10 paid 11 return made for a superb debut. It was also in this match that Gordon Kennett set up a new National League track record with a time of 59.64 seconds. Jamie Luckhurst of Wimbledon won the restaged Championship of Sussex before a real cut-and-thrust local derby at Rye House saw the Rockets scrape home 39-37. The next event was the National League Fours with Eastbourne drawn against Hackney, Canterbury and Poole in the first round. The first leg at Hackney was rained off but at Kingsmead, home of the Canterbury Crusaders, the Eagles won with 26 points from Hackney and Poole on 24 and the home side Canterbury on 22. However, on their home track at Arlington the Eagles could only manage to win one race on their way to a miserable total of 18. The leg was won by Poole on 28. Hackney with 27 and Canterbury 23 completed the scores. On the same day an 11 a.m. start saw a Junior Fours at Arlington won by the Eagles with 34 points, Dugard scoring a maximum 12, Ray Morton 9, Bob Kinning 8 and Garry Tagg 5. Wimbledon were second with 27, Hackney third on 21 and Arena-Essex last with 12.

Back in the main event, the final leg at Poole, 23 points put the Eagles equal second on the night but out of the competition. League defeats at Middlesbrough, 45-33, and Ellesmere Port, 50-28, followed. But a thumping 50-28 win over Glasgow with both Richardson and Kennett unbeaten restored some confidence. The pair were unbeaten again seven days later as Exeter were walloped 52-26. Martin Dugard made his first-team debut in this match, recording a score of 5 paid 7. Twenty-four hours later the Eagles went down to a 42-35 defeat at Exeter's County Ground. At Birmingham the Eagles recorded a 39-39 draw with Pritchard and Buck top scoring with 10 each. Dean Standing made his debut in the next match against a dogged Long Eaton as the Eagles ran out 43-35 victors.

The Knock-Out Cup quarter-finals saw Eastbourne victorious as they dumped Wimbledon out, 39-39 away and 44-33 at home. Arena-Essex came to Arlington as the Eagles returned from a Northern tour that had seen them win away at Berwick 39-38 after the match at Edinburgh had been rained off. The match against the Hammers was a real classic, with ex-Eagles Neil Middleditch and Martin Goodwin pushing the home side all the way, but with Gordon Kennett recording another maximum and setting yet another new track record with a time of 58.2 seconds, the home side got through 42-36. The Knock-Out Cup semi-final saw the Eagles and Middlesbrough come face to face. In the first leg at Arlington, the Eagles were rampant and won 49-29 with everyone in the team winning at least one race. The second leg at Middlesbrough turned out to be a real nail-biter as Boro won 48-30, leaving Eastbourne to go through to the final by the narrowest of margins, 79-77 on aggregate. Two close away matches followed as the Eagles beat Glasgow 39-38 and then were just narrowly defeated 40-38 in a classic match at Stoke. In the league, Eastbourne were generally just about holding their own, following the normal pattern of winning most at home and losing most away. In the end they were to finish the season in a mid-table tenth position, but perhaps somewhat surprisingly they now found themselves in the Knock-Out Cup final. Their opponents were Ellesmere Port, who had turned out to be the real powerhouse team of the 1985 National League, winning the league after recording 8 away victories and 2 draws. Now looking for the double, the Gunners began the final as the clear favourites, especially as one of those away draws had been at Arlington. However, Eastbourne had failed to read the script and in the first leg at home they stormed into a 35-13 lead after eight heats. The Gunners managed to pull this back in the second half of the match, however, with three shared heats and two 5-1s leaving the tie in the balance at 46-32. Before the second leg the Eagles travelled to Edinburgh for the rearranged league match and took the points with a 41-36 win. Then it was down to Merseyside via Blackpool for the final in front of a large morning crowd. Fired up for their first final in seven years, the Eagles took to the big, fast Thornton Road track right from the off as Kennett won heat one and a Dugard-Mulvihill 5-1 in the second set the tone. By heat seven the score was 24-18 to the Eagles and the league leaders were chasing shadows. By heat ten the destination of the cup was known – it was heading for Sussex. For the record, Ellesmere Port eventually won on the night 41-37, but the aggregate score was 83-73 to the Eagles. It was a fairytale return to the National League. They had left it as Knock-Out Cup champions and had now returned to take up where they had left off. The Eastbourne scorers on that heroic night were Kennett with a 12-point maximum, Buck 9, Richardson 7, Dugard 4, Clarke 2+1, Mulvihill 2+1 and Pritchard 1.

The final action for 1985 was the Steve Weatherley Benefit Meeting, a pairs event won by Kennett and Dugard. Towards the end of the year, Russell Lanning signed a further two-year contract as general manager. The switch to the National League had been a success and had made a big difference to the club. 'There is so much keenness around the place,' said Lanning. 'People are looking forward to next season in a way they haven't done for years.'

1985 – National League

Date	H/A	Against	W/L	Score
14 April	Home	Stoke	Won	41-37
21 April	Home	Barrow	Won	51-27
26 April	Away	Hackney	Lost	28-50
5 May	Home	Poole	Won	42-35
12 May	Home	Ellesmere Port	Drew	39-39
19 May	Home	Peterborough	Won	41-37
28 May	Away	Poole	Lost	27-51
31 May	Away	Peterborough	Lost	35-43
2 June	Home	Birmingham	Won	41-37
16 June	Away	Rye House	Lost	37-39
27 June	Away	Middlesbrough	Lost	33-45
28 June	Away	Ellesmere Port	Lost	28-50
30 June	Home	Glasgow	Won	50-28
7 July	Home	Exeter	Won	52-26
8 July	Away	Exeter	Lost	35-42
12 July	Away	Birmingham	Drew	39-39
14 July	Away	Long Eaton	Won	43-35
11 August	Home	Edinburgh	Won	58-20
17 August	Away	Berwick	Won	39-38
18 August	Home	Arena-Essex	Won	42-36
21 August	Away	Wimbledon	Lost	34-44
24 August	Away	Canterbury	Lost	35-43
29 August	Away	Arena-Essex	Lost	37-41
1 September	Home	Milton Keynes	Won	43-35
7 September	Home	Rye House	Lost	38-40
8 September	Home	Wimbledon	Lost	37-41
11 September	Away	Long Eaton	Won	40-38
13 September	Away	Glasgow	Won	39-38
14 September	Away	Stoke	Lost	38-40
21 September	Home	Mildenhall	Won	46-31
22 September	Away	Mildenhall	Lost	33-45
24 September	Away	Milton Keynes	Lost	37-39
29 September	Home	Hackney	Won	44-34
6 October	Home	Canterbury	Won	43-35
16 October	Away	Edinburgh	Won	41-36
20 October	Home	Berwick	Won	47-31

P36 W18 D2 L16 For 1,424 Against 1,374 Pts 38 Position 10th (out of 19)

Knock-Out Cup

First Round

Date	H/A	Against	W/L	Score
28 April	Home	Canterbury	Won	47-31
6 May	Away	Canterbury	Lost	33-45

Won 80-76 on aggregate

Second Round

Date	H/A	Against	W/L	Score
14 May	Away	Milton Keynes	Won	42-35
26 May	Home	Milton Keynes	Won	50-28

Won 92-63 on aggregate

Third Round

Date	H/A	Against	W/L	Score
7 August	Away	Wimbledon	Drew	39-39
11 August	Home	Wimbledon	Won	44-33

Won 83-72 on aggregate

Semi-final

Date	H/A	Against	W/L	Score
25 August	Home	Middlesbrough	Won	49-29
12 September	Away	Middlesbrough	Lost	30-48

Won 79-77 on aggregate

Final

Date	H/A	Against	W/L	Score
13 October	Home	Ellesmere Port	Won	46-32
18 October	Away	Ellesmere Port	Lost	37-41

Won 83-73 on aggregate

1985 – National League and Knock-Out Cup

Rider	Matches	Rides	Points	BP	Total	Average
Gordon Kennett	44	186	480	7	487	10.47
Colin Richardson	45	189	392	17	409	8.66
Andy Buck	39	163	272	24	296	7.26
Martin Dugard	28	102	120	25	145	5.69
Keith Pritchard	46	184	227	32	259	5.63
Paul Clarke	38	150	176	30	206	5.49
Mick Hines	6	22	25	5	30	5.46
Chris Mulvihill	38	115	100	26	126	4.38
Derek Harrison	11	34	21	6	27	3.18
Dean Standing	14	33	8	2	10	1.21

1986

Lanning was right. After finishing on such a high in 1985, there was a buzz of expectancy about the place and a real feeling that the good times were about to return to Arlington. Only one major change was made to the team as Dean Standing was brought on board full time, taking the place of Paul Clarke, who was released. The season started with little hint of what was to come as in the first meeting, a challenge match at Plough Lane on 26 March, the Eagles went down 40-38 as the winter rust was removed. Forty-eight hours later, however, the Dons came to Arlington on Good Friday and the Eagles exacted sweet revenge, with Andy Buck hitting a maximum in a 50-28 win. Then it was off to Canterbury for the Easter Trophy, where a last-race 4-2 gave the home side a 39-38 win. Easter Sunday saw the Eagles storm to a 51-37 win with Martin Dugard the lowest scorer with paid 8. When Middlesbrough came for the first league match on 20 April, it had all the makings of a classic and it didn't disappoint. Gary Havelock took heat one, heading home Kennett, Martin Dixon and Dugard as the Tigers took a 4-2. For Middlesbrough, Havelock won his first three races in brilliant style while the exciting Mark Courtney dropped just 1 point out of 15. Nevertheless, the Eagles managed to build up a 34-26 lead. However, good use of tactical substitutes with a helping hand from referee Graham Brodie, who failed to stop heat twelve when Kennett was shown the safety fence, saw the visitors take home a 39-39 draw. This was the last time all season that any team was to take a point away from Arlington. They weren't about to lose many matches away from home either as the next match showed, with Eastbourne gaining a 41-37 victory at Glasgow.

Meanwhile the Eagles' management were taking every opportunity of gaining publicity, especially for their training school as six of the club's teenagers appeared on TVS's *Coast to Coast* news programme, explaining how the five-year marriage ban introduced by the management would keep them in line.

A disappointing 40-37 defeat at Arena-Essex was followed by a double over Rye House, 41-37 at home and a comfortable 42-36 win away as the Eagles hit three 5-1s and a 4-2 between heats nine and twelve. Next Berwick were taken to the cleaners 58-20 as the Eagles began to hit top form. Peterborough fared little better, going down 54-23 with every member of the Eastbourne team winning at will. When the team travelled up to Brough Park, Newcastle, many expected a home win, but no-one told the Eagles, who turned in a 50-28 away win with eleven heat wins out of the thirteen. By this time, Eastbourne had already reached the top of the League with 15 points from 9 matches. Stoke were second on 14, also from 9. Arena-Essex's former Eagle Neil Middleditch won the Championship of Sussex with a faultless 15-point maximum from Richardson with 14 and Kennett 12. A magnificent 40-38 win at Exeter followed, albeit with a bit of luck after the Falcons' Kevin Price ground to a halt in the last heat. However, at Arlington luck had nothing to do with it as the Eagles ran out 59-19 winners, with maximums for Dugard and Pritchard and paid ones for Kennett, Richardson and Standing. The National League Fours saw the Eagles win at Canterbury before recording a magnificent 42 points out of a possible 48 at home. Second place at Exeter with 24 and second again at Poole with 19 saw the Eagles make the finals with ease.

It was the round at Exeter that saw Colin Richardson suffer serious life-threatening injuries that clearly shook not only the team but speedway in general. Richardson broke three vertebrae, his collarbone and his right shoulder blade. The accident pushed his whole shoulder into his chest six inches, tore all the ribs off his spine and broke all the ribs on the front of his chest so that effectively the whole right side of his upper body was detached. He severed all the nerves on his hip, losing all the feeling in his hip area down to his groin and across the right side of his buttocks. He chipped his heel and wrist and his right lung completely collapsed. He lost a total of twelve pints of blood into the chest cavity. He was paralysed from the neck downwards for a week while the doctors were unsure of the extent of the damage to the spine. Richardson later said, 'The worse thing was I was conscious throughout the whole ordeal, including having chest drains fitted. I don't like thinking about it too much. All I can say is it wasn't funny. I had to sleep propped up with pillows for four weeks afterwards. Once I laid down I couldn't get up again. It was a nightmare.' Although, somewhat amazingly, Richardson made a return to speedway later in the year, this accident effectively ended his career.

The top-of-the-table clash with Stoke at Arlington saw Paul Thorp record a 15-point maximum for the Potters and with Nigel Crabtree scoring 13 it took a last-race win from Dugard to ensure the 42-36 win. The winning streak continued at Long Eaton as Dugard slammed in a 15-point maximum with Standing's 9 paid 12 from reserve also vital in the 46-32 victory. The away encounter at Stoke saw Kennett and Potter Daz Sumner come to blows, but that was nothing compared to Bob Dugard and a member of the Stoke track staff as tempers flared. It was a Crabtree-Thorp 5-1 in heat thirteen that saw the Eagles' winning run at last come to an end, 43-35. A 42-36 win at Wimbledon in the Knock-Out Cup on 2 July meant the second leg was a formality as only Roger Johns with 12 and Jamie Luckhurst with 13 put up any resistance in another rout. Steve Chambers was given his debut as Glasgow were whipped 54-24 before another brilliant away win, 48-30, at Milton Keynes. In the quarter-final of the Knock-Out Cup, Les Collins' Edinburgh put up a good battle before eventually going down 48-28, Gordon Kennett scoring a low 6 points in the first leg. The second leg at Edinburgh saw the Eagles safely through with a 40-38 win. Top of the league and through to the semi-finals of the Knock-Out Cup, Eastbourne were riding high but in the National League Fours final at Peterborough the Eagles somehow failed to show to their advantage and lost out in the first semi-final with rivals Middlesbrough, the only team to take a point from them at Arlington all year, taking the honours.

Richardson made a remarkable comeback from his injuries against Canterbury but, clearly unfit, he could manage only 1 point, although the final 46-32 score was comfortable enough. In the second half of this match an Eagles junior team beat the Crusaders 17-7, Darren Standing and yet another new discovery, Dean Barker, shining in this one. Martin Dugard won the Southern Riders' Championship at Poole against a top-class field, but even he couldn't prevent a league defeat at the hands of Peterborough 42-36. A local derby against Canterbury was always going to be hotly contested and so it proved, as the Eagles turned on the style to record a league double in just twenty-four hours, 45-33 away and 46-32 at home. The away win at Kingsmead was a significant away victory as the other title challengers Middlesbrough, Stoke and Arena-Essex had all fallen to defeat on the Kent circuit. One of those challengers, Arena-Essex, was the next team to visit Arlington. The Hammers were expected to push the Eagles all the way as they included Neil Middleditch, Andrew Silver and Martin Goodwin, all Eastbourne track specialists, in their side. After four heats the visitors were in front and after six it was level. At this point the Eagles moved up a gear with Dean Standing recording a brilliant 15-point maximum from reserve as the home side ran out 47-31 winners. Wimbledon came next and once again the Eagles were really pushed in the early heats, but took control from heat seven to run out victors 42-36, but they certainly knew they had been in a match. This match saw yet another debut for a junior off the Eastbourne training production line. His name was Dean Barker.

The first leg of the Knock-Out Cup semi-final was a home tie against Peterborough and saw Dean Standing move to a heat-leader position. It proved to be an easy victory as Dugard with 15 and Kennett with 13, helped by Buck's 9.5 and Pritchard's 9, saw the Eagles win 49.5-28.5. Following the next two league matches, a home victory over Long Eaton and an away one at Birmingham, which saw Dugard smash the track record, Eastbourne found themselves in second place, two points behind Middlesbrough but with five matches in hand. Next up were Edinburgh, who were beaten 47-31, before the Eagles travelled to the East End of London to take on Hackney. In a real nail-biter the Eagles gave chase as the Kestrels took an early lead. Dugard hit a maximum but the real hero was Keith Pritchard, who teamed up with the teenager to record a match-winning 5-1 in heat twelve over Malcolm Simmons. In a remarkable 41-37 win, it was skipper Kennett and Buck who made sure of the points in the last heat. This made six wins in a row as the Eagles went to the top of the table. Dugard also won the Silver Helmet, beating Alan Mogridge.

Six thousand spectators turned up at Arlington to see the next meeting, which was a double-header against Hackney and Newcastle. The reason for the great interest was because if Eastbourne could win both matches they would win the league title. In the first match against Hackney, Dugard again hit a maximum in a 47-31 win over the Kestrels. Against the Diamonds, Standing hit 15 and Kennett and Dugard also went through the card unbeaten in a 52-26 win. They had done it! The Eagles were league champions for the first time since 1977. Just for good measure that day, Dugard retained the Silver Helmet against Mogridge and David Blackburn.

However, there was still the chance of the double as Eastbourne moved on to Peterborough for the Knock Out Cup semi-final second leg and, in another stunning performance, took the Panthers out 41-37 to move into the final. And so there were just two matches left to decide the destination of the last piece of silverware in 1986, the Knock-Out Cup, Eastbourne v. Mildenhall. The first leg was at Arlington on 26 October, with the Eagles winning an epic battle 51-25. The second leg was staged at West Row on 2 November, again in front of 6,000 fans, many of whom had travelled up from Sussex to take over the terracing on turns one and two. In a carnival atmosphere the Fen Tigers took an early lead with a heat-one 5-1. The Eagles were level, though, by heat five, before a controversial exclusion for Dugard saw the home side go back in front 20-16. Again the Eagles hit back and by heat eight the score was 24-24 and the blue and yellow flags and banners were flying high as ticker tape fell like a snowstorm. The match went down to the wire with Andy Buck and Gordon Kennett rounding off with a 4-2 to earn a 39-39 draw and a 90-64 win on aggregate to complete a brilliant league and cup double. The Eagles' scorers in the second leg were: Dugard 8, Standing 8, Kennett 7, Buck 6+1, Pritchard 5, Chambers 3 and Barker 2+1.

Eastbourne's resurrection in the National League was complete. They had won the league by six points and had not lost one match in the Knock-Out Cup, home or away. It was certainly a return to the good old days in more ways than one as once again the Eastbourne junior production line came into its own. One of its first discoveries, Gordon Kennett topped the team's averages with 9.87 with the latest star to roll off the line, Martin Dugard, just behind on 9.76. Both scored eleven maximums during the season. Yet another training school protégé, Dean Standing, broke into the team and made it to heat leader, finishing with an average of 7.06, while Dean Barker also became a team regular.

1986 – National League

Date	H/A	Against	W/L	Score
20 April	Home	Middlesbrough	Drew	39-39
25 April	Away	Glasgow	Won	41-37
26 April	Away	Berwick	Lost	38-40
27 April	Home	Birmingham	Won	47-31
1 May	Away	Arena-Essex	Lost	37-40
4 May	Home	Rye House	Won	41-37
5 May	Away	Rye House	Won	42-36
11 May	Home	Berwick	Won	58-20
18 May	Home	Peterborough	Won	54-23
19 May	Home	Newcastle	Won	50-28
26 May	Away	Exeter	Won	40-38
15 June	Home	Stoke	Won	42-36
18 June	Away	Long Eaton	Won	46-32
21 June	Away	Stoke	Lost	35-43
29 June	Home	Milton Keynes	Won	54-24
9 July	Away	Mildenhall	Lost	36-42
12 July	Home	Mildenhall	Won	44-34
20 July	Home	Glasgow	Won	54-24
22 July	Away	Milton Keynes	Won	48-30
27 July	Home	Edinburgh	Won	47-31
3 August	Home	Poole	Won	51-27
6 August	Away	Wimbledon	Lost	35-43
9 August	Home	Boston	Won	50-28
16 August	Away	Canterbury	Won	45-33
17 August	Home	Canterbury	Won	46-32
23 August	Away	Boston	Lost	33-45
29 August	Away	Peterborough	Lost	32-46
31 August	Home	Arena-Essex	Won	47-31
7 September	Home	Exeter	Won	59-19
12 September	Away	Hackney	Won	41-37
14 September	Home	Long Eaton	Won	57-21
18 September	Away	Middlesbrough	Lost	33-44
19 September	Away	Edinburgh	Won	40-37
21 September	Home	Wimbledon	Won	42-36
26 September	Away	Birmingham	Won	48-30
7 October	Away	Poole	Lost	34-44
12 October	Home	Newcastle	Won	52-26
12 October	Home	Hackney	Won	46-32

P38 W28 D1 L9 For 1,688 Against 1,272 Pts 57 Position 1st (out of 20)

Knock-Out Cup

First Round
Bye

Second Round

Date	H/A	Against	W/L	Score
2 July	Away	Wimbledon	Won	42-36
6 July	Home	Wimbledon	Won	48-30

Won 90-66 on aggregate

Third Round

Date	H/A	Against	W/L	Score
1 August	Away	Edinburgh	Won	40-38
27 September	Home	Edinburgh	Won	48-28

Won 88-66 on aggregate

The 1986 double-winning Eastbourne Eagles. From left to right: Martin Dugard, Keith Pritchard, Gordon Kennett, Andy Buck, Dean Standing, Chris Mulvihill, Dean Barker

Semi-Final

Date	H/A	Against	W/L	Score
21 September	Away	Peterborough	Won	41-37
17 October	Home	Peterborough	Won	49.5-28.5

Won 90.5-65.5 on aggregate

Final

Date	H/A	Against	W/L	Score
26 October	Home	Mildenhall	Won	51-25
2 November	Away	Mildenhall	Drew	39-39

Won 90-64 on aggregate.

1986 – National League and Knock-Out Cup

Rider	Matches	Rides	Points	BP	Total	Average
Gordon Kennett	46	210	487	31	518	9.87
Martin Dugard	46	212	483	34	517	9.76
Colin Richardson	16	62	102	23	125	8.07
Keith Pritchard	46	194	298	52	350	7.22
Andy Buck	46	199	296.5	56	352.5	7.09
Dean Standing	44	178	274	40	314	7.06
Chris Mulvihill	32	82	72	14	86	4.20
Dean Barker	14	45	27	8	35	3.11

1987

To pull off the league and cup double in 1986 was a great achievement, but it had been done before. Belle Vue Colts, Crewe, Boston, Birmingham and Eastbourne themselves had all performed this feat in the Second Division/National League in recent years. What had not been done before was to follow it up a year later by doing it again. There were high hopes at Arlington that the Eagles could be the first. There were not too many changes to the team. Following his horrific injuries, Richardson had decided to call it a day and Mulvihill left to be replaced by Kevin Pitts, but essentially it was the same team that had won the double in 1986 that started the new season with Kennett, Dugard, Buck, Pritchard, both Standings and Barker all raring to go.

The writing was on the wall for the other teams as soon as the season started. In the opening league match Peterborough were thumped 52-26 with Kennett, Pritchard, Dugard and Buck going through the card. The Eagles won by an even bigger margin in their next match as Good Friday's meeting against Boston was a complete mismatch, the Eagles winning 57-21, with Darren Standing contributing a reserve's maximum with 5 paid 6. The first away fixture followed but this made no difference to Eastbourne's winning ways as they took on and beat Milton Keynes 42-36. There was a short respite from league action as the Eagles took part in the National League Fours first round. Winning all four matches, Eastbourne finished up with a stunning total of 148 points to Rye House's 83, Arena-Essex's 81 and Canterbury's 67.

As the season progressed it became more than obvious that no team stood a chance against the Eagles at 'Fortress Arlington'. Following the 52-26 defeat of Peterborough and the 57-21 defeat of Boston, the next six home league matches also resulted in scores of over 50 for Eastbourne: 55-23 against Rye House, 56-22 against Exeter, 54-23 against Long Eaton, 53-25 against Berwick, 53-25 against Middlesbrough and 57-21 against local rivals Canterbury. As if this wasn't bad enough for the rest of the league, Eastbourne followed all this up with a crushing 62-33 defeat of Poole in the second round of the Knock-Out Cup. Away from home, although the final totals were smaller, the Eagles were also winning every match, including a 39-38 thriller at Edinburgh thanks to a last-race 5-1 from Buck and Kennett. At this stage of the season the Eagles had a record in all competitions that read: raced 14 won 14.

The run finally came to an end at Stoke as Eastbourne went down to the Potters 43-35 but by now there was little doubt in most minds that Eastbourne would retain the league title. Mildenhall and Stoke had not given up, but in reality only a slip-up from the powerful Eagles would put them back in with a chance. The main question now was: could they add the Knock-Out Cup again and perform the so far unheard of double double? Although Eastbourne lost another match in the second-round second-leg match at Poole, 51-45, they were safely through to the quarter-finals.

To warm up for the next round of the cup, the Eagles took on Glasgow at Arlington and slaughtered them 60-18. Then came the visit of their fellow Scots Edinburgh in the quarter-final. This proved to be slightly closer but was still a good win for the Eagles, 56-40. The return at Powderhall proved to be no problem for Eastbourne as they cruised through 50-45, taking the quarter-final 106-85 on aggregate. Eastbourne then had to face the two teams that were dogging them in the league and hoping for a mistake. First up was Mildenhall at the latter's own track. The result was to give the Fen Tigers some hope as they defeated the Eagles by the fairly comfortable score of 45-33. Then came Stoke in the semi-finals of the cup. The first-leg match at Stoke saw a massive crowd witness a superb advert for National League speedway with the Potters winning 53-42 to set up an interesting second leg. But before the second leg could be run, Arlington played host to the return visit of Mildenhall who came to Sussex in search of the National League points that would put them in the driving seat ahead of Eastbourne. They very nearly got them too as only an exclusion for Dave Jackson in the final heat gave the Eagles a 40-38 win. The eagerly awaited cup semi-final second leg was next and what a match it was, as scores of 15 for Dugard, 12 for Kennett and Pritchard, paid 11 for Dean Standing and 10 for Buck sent the home fans wild with a 57-39 win, 99-92 on aggregate. While all the league and cup excitement was going on, Stoke's Nigel Crabtree won the Championship of Sussex with 14 points, four more than his nearest rival and the Eagles' Andy Buck become Southern Riders' Champion at Poole with 14 points.

With Stoke and Mildenhall still keeping up the challenge, Wednesday 9 September saw the Eagles gain a 40-38 win at Wimbledon. This was a real corker with never more than four points in it. Wimbledon took the early lead but the Eagles drew level in heat nine and then a brilliant ride by Dean Standing in heat twelve with Dugard holding out Neville Tatum saw the Eagles go in front 37-35. As the tapes rose for the final heat it was the Dons who were away first and a 5-1 for them looked a distinct possibility, giving them the match 40-38. But Kennett and Buck did not give up as first Kennett and then Buck pushed homester Kevin Jolly to the back for a 3-3 and a 40-38 to the Eagles. This turned out to be the first match in a good week for Eastbourne as Arena-Essex were then thumped 50-28 with Keith Pritchard taking the Silver Helmet for good measure and then, in the second part of the night's double-header, Newcastle were whipped by an identical 50-28 scoreline.

Now three points clear at the top of the league, the Eagles moved on to the first leg of the Knock-Out Cup final, a repeat of the 1986 one as the Eagles travelled to West Row to take on Mildenhall. It was another top-notch match with the sun-drenched crowd being treated to some great racing. Heat one saw Kennett storm past ex-Eagle Dave Jessup on the way to a paid 14-point haul, matched by Dugard, but it was a superb Mel Taylor and Glen Baxter who helped the home side to a narrow 50-46 win. The second leg was held on 4 October and it was a massive crowd that witnessed the Eagles win 54-41 to give them the cup 100-91 on aggregate despite another superb showing by Jessup, Taylor and Jackson. The Eagles' scorers were: Dean Standing 11+2, Buck 11+1, Kennett 10+1, Dugard 9+1, Dean Barker 6, Pritchard 5+3 and Darren Standing 2.

Stoke Potters came on 11 October but by now they were down to fourth spot as Milton Keynes were climbing the league at a rate of knots. The Eagles duly won 57-21 in another powerhouse performance. With Stoke now out of it the only team who could beat Eastbourne to the league title were Mildenhall. With one home match left each, the position was that if Mildenhall beat the rapidly improving Milton Keynes then Eastbourne would need to beat Edinburgh to retain the title. Ken Burnett travelled to West Row to witness an unbelievable finish as the Milton Keynes Knights handed the championship to the Eagles with a stunning 40-38 victory. Ken says, 'I phoned Russell Lanning from the track to tell him the news, but the Eagles manager didn't believe me, insisting that I was winding him up! Eventually he did believe me and came to terms with the fact that Eastbourne had completed the incredible double double without turning a wheel.'

As it happened, even if Mildenhall had won, the Eagles would have still won the league as they hammered Edinburgh 55-22 in their last league match. Mildenhall did, however, have one last trick up their sleeve as they stopped the Eagles from doing the treble by winning the National Fours final from the Eagles at Hackney on 16 October. It had been yet another amazing season for the Eagles. They had won every one of their home league matches as well as 7 away. But their cup performance was in many ways even more astonishing, as it meant that not only had they won the cup three years in succession, but that they had not lost a National League Cup tie since 1976. In recognition of this outstanding accomplishment, the trophy was awarded to Eastbourne outright.

Although it becomes somewhat repetitious to say it, once again much of the success was due to the famous Arlington training school. Dugard moved to the top of the averages with a brilliant 10.45, the second best in the whole league, while Dean Standing contributed 7.33 and Dean Barker, in his first full season, 5.16. Kennett continued to score prolifically, giving strong support to Dugard with 9.40 and the supporters' Rider of the Year, Buck, improved his average by over 1.5 points per match to 8.66. The rest of the regular team members, Pritchard, Darren Standing and Steve Chambers, all did their bit to make this a year to remember for the Eastbourne Eagles.

In their first period in the Second Division/National League, Eastbourne were the most consistent and best team, but in the three years since their return, the team had done even better and had totally dominated the league with two championships and three cup wins. In a total of thirteen years of Second Division/National League racing, the Eagles had lost just 8 home matches and had recorded 71 away wins. No other team came anywhere close to equalling, let alone beating, this unbelievable record.

1987 – National League

Date	H/A	Against	W/L	Score
12 April	Home	Peterborough	Won	52-26

Date	H/A	Against	W/L	Score
17 April	Home	Boston	Won	57-21
21 April	Away	Milton Keynes	Won	42-36
3 May	Home	Rye House	Won	55-23
9 May	Home	Exeter	Won	56-22
17 May	Home	Long Eaton	Won	54-23
22 May	Away	Edinburgh	Won	39-38
23 May	Away	Stoke	Lost	35-43
24 May	Home	Berwick	Won	53-25
31 May	Home	Middlesbrough	Won	53-25
7 June	Home	Canterbury	Won	57-21
27 June	Home	Milton Keynes	Won	43-35
3 July	Away	Peterborough	Lost	38-40
5 July	Home	Wimbledon	Won	42-36
11 July	Away	Berwick	Lost	35-42
12 July	Home	Glasgow	Won	60-18
10 August	Away	Mildenhall	Lost	33-45
16 August	Home	Mildenhall	Won	40-38
19 August	Away	Long Eaton	Lost	35-42
20 August	Away	Middlesbrough	Won	45-33
23 August	Home	Newcastle	Won	50-28
29 August	Home	Arena-Essex	Won	50-28
5 September	Away	Canterbury	Lost	35-43
6 September	Home	Edinburgh	Won	55-22
9 September	Away	Wimbledon	Won	40-38
15 September	Away	Poole	Lost	34-44
21 September	Away	Newcastle	Won	44-33
27 September	Away	Rye House	Won	45-33
28 September	Away	Exeter	Lost	37-41
11 October	Home	Stoke	Won	57-21

P30 W22 D0 L8 For 1,348 Against 987 Pts 44 Position 1st (out of 16)

Knock-Out Cup

First Round
Bye

Second Round

Date	H/A	Against	W/L	Score
14 June	Home	Poole	Won	62-33
16 June	Away	Poole	Lost	45-51

Won 107-84 on aggregate

Third Round

Date	H/A	Against	W/L	Score
25 July	Home	Edinburgh	Won	56-40
31 July	Away	Edinburgh	Won	50-45

Won 106-85 on aggregate

Semi-final

Date	H/A	Against	W/L	Score
15 August	Away	Stoke	Lost	42-53
20 September	Home	Stoke	Won	57-39

Won 99-92 on aggregate

Final

Date	H/A	Against	W/L	Score
27 September	Away	Mildenhall	Lost	46-50
4 October	Home	Mildenhall	Won	54-41

Won 100-91 on aggregate
Eastbourne won the league and cup double

1987 – National League and Knock-Out Cup

Rider	Matches	Rides	Points	BP	Total	Average
Martin Dugard	38	168	429	8	437	10.41
Gordon Kennett	38	166	368	22	390	9.40
Andy Buck	38	163	324	29	353	8.66
Dean Standing	37	156	222	64	286	7.33
Keith Pritchard	36	143	199	52	251	7.02
Dean Barker	21	76	85	13	98	5.16
Darren Standing	33	93	82	18	100	4.30
Steve Chambers	13	38	31	7	38	4.00
Kevin Pitts	6	20	11	2	13	2.60

1988

With Eastbourne now on top of the world, the news came as a bombshell when, in January 1988, Bob Dugard announced that Eastbourne would be closing down for at least a year in protest at the National League promoters insisting that the Eagles had to abide by the 42-point limit. With Dean Standing requesting a transfer, Eastbourne's average had come down to fractionally above the limit at 42.08, but the promoters' management committee was still pressing for them to lose another rider. Dugard was incensed that they should stick so rigidly to the letter of the law. 'I'm not prepared,' he said, 'to con the public by putting out a below-quality side simply to satisfy this particular rule. We are having to increase admission prices, but I am being asked to reduce the quality of the product for the supporters. I know they will not stand for it. It would be financial lunacy to run under the circumstances. We have had a wonderful three years and are quite rightly expected by our public to maintain certain standards. I have not got the heart to continue. If we can't keep our three heat leaders, we will not open this season.' Dugard went on to say that he believed the loss of one of his star riders would trigger a twenty per cent fall in attendance. He said he intended to loan out all his riders in 1988 with a view to a possible relaunch in 1989. Russell Lanning, who had left Eastbourne at the end of the 1987 season to join Wimbledon, contacted Dugard immediately, offering his support and saying he would work hard to find a solution to the problem.

Fortunately a solution to the impasse was reached before the start of the season when Gareth Rogers agreed to take over the running of the club for the next twelve months. Under the terms of the deal, Rogers agreed to rent Eastbourne Speedway from the Dugard family's Oxspeed Company with Bob Dugard continuing to handle all contractual matters and acting in an advisory capacity while Rogers took over as promoter. It was agreed that the Eagles would retain Dean Standing, who decided to stay, as well as Gordon Kennett, Andy Buck, Keith Pritchard, Darren Standing and Dean Barker but that Martin Dugard would move up to First Division Oxford.

All this close-season wrangling left its mark on the team, who got off to a bad start with defeats at Hackney and Stoke and a draw at home to Milton Keynes. By mid-season, the Eagles were in the unaccustomed position of being in the bottom half of the table. Some victories followed the early reverses, notably in the National League Fours first round, which they won by one point, 121 to 120 from Poole with Wimbledon and Exeter languishing well behind on 97 and 46 respectively, but an emphatic home defeat, 55-41, at the hands of Hackney, coupled with a much-publicised walkout by heat leader Andy Buck, who had suffered greatly with bike problems, left the Eagles reeling. He returned two nights later with a superb 15-point maximum, but even this wasn't enough to prevent his team slipping to a 50.5-45.5 reverse. But if the match against Hackney on 22 May had seen them at a low ebb, the match on 21 August certainly proved one of the highlights of the season as the Eagles' 60-35 defeat of Stoke saw the debut of sixteen-year-old David Norris, who scored a paid 10-point return, thus taking the first step on the ladder that was to install him as an Eastbourne legend.

By that time, however, Eastbourne's proud National League Knock-Out Cup record had come to an end as they lost in the second round to Berwick, 101-91 on aggregate, the damage being done on the away visit to Berwick's Shielfield Park track where the Eagles went down 56-40. Following home wins against both Arena-Essex, 58-38, and Long Eaton, 66-30, the Eagles exacted some revenge over Berwick with a 64-32 defeat of the border side at Arlington. They were to remain unbeaten at home thereafter, though a draw with Wimbledon in mid-September proved something of a disappointment. Away from Sussex the wins didn't come quite as readily as they had previously but a draw at Arena-Essex and narrow victories at both Rye House, 48-47, and Mildenhall, 51-45, saw the Eagles claw their way gradually up the table. Eastbourne came close to glory in the National League Fours final at Peterborough, finishing in equal second place with Mildenhall behind the winners Peterborough, though victory by Mildenhall's Mel Taylor over Andy Buck in the run-off relegated the Eagles to third place overall. They also came close in the National League Pairs Championship at Poole, with Kennett and Buck reaching the semi-final, only to lose out to Stoke 5-4, with Kennett winning the race but Buck dropping out with engine trouble.

In spite of a difficult start to the season, the Eastbourne spirit had seen the Eagles reassert themselves and, in the end, third place in the league was a very creditable performance. Once again it was Gordon Kennett who took responsibility for guiding the team through the lowlands of the first half of the season into the sunnier uplands of their final position. He proved to be a great ambassador for the sport and once more he topped the Eagles' standings with an average of 9.97, just a short head above Buck who finished the year on 9.57. Dean Standing was the third heat leader and though he was inconsistent at times, he was a rider of genuine quality. Sadly he once again expressed his intention to leave at the end of the season and was ruled out of team-building plans for the following year. Dean Barker, Darren Standing and Keith Pritchard all gave solid support. The latest production-line junior, David Norris, rode in 12 matches for an average of 5.00. After his debut match against Stoke, Rogers commented that the sight of this youngster in full hair-raising flight around the track was 'a real golden moment that will live in my memory as long as I'm in speedway.'

1988 – National League

Date	H/A	Against	W/L	Score
15 April	Away	Hackney	Lost	44-50
30 April	Away	Stoke	Lost	43-52
1 May	Home	Edinburgh	Won	60-36
8 May	Home	Mildenhall	Won	58-36
10 May	Away	Milton Keynes	Lost	45-51
22 May	Home	Hackney	Lost	41-55
24 May	Away	Poole	Won	58.5-37.5
29 May	Home	Glasgow	Won	57-38
30 May	Away	Rye House	Won	48-47
22 June	Away	Long Eaton	Lost	45-51
23 June	Away	Middlesbrough	Won	49-46
24 June	Away	Edinburgh	Won	49-47
26 June	Home	Milton Keynes	Won	62-34
3 July	Home	Middlesbrough	Won	51-45
8 July	Away	Glasgow	Lost	46-50
9 July	Away	Berwick	Lost	44-52
10 July	Home	Arena-Essex	Won	58-38
17 July	Home	Long Eaton	Won	66-30
31 July	Home	Berwick	Won	64-32
6 August	Home	Exeter	Won	67-29
12 August	Away	Peterborough	Lost	39-57
21 August	Home	Stoke	Won	60-35
27 August	Away	Arena-Essex	Drew	48-48
28 August	Home	Rye House	Won	60-34

11 September	Home	Wimbledon	Drew	48-48
12 September	Away	Exeter	Lost	47-49
17 September	Away	Peterborough	Lost	39-57
18 September	Away	Mildenhall	Won	51-45
25 September	Home	Poole	Won	56-40
28 September	Away	Wimbledon	Lost	43-53

P30 W17 D2 L11 For 1,546.5 Against 1,322.5 Pts 36 Position 3rd (out of 16)

Knock-Out Cup

First Round

Date	H/A	Against	W/L	Score
15 May	Home	Exeter	Won	66-29
16 May	Away	Exeter	Won	50-46

Won 116-75 on aggregate

Second Round

Date	H/A	Against	W/L	Score
18 June	Away	Berwick	Lost	40-56
19 June	Home	Berwick	Won	51-45

Lost 91-101 on aggregate

1988 – National League and Knock-Out Cup

Rider	Matches	Rides	Points	BP	Total	Average
Gordon Kennett	34	178	424.5	19	443.5	9.97
Andy Buck	32	161	363	22	385	9.57
Dean Standing	34	166	297	23	320	7.71
Dean Barker	32	164	251	51	302	7.37
Keith Pritchard	31	151	175	37	212	5.62
David Norris	12	48	53	7	60	5.00
Jon Surman	22	91	84	17	101	4.44
Darren Standing	29	99	84	23	107	4.32

1989

Following a season that had turned out reasonably well in spite of the poor start, newly installed promoter Gareth Rogers was looking to draw on his experiences, both good and bad, to take into the 1989 season, one that he hoped would form a firm foundation on which the club could build heading into the 1990s. In the event, what followed proved to be a turbulent campaign, one that witnessed little in the way of success on the track and culminated in an unsightly brawl at the end-of-season dinner and dance, prompting a transfer request from two of the team's rising stars and Rogers questioning his involvement at the Sussex venue.

There was little hint at the depression to follow as Rogers readied himself for a second season at the helm. He had found a much-needed co-promoter in former Canterbury boss Chris Galvin, which gave him more time to concentrate on administration matters and although Martin Dugard had long since departed to Oxford, Rogers hoped that sibling Paul would prove just as great a draw as his elder brother had. That was to prove his first disappointment as Paul opted to join Martin at Cowley, and then his fall-back option, Gary Tagg, also turned him down, preferring to team up with league champions Hackney. Of the team which had finished the previous season with such a flourish, Gordon Kennett, Andy Buck, Keith Pritchard, who had had a much deserved testimonial in 1988, Dean Barker, David Norris and Darren Standing returned to see action, Standing's elder brother Dean having departed to join Ipswich. The number seven berth was to prove the stumbling block to start with but Oxford youngster

Jon Surman, who had ridden for the Eagles in 1988 on loan, was once again engaged to fill the void and the way he started rattling up the points certainly seemed to justify the faith shown in him. It wasn't set to last, however, as the Cheetahs' loanee broke a scaphoid against Milton Keynes in early June, thus bringing to an end his all-too-brief spell with the Eagles. Though Surman was eventually to play a bit-part role for Poole in the twilight of the season, the Eagles saw out the year with Steve Masters and Darren Grayling fulfilling the reserve role.

The season began in encouraging fashion, a three-cornered success in the Easter Trophy against Arena-Essex and Hackney kicked it all off, then challenge match wins against Ipswich 54-40, Wimbledon 53-42 and Kulsvierne of Denmark 63-33 seemingly prepared them for the real business that lay ahead. Exeter, 67-29, and Berwick, 49-47, were the first to fall in the League at Arlington while Glasgow were unable to prevent the Eagles from winning through into the next round of the Knock-Out Cup. And then, despite early defeats for the Eagles at both Stoke and Poole, the Peterborough Panthers were soon to feel the might of the Eastbourne roadshow as the Sussex side raced to a 50-45 win at Alwalton. Eastbourne qualified for the final of the National League Fours with a group success over Exeter, 108, Poole, 101 and Wimbledon, 60, the Eagles having amassed 115 points from the four rounds. Back to the league and victories over Ipswich 55-41, Milton Keynes 65-30 and Wimbledon 48-47 at Arlington followed while the Sussex travellers tasted success away at Milton Keynes.

It was during this productive time for the Eagles on the track that things started to go badly wrong off the track. Barker's early-season form was such that he was chosen to ride for England against Australia in a Test match at Edinburgh. Instead of taking his place in the England line-up, however, he chose to ride in an open meeting at Oxford, for which he claimed he had a prior booking. The National League management committee slapped a £500 fine on Rogers for giving Barker permission to ride at Oxford rather than in the Test match and Barker himself was warned that he could face disciplinary action. To complicate matters, Bob Dugard, no doubt fuelled by the resentment that had simmered since he had threatened to pull the 1988 Eagles from the league over the 42-points limit affair, went public with a scathing attack on National League chairman Mervyn Stewkesbury. Barker was eventually cleared of wrong-doing but Rogers agreed to pay his fine. Rogers' action infuriated Dugard still further as he felt it completely undermined the principled stand the club had made on the issue.

All this had its effect on the track as Poole were the first to heap disappointment on the Eagles, winning both legs to knock them out of the cup, and then came the Northern tour that was to have a damning and detrimental affect on team morale. A fall-out between Gordon Kennett and Andy Buck at Glasgow in early July led to Buck walking out of the club and team manager Barney Kennett resigning his position. The troubles persisted as riders and supporters voiced their feelings openly through the media about the way the club was being run and it didn't help when Mildenhall came and won 49-47 at Arlington.

The Eagles won through from their semi-final but finished fourth in the final of the National League Fours with 7 points, behind Peterborough on 15, Stoke on 14 and Exeter on 12. They were to fare no better in the National League Pairs, Buck and Kennett getting a combined total of 13 points in their group but this being insufficient to prevent Mildenhall, on 18, progressing to the later stages. The culmination of the club's problems came on 28 October at the annual end-of-season dinner and dance when an unseemly fracas between Norris and Barker took place and fists flew. David Norris collected minor injuries during the scuffle and immediately banged in a transfer request, stating that he would never ride for Eastbourne again. Barker had already signed for Oxford for the following year.

In spite of everything, the Eagles still managed to finish the season in a fairly respectable seventh place. Much of this was due once again to Gordon Kennett, who led his team through all the troubles to finish with a 9.60 average. Behind him was the ever-improving Dean Barker, who also recorded a 9-plus average. Unfortunately his season was cut short when he received multiple injuries following an horrific pile-up at Hackney on 8 September. David Norris had a good season, his average going up to 7.04. He also achieved personal success in the Silver

Helmet with wins against Jens Rasmussen at Rye House and Trevor Banks of Milton Keynes at Arlington before losing the honour to Preben Eriksen at Mildenhall. This year's junior discoveries were Ben Howe and David Mason.

Rogers summed up his second season in charge by saying, 'The continued development of junior talent is one of the most positive points I can look back on. In honesty, though, 1989 will not go down as one of Gareth Rogers' – or Eastbourne's – favourite years. My motivation is very low. Bob Dugard has said "don't throw the towel in." But a certain faction have demoralised me. You don't mind if people aren't going to row the boat with you, but you don't need the abuse.' Despite everything the Eagles had gone through, the end-of-season figures revealed that there had been an 11.79 per cent increase in attendance figures, giving a total of 26,820 cash customers with the average attendance rising from 992 to 1,090.

1989 – National League

Date	H/A	Against	W/L	Score
23 April	Home	Exeter	Won	67-29
30 April	Home	Berwick	Won	49-47
6 May	Away	Stoke	Lost	40-56
7 May	Home	Edinburgh	Won	66-30
9 May	Away	Poole	Lost	39-57
19 May	Away	Peterborough	Won	50-45
28 May	Home	Ipswich	Won	55-41
29 May	Away	Rye House	Lost	45-51
3 June	Home	Milton Keynes	Won	65-30
4 June	Away	Mildenhall	Won	53-43
19 June	Away	Newcastle	Lost	47-49
20 June	Away	Milton Keynes	Won	51-45

David Norris first rode for Eastbourne in 1988 as a sixteen-year-old. In 2004 he became a Team GB regular.

EASTBOURNE

Meeting No.12
**UNDER 21 CHAMPIONSHIP OF
GREAT BRITAIN**
Sunday 12 June 1988 at 3:30pm
In association with: Speedway Mail International

The programme cover for the 1988
Under-21 Championship of Great
Britain, held at Arlington.

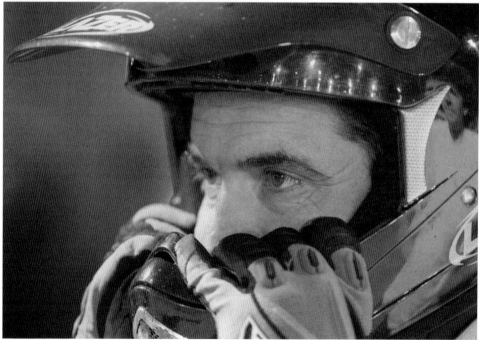

Eastbourne discovery and stalwart Dean Barker has had several spells with the club, from 1986 to 1989
and 1993 to 2003. He returned again in 2005.

22 June	Away	Arena-Essex	Lost	45-50
25 June	Home	Wimbledon	Won	48-47
7 July	Away	Glasgow	Lost	40-56
8 July	Away	Berwick	Lost	32-62
9 July	Home	Mildenhall	Lost	47-49
16 July	Home	Newcastle	Won	67-28
22 July	Home	Poole	Won	52-44
26 July	Away	Long Eaton	Lost	37-59
27 July	Away	Middlesbrough	Won	50-45
28 July	Away	Edinburgh	Lost	43-53
30 July	Home	Arena-Essex	Won	62-34
6 August	Home	Middlesbrough	Won	62-34
13 August	Home	Hackney	Won	52-44
16 August	Away	Wimbledon	Lost	45-51
20 August	Home	Stoke	Won	59-37
27 August	Home	Rye House	Won	59-37
3 September	Home	Glasgow	Won	55-39
8 September	Away	Hackney	Lost	29-67
10 September	Home	Peterborough	Lost	43-53
17 September	Home	Long Eaton	Won	61-35
18 September	Away	Exeter	Lost	24-72
28 September	Away	Ipswich	Lost	66-30

P34 W19 D0 L15 For 1,667 Against 1,587 Pts 38 Position 7th (out of 18)

Knock-Out Cup

First Round
Bye

Second Round

Date	H/A	Against	W/L	Score
12 May	Away	Glasgow	Drew	48-48
14 May	Home	Glasgow	Won	64-32

Won 112-80 on aggregate

Third Round

Date	H/A	Against	W/L	Score
2 July	Home	Poole	Lost	43-53
4 July	Away	Poole	Lost	36-60

Lost 79-113 on aggregate

1989 – National League and Knock-Out Cup

Rider	Matches	Rides	Points	BP	Total	Average
Gordon Kennett	38	207	473	24	497	9.60
Dean Barker	24	114	238	19	257	9.02
Andy Buck	36	192	375	19	394	8.21
David Norris	38	201	284	70	354	7.05
Keith Pritchard	38	192	233	47	280	5.83
Darren Standing	38	166	158	36	194	4.68
Jon Surman	11	35	34	4	38	4.34
Steve Masters	18	55	33	10	43	3.13
Darren Grayling	18	56	30	6	36	2.57

THE 1990s

1990

In the end Rogers decided to carry on. As he told the supporters in the first programme of the new season, 'The past problems have to be put to the back of our minds.' David Norris kept to his word, at least for the time being, and left Eastbourne for Ipswich for a transfer fee of £12,000. With two of his brightest prospects, Norris and Barker, now gone, Rogers had to look round for some worthy replacements. His first signing went down well with the Arlington faithful as he brought back former favourite Paul Woods. His second capture was an Australian by the name of Tony Primmer. Although Rogers had plugged the gaps, the season started off disastrously when the Eagles' kingpin Gordon Kennett injured his shoulder in practice and was forced to miss the first month of the season. Keith Pritchard was appointed temporary captain.

A 'don't panic' directive was issued as the Eagles hit an all-time low with a 74-22 defeat at Peterborough and a 63-32 home challenge match hammering against Wimbledon. The pressure eased slightly when Kennett's return coincided with a narrow 49-47 victory over Long Eaton. However, his shoulder was still giving him trouble and when he started to tire in the latter stages of the home match against Middlesbrough the Bears took full advantage and stole the first league points from Arlington. Rogers made an audacious bid to sign Bo Petersen, but following weeks of speculation his attempts finally came to nothing. However, by now, the team was starting to string some good results together and the signs were beginning to look good but the Eagles couldn't maintain their progress as they crashed out of the H.E.A.T.-sponsored National League Fours, finishing a distant last with just 58 points to Poole on 121, Wimbledon 104 and Exeter 101, and the Knock-Out Cup in quick succession, Hackney enjoying an easy double in the second round.

Ironically, that was followed by the Sussex club's best form of the season, a run of six straight wins including impressive away victories at Milton Keynes and Arena-Essex as well as a confidence boosting home win, 54-42, against Wimbledon. A 63-32 defeat at Exeter brought that sequence to an end, and then Arena arrived in Sussex with all guns blazing, gaining revenge for their Purfleet reverse by stinging the Eagles on their home shale by a 56-39 margin. Kennett was again sidelined with injury soon after, putting a dampener on the Eagles' 61-34 win over Rye House and, despite free-scoring displays from Primmer, without their inspirational leader the club slumped to successive defeats at Glasgow 66-30, Middlesbrough 61-35 and Edinburgh 60-36 on their Northern tour.

Though the team responded in fighting style as they turned things around against the Monarchs with a 62-34 win at Arlington two days later, and Kennett returned to motivate them to a 49-46 victory against Newcastle, things were never quite the same again and the club embarked on a confidence-sapping run of five consecutive losses. The first of these proved a bitter pill as Ipswich, inspired by former Eagle Norris, triumphed 49-46 in Sussex before a swift away 71-25 and home 61-35 double reverse by Poole Pirates proved the lowest point of the season. A late rally saw the Eagles win their final two league engagements, both at home, against Milton Keynes 56-39 and Hackney 51-45, but it wasn't sufficient to prevent them finishing in eleventh place (out of seventeen) in the table, their worst placing since joining the league in 1969. In addition to their Fours and Knock-Out Cup exits, the Best Pairs Championship also failed to offer any silverware as a combined total of 5 points from a below-par Kennett with 3 and Justin Walker with 2 saw them crash out at the group stages.

It had been a poor season for the Eagles. The problem was that there was no real heat-leader support for Kennett, who himself was troubled by his shoulder all season, finishing on a below-par 8.94 average. Andy Buck struggled against a viral infection that finally forced him to retire in September and although Tony Primmer and Paul Woods did their best they still finished up with averages only just over the 6-point mark. The one bright spot was the form of new Aussie Brian Nixon, brought in to the team midway through the season, making everyone wonder why he hadn't been brought in before. One brief glimpse of a trophy came in the form of the Silver Helmet as Paul Woods triumphed over Rye House's Scott Humphries at Arlington. But it was just a brief glimpse as he lost it a mere four days later to Steve Lawson at Glasgow. Further attempts by Buck, against Dean Standing at Ipswich, and Kennett, against David Bargh at Newcastle, met with failure.

As the 1990 season came to an end, Gareth Rogers again expressed his doubts about whether Arlington could continue to stage speedway. It looked at first as if Bob Dugard had come to the rescue as he managed to obtain a good financial sponsorship deal, allowing Eastbourne to return to the Sunbrite British League. Dugard named his team and went ahead with the application, confident that it would be accepted. No sooner had he done this, however, then Mervyn Stewkesbury came up with a plan for evening up the league strengths (there were currently nine teams in the British League and seventeen in the National League) together with automatic promotion and relegation. This plan received the backing of the National League promoters on 6 December, who further agreed that the teams to be promoted in the first instance to even up the leagues would be Poole, Ipswich, Berwick and Wimbledon with Eastbourne on 'stand-by'. Dugard insisted that for him it was 'First Division or bust', to which Rogers added, 'The message is clear from my own bankers. I can't afford another season in the Second Division.' Following further discussions between the Eastbourne management and the National League, Dugard announced on 21 December that the track would close as they had not been given any assurances about automatic promotion. Although he agreed to defer a final decision, there was to be no change of heart and Dugard and Rogers carried out their threat to close down speedway operations at Arlington.

1990 – National League

Date	H/A	Against	W/L	Score
13 April	Away	Peterborough	Lost	22-74
25 April	Away	Wimbledon	Lost	29-66
27 April	Away	Hackney	Lost	33-62
29 April	Home	Long Eaton	Won	49-47
5 May	Away	Berwick	Lost	35-61
6 May	Home	Middlesbrough	Lost	42-54
12 May	Away	Arena-Essex	Won	58-38
13 May	Home	Stoke	Won	54-42
19 May	Away	Stoke	Lost	42-54
20 May	Home	Exeter	Won	66-30
14 June	Away	Ipswich	Lost	33-63
24 June	Home	Peterborough	Won	53-43
26 June	Away	Milton Keynes	Won	55-41

1 July	Home	Wimbledon	Won	54-42
8 July	Home	Berwick	Won	58-38
12 July	Away	Long Eaton	Won	55-41
15 July	Home	Glasgow	Won	53-42
16 July	Away	Exeter	Lost	32-63
29 July	Home	Arena-Essex	Lost	39-56
4 August	Home	Rye House	Won	61-34
8 August	Away	Glasgow	Lost	30-66
9 August	Away	Middlesbrough	Lost	35-61
10 August	Away	Edinburgh	Lost	36-60
12 August	Home	Edinburgh	Won	62-34
26 August	Home	Newcastle	Won	49-46
2 September	Home	Ipswich	Lost	46-49
9 September	Away	Rye House	Lost	32-63
11 September	Away	Poole	Lost	25-71
16 September	Home	Poole	Lost	35-61
17 September	Away	Newcastle	Lost	45-51
30 September	Home	Milton Keynes	Won	56-39
7 October	Home	Hackney	Won	51-45

P32 W15 D0 L17 For 1,426 Against 1,636 Pts 30 Position 11th (out of 17)

Knock-Out Cup

First Round
Bye

Second Round

Date	H/A	Against	W/L	Score
10 June	Home	Hackney	Lost	40-56
15 June	Away	Hackney	Lost	32-64

Lost 72-120 on aggregate

1990 – National League and Knock-Out Cup

Rider	Matches	Rides	Points	BP	Total	Average
Gordon Kennett	27	140	303	10	313	8.94
Andy Buck	30	154	257	12	269	6.99
Tony Primmer	34	177	240	47	287	6.49
Paul Woods	34	193	262	39	301	6.24
Darren Standing	11	41	47	12	59	5.76
Keith Pritchard	34	168	193	39	232	5.52
Brian Nixon	7	29	34	6	40	5.52
Justin Walker	23	73	69	19	88	4.82
Darren Grayling	27	100	90	13	103	4.12

1991

For a time it appeared that only the stock cars would roar at Arlington in 1991 but, behind the scenes, another team's misfortune was about to prompt the rebirth of the Eastbourne speedway team. On 5 June 1991, Wimbledon managing director Don Scarf announced that 'during the winter as amalgamation got underway it became obvious to me that we had to go First Division or close, so we decided to give it a go. Despite all our efforts, we failed to find a team sponsor and although our attendances have been slightly higher than last year, we have been losing over £2,000 per meeting, a situation that obviously could not continue. In order to honour our commitments we are moving our operation to Arlington.' Although a tragedy for Wimbledon it was a reprieve for the Eastbourne faithful as speedway began again on 30 June. Although invited to Arlington by Bob Dugard, the Wimbledon team kept their nickname and their riders, so for the rest of the season the team became known as the Eastbourne Dons and a complete set of new riders was introduced to the fans.

The amalgamation wasn't without its problems in the early days, however. The Dons' management, on a budget, had originally picked a team capable of winning home matches at Wimbledon and some of their number clearly didn't relish the impromptu change of venue. American Bobby Ott and England international Andy Grahame, along with New Zealander Nathan Simpson, South African Deon Prinsloo and Dane Jesper Olsen soon settled in their new surroundings to form the basis of a cosmopolitan, if not title-chasing, line-up, but for both John Davis and Neville Tatum the transition was never easy and each rider soon departed for pastures new.

The Dons had already had a poor start to the season at Wimbledon and things did not get much better in their new home. The new era began with a visit from the Berwick Bandits, but hopes of a successful dawning were dashed as a 12-point maximum from Kelvin Tatum inspired the Border club to a 48-42 Arlington victory. Significant losses at both Reading, 56-34 in the Knock-Out Cup, and King's Lynn, 51-39 in the Sunbrite British League, sandwiched a heavy home defeat against Wolverhampton, 53-37, and in the meantime the Dons also crashed out of the H.E.A.T. Four-Team Tournament, finishing last with 82 points in a group that included Reading with 114, Poole 95 and Swindon 93. Problems continued to mount for the new promotion. Davis fell in the first race against Wolverhampton and the groin injury he sustained subsequently became infected, causing a longer lay-off than was first expected. Scarf warned his riders, 'We must start winning soon, that is obvious to everyone.' Grahame hit 15 as the Dons lost by eight, 49-41, at Monmore Green; Tatum failed to score that night and left the team, making way for the return to Arlington of Eagles' legend Gordon Kennett. A home draw with Poole made it a total of just 2 points from 8 league matches and lower sphere Arena-Essex then dumped them out of the BSPA Cup with a 55-35 victory over the Dons at the Essex Raceway. There was no let-up in the troubles afflicting them as Davis quit the side following an unsatisfactory comeback and then they lost by eleven points, 50-39, at home to an improving Ipswich side. By now, Eastbourne were bottom of the league with just 2 points. Mitch Shirra was targeted as a replacement for Davis but his average was too high, so attention was turned to Mikael Blixt. Eastbourne, however, were too late as Berwick signed him up first.

Some relief came as Reading were beaten by ten points, 50-40, at Arlington in the *Speedway Star* Cup but the Racers had arrived with a twenty-two-point first-leg lead in the bag. The result did at least relieve the pressure as Andy Grahame celebrated his captain's role with an 18-point maximum, one of three full-houses (two full, one paid) that he scored during the season. Ott starred with 17 at Ipswich as Eastbourne crashed 57-33 but then they sprang a shock as they recorded an away victory at Coventry 49-41. A big win at home to King's Lynn, 55-35, and another travelling success at Swindon, 47-43, saw the Dons go three matches unbeaten, elevating them above Reading in the table. The rider replacement facility for Davis expired, but the club moved swiftly to engage the services of Armando Castagna on loan from Reading. The arrival of the Italian breathed new life into the Arlington operation and together with Ott (even though the American apparently wasn't entirely happy), Grahame and Nathan Simpson, who had now returned from a sabbatical in his homeland to visit his seriously ill father, the quartet were largely responsible for carving out the results that saw the team finish five points above Swindon in the final table. A 50-40 home win against the Robins and then respective victories against Coventry, 53-36, and Cradley Heath, 49-41, proved the key and although Oxford, including Champion of Sussex Martin Dugard and fellow former Eagle Dean Barker, ended the Dons' home dominance with a 47-42 success in the final league match of the season, twelfth place (out of thirteen) was already secure with the Dons successfully avoiding relegation. Andy Graham finished the season as top Don with an average of 9.44.

1991 – British League

Date	H/A	Against	W/L	Score
18 May	Away	Cradley Heath	Lost	37-53*
29 May	Home	Belle Vue	Drew	45-45*
30 June	Home	Berwick	Lost	42-48
6 July	Away	King's Lynn	Lost	39-51
12 July	Home	Wolverhampton	Lost	37-53
13 July	Away	Berwick	Lost	35-53
15 July	Away	Wolverhampton	Lost	41-49
19 July	Home	Poole	Drew	45-45
26 July	Home	Ipswich	Lost	39-50
8 August	Away	Ipswich	Lost	33-57
9 August	Away	Oxford	Lost	43-47
10 August	Away	Coventry	Won	49-41
16 August	Home	King's Lynn	Won	55-35
17 August	Away	Swindon	Won	47-43
20 August	Away	Poole	Lost	40-50
6 September	Home	Bradford	Drew	45-45
11 September	Away	Bradford	Lost	40-50
13 September	Home	Reading	Lost	43-47
20 September	Away	Belle Vue	Lost	41-49
27 September	Home	Swindon	Won	50-40
30 September	Away	Reading	Lost	37-50
6 October	Home	Coventry	Won	53-36
18 October	Home	Cradley Heath	Won	49-41
25 October	Home	Oxford	Lost	42-47

*Raced as Wimbledon

P24 W6 D3 L15 For 1,027 Against 1,125 Pts 15 BP 3 Position 12 (out of 13)

Knock-Out Cup

First Round

Date	H/A	Against	W/L	Score
27 April	Away	King's Lynn	Won	50-40*
22 May	Home	King's Lynn	Won	52-38*

Won 102-78 on aggregate

Second Round

Date	H/A	Against	W/L	Score
1 July	Away	Reading	Lost	34-56
2 August	Home	Reading	Won	50-40

Lost 84-96 on aggregate
*Raced as Wimbledon

1991 – British League and Knock-Out Cup

Rider	Matches	Rides	Points	BP	Total	Average
Andy Graham	27	144	330	10	340	9.44
Bobby Ott	28	160	319	20	339	8.48
Armando Castagna	7	30	48	2	50	6.67
John Davis	9	34	50	6	56	6.59
Nathan Simpson	24	119	147	28	175	5.88
Gordon Kennett	18	82	83	19	102	4.98
Deon Prinsloo	28	122	122	23	145	4.75
Neville Tatum	10	41	37	7	44	4.29
Jesper Olsen	27	98	74	14	88	3.59

Bobby Ott, seen here in 1991 Wimbledon colours shortly before they closed down and moved en bloc to Eastbourne.

1992

The 1992 season proved to be a year of high drama at Arlington, the track that had provided a home for the once-mighty Wimbledon Dons the previous summer. Twelve turbulent months witnessed just about every possible scenario that the Sussex club could have experienced. They survived a bid to wind-up the promoting company, went two full months without a win at senior level and were forced to restructure the pay deals of their riders as attendances slumped. They protested in advance of Paul Dugard's suspension for a positive sample containing a banned substance, they escaped relegation in the very last race of the very last match and then the closing chapter saw Len Silver arrive as a promoter to a team that would henceforth be run on Swedish lines.

As 1992 dawned the club was saved when former shareholders of Wimbledon Speedway 1987 Ltd eventually accepted 20p per share. Though they were largely regarded as worthless, Bob Dugard offered 10p a share but it still took the intervention of long-time Dons benefactor John Cearns at a meeting at Wimbledon's original Plough Lane stadium to help keep the club afloat. Although Wimbledon's misfortune in 1991 had proved to be Eastbourne's good fortune, the name Dons had not become a vote-winner among the Sussex fraternity and was duly consigned to history at the start of 1992. And so the Eastbourne Eagles were reborn.

It was all change as far as riding personnel were concerned. A deal was struck with Oxford to make Andy Grahame's move permanent while Nathan Simpson was the only other member of the 1991 team to remain on the retained list. There was no place for Bobby Ott, who had fallen out with the management the previous year and had demanded a transfer request, Armando Castagna returned to action at Reading while both Gordon Kennett and Deon Prinsloo made the drop to the lower league, moving to Milton Keynes and Long Eaton respectively. In came former National League hot shot Andrew Silver, who signed following a troubled spell at Swindon, while Aussie Glenn Doyle was recruited from Bradford. The Eagles also opted to bring Olli Tyrvainen back to the club after a break approaching a decade.

With the name Eagles now back in force, the club soared to victory in an opening challenge match against a team called the Anzacs, but problems were soon to surface as they hit the Gold Cup trail. A win in their first encounter against Arena-Essex, 52-38, raised hopes for the season ahead but it was a false dawn as the Hammers exacted quick revenge and took the bonus point with a 56-34 victory at Purfleet. Then, the next evening, the Eagles slipped to a 48-41 defeat in their first league match at Cradley Heath. Back at Arlington for their third meeting in as many days, the Eagles blew a ten-point lead to be pipped 46-44 by Poole. A devastating run then failed to see them win another Gold Cup match as they slipped to double defeats against Reading, King's Lynn, Swindon and Ipswich as well as the Pirates. The Homefire British League failed to offer better fortunes in the early days as they succumbed to a hefty Arlington reverse at the hands of Wolverhampton, 53-37, while Bradford also tasted victory in Sussex 46-44. A 51-39 win at Long Eaton in the BSPA Cup offered the Eagles a glimpse of success but that was all that was on the horizon until the Eagles triumphed over Belle Vue in the league 46-44 some three weeks later. Though they hoped that result would mark a change in their luck, they were to be disappointed as they embarked on a run of six straight defeats. Draws at home to Poole and away at Swindon at least put some points on the board but it was to be a full six weeks after their success against the Aces before their next win, a 46-44 victory against Arena, furthered their interest in the BSPA Cup.

By this time attendances had dropped alarmingly and a crisis meeting was held at the club. A new pay structure was put in place, which related riders' earnings to crowd levels at home matches. Team changes were urgently needed and Swede Stefan Danno was signed up. A paid 10 on his debut was a promising start but shortly afterwards Andy Grahame, captain and top scorer, asked for a move to Cradley Heath. His place was taken for one meeting by Bobby Schwartz and then permanently by Peter Nahlin. In September another old favourite returned to Arlington when Paul Woods made a brief comeback for the team. The Swedes added a touch of colour to the place but the Eagles still weren't winning regularly enough to allay relegation fears. Bradford put an end to their Knock-Out Cup hopes with an aggregate victory while once again the Eagles finished bottom of their group in the fours on 77 points, behind Ipswich (124), Arena-Essex (99) and King's Lynn (84). It seemed their best hope of silverware was in the BSPA Cup but a home defeat against Poole 49-41 put paid to such hopes. Home wins against King's Lynn, Oxford and Ipswich gave them hope but in a season that had seen them lose every single away match as well as five of their home matches it all came down to the very last match of the season. With automatic promotion and relegation now the order of the day, Eastbourne found themselves in a position where they had to win their last home match against Arena-Essex on 25 October to stay in the First Division. Reserve Tyrvainen gave one of his best performances of the season, scoring 10 paid 12 points. In spite of this, it looked all over for Eastbourne as at one point, they trailed the Hammers by 7 points. With one heat to go, however, the Eagles had pegged back the deficit and were leading by three points, 43-40. In the last race, Arena-Essex's Brian Karger shot away from the gate but, in a nail-biting effort, Andrew Silver and Peter Nahlin managed to grab a share of the points to save the match and First Division status for the Eagles. This victory consigned Swindon to bottom place in the League. It was the final irony that the two men who had done this, Andrew Silver and Peter Nahlin, had both been signed from Swindon. At the end of the season Nahlin proved to have been Eastbourne's top rider, turning in an average of 8.63 with Graham on 7.18 and Silver on 6.58.

Not only did a member of the Silver family help to save Eastbourne's First Division place on 25 October, but that was also the day when another member of the Silver family, Andrew's father Len, saved the club from closing down. The poor attendances had once again raised doubts over whether Eastbourne could continue in 1993, but Len Silver agreed to take over as promoter along with Jon Cook, and promised that Arlington would stay open. Silver, of course, was one of the best known and most successful promoters in the history of speedway with many years' experience promoting at Hackney, Rayleigh and Rye House, though he had been absent from speedway for seven years looking after his skiing business. He looked forward to the new challenge with relish. 'We have to be much more positive in our publicity and get away from abusing our own sport at every opportunity,' he said. 'It's a great sport and we have to start selling it to the public at large as that. If anybody wants to kick up a fuss from the centre green phone they should be allowed to do so – the crowd love that sort of thing – but if someone tries it as things stand at the moment they get fined, which can't be right.' 'Leaping Len', the flamboyant showman, was back!

At a supporters' club meeting at the end of the season, a positive vote was taken on moving the Eagles' race night to Saturday. Silver agreed and Eastbourne's regular race night was changed, although there were still eight Sunday dates pencilled in. The Dugard family too played its part by agreeing to invest in excess of £25,000 on upgrading the floodlights. One of Len Silver's new ideas for publicity resulted in the appointment of a community relations officer, whose job it was to approach local councils with a view to arranging school visits in order to raise the club's profile. He was also to be responsible for investigating the possibility of obtaining grants. The man appointed to this role was local policeman Peter Brown.

1992 – British League

Date	H/A	Against	W/L	Score
11 April	Away	Cradley Heath	Lost	41-48
10 May	Home	Wolverhampton	Lost	37-53
24 May	Home	Bradford	Lost	44-46
7 June	Home	Belle Vue	Won	46-44
13 June	Away	Bradford	Lost	26-64
15 June	Away	Wolverhampton	Lost	40-49
5 July	Home	Coventry	Lost	40-50
12 July	Home	Poole	Drew	45-45
16 July	Away	Swindon	Drew	45-45
22 July	Away	Poole	Lost	38-52
2 August	Home	King's Lynn	Won	48-42
8 August	Away	King's Lynn	Lost	42-48
14 August	Away	Belle Vue	Lost	36-54
16 August	Home	Oxford	Won	49-41
22 August	Away	Coventry	Lost	41-48
23 August	Home	Ipswich	Won	49-41
3 September	Away	Ipswich	Lost	31-58
4 September	Away	Arena-Essex	Lost	32-58
26 September	Home	Swindon	Won	49-41
30 September	Away	Oxford	Lost	32-58
11 October	Home	Reading	Lost	41-49
12 October	Away	Reading	Lost	32-58
18 October	Home	Cradley Heath	Lost	35-55
25 October	Home	Arena-Essex	Won	46-43

P24 W6 D2 L16 For 965 Against 1,190 Pts 14 BP 1 Position 12th (out of 13)

Knock-Out Cup

First Round
Bye

Second Round

Date	H/A	Against	W/L	Score
21 June	Away	Bradford	Lost	31-59
24 June	Home	Bradford	Won	48-42

Lost 79-101 on aggregate

1992 – British League and Knock-Out Cup

Rider	Matches	Rides	Points	BP	Total	Average
Peter Nahlin	18	101	207	11	218	8.63
Andy Grahame	6	34	60	1	61	7.18
Andrew Silver	26	144	216	21	237	6.58
Olli Tyrvainen	22	85	103	21	124	5.84
Glenn Doyle	19	84	112	10	122	5.81
Stefan Danno	21	91	111	19	130	5.71
Nathan Simpson	26	120	135	32	167	5.57
Paul Dugard	20	75	68	21	89	4.75
Darren Grayling	6	16	5	1	6	1.50

1993

1993 truly marked the dawning of a new era at Arlington. The Eagles' highest placing ever in the First Division, the club back on a sound financial footing and the relaunch of the famed Eastbourne training track meant there was much to savour in a memorable year in Sussex.

With all the pieces starting to fall into place behind the scenes at the start of 1993, the team then became the priority and Andrew Silver, having installed himself as an Arlington favourite in 1992, became the first to sign on the dotted line. At the end of January, rider number two was added to the squad as Dean Barker rejoined for an undisclosed fee, described as 'substantial'. He had spent three years with Oxford but was now back where it had all started for him in 1986. Stefan Danno was the next name to go down on the Eastbourne team sheet and then, at the beginning of March, Silver finally got the man he had been gunning for as Peter Nahlin re-signed on a year's loan from Swindon. John Wainwright signed on a free transfer from Rye House and, taking care of the lower order, Darren Grayling, Scott Swain, Mark Bruton, Nathan Gaymer and Paul Mitchell were all in contention to share the number seven and eight berths. Events then took an unexpected turn as the Oxford management delivered the unexpected news that the Cheetahs were to close and all their assets circulated for transfer. Immediately Martin Dugard was linked with the Eagles and seven days later the rumour became a reality as the master of Arlington joined his good friend Barker in returning to the club. Yet another former Eagle then entered the frame when David Norris suddenly demanded a transfer from Ipswich. Despite mutterings of an illegal approach emanating from Foxhall the Eagles' hierarchy insisted they had done nothing wrong as, in spite of the politics, Norris completed a hat-trick of returning 'old boys', making the move in a deal thought to be slightly less than the £20,000 asked for. A bid by Len Silver to buy Savalas Clouting from Ipswich for £15,000 was turned down. Nevertheless, the Eagles now looked rather more like the sort of team the Arlington faithful were used to and there were great hopes for the forthcoming season.

The first encounter ended prematurely at King's Lynn as heavy rain called a halt with the scores standing at 36-36, Norris with three wins out of three. Under the new rules the scores stood as the match had reached heat twelve. News of Len Silver's new team had spread quickly and it was a good-sized crowd that greeted them the following afternoon at Arlington for the first home match of the season as the Eagles sent Cradley Heath packing to the tune of 62-46.

Sadly this was to prove the final time that Charlie Dugard would see his grandson Martin in action. Charlie had been at Eastbourne since the early 1930s, passing on his love of speedway to his three sons, Bob, John and Eric, and succeeding grandsons, Martin and Paul, all of whom had ridden for his beloved Eagles. The name Dugard had been synonymous with Eastbourne speedway almost since its inception, a proud tradition that still continues. The Dugard family had stepped in many times over the years to rescue Eastbourne financially and to pour money in from their own pockets to keep the track going when it would otherwise have closed.

Charlie's final wish was to see his Martin and one of his discoveries, Dean Barker, ride for Eastbourne once again, which he did before passing away on Thursday 8 April at the age of eighty-one.

Of course, Charlie would have wanted the show to go on, and it did in style with a follow-up 70-38 thrashing of Bradford in front of a huge Arlington crowd, and then King's Lynn were next on the chopping block, going down 82-26, though Silver had some sympathy for their plight as injuries had ravaged their side. In contrast to 1991 and 1992, home wins were the norm with only Coventry, 55-53 on 1 May, and Wolverhampton, 61-45 in early August, coming away from Arlington with the points. Once again it was Bradford who were on hand to condemn Eastbourne to an early Knock-Out Cup exit as the Dukes won through in their second-round clash by a 6-point aggregate margin. The Eagles lost out again in the H.E.A.T. Fours competition, but it was a much better showing this year as they lost out by just three points to group leaders Arena-Essex. The final scores were Arena-Essex 114, Eastbourne 111, Ipswich 83, King's Lynn 76. In the league, the Eagles were having their best ever season as a First Division team, which turned into something of a three-horse race with Eastbourne vying with Belle Vue and Wolverhampton for top honours. In spite of a brace of victories away at Arena-Essex and Reading and a late-season win away at Coventry, the Eagles just missed out and had to be content with third place on 61 points, just two behind champions Belle Vue and runners-up Wolverhampton. The fourth-placed team, Arena-Essex, were a further eight points adrift. Dugard's return saw him as top scorer for the team with an average of 8.98, just in front of Nahlin on 8.02. David Norris took the third heat leader spot.

The Finn Olli Tyrvainen had two spells as a rider for Eastbourne in the 1980s and 1990s and later returned as team manager.

Andrew Silver, son of former Eastbourne promoter
Len, rode for the club from 1992-1993.

At the end of the season, the Eastbourne management announced that they had managed
to land a £40,000 sponsorship deal to help youth development at Arlington. Although
sponsorship was nothing new in speedway, this deal was unique as it represented the first major
investment by the government through the Business Sponsorship Incentive Scheme for Sport.
The deal was that the fund would match pound for pound the investment put in by two major
companies, Len Silver's Silverski Holidays and the Dugards' Machine Tools Ltd.

1993 – British League

Date	H/A	Against	W/L	Score
3 April	Away	King's Lynn	Drew	36-36
4 April	Home	Cradley Heath	Won	62-46
10 April	Away	Cradley Heath	Lost	50-58
11 April	Home	Bradford	Won	70-38
17 April	Away	Bradford	Lost	40-68
18 April	Home	King's Lynn	Won	82-26
24 April	Away	Coventry	Lost	46-62
28 April	Away	Poole	Lost	52-56
1 May	Home	Coventry	Lost	53-55
8 May	Home	Belle Vue	Won	63-45
15 May	Home	Arena-Essex	Won	57-51
22 May	Home	Wolverhampton	Won	56-52
24 May	Away	Reading	Won	59-49
29 May	Home	Reading	Won	62-46
3 June	Away	Ipswich	Lost	50-58
7 June	Away	Wolverhampton	Lost	44-64
18 June	Away	Belle Vue	Lost	46-62
3 July	Home	Coventry	Won	62-45
16 July	Away	Arena-Essex	Won	54-53
24 July	Home	Poole	Won	60-48

31 July	Home	Arena-Essex	Won	60-48
2 August	Away	Wolverhampton	Lost	46-61
6 August	Away	Arena-Essex	Won	54-53
7 August	Home	Wolverhampton	Lost	45-61
13 August	Away	Belle Vue	Lost	50-58
14 August	Home	Ipswich	Won	62-46
21 August	Home	Belle Vue	Won	62-46
28 August	Home	Poole	Won	62-46
30 August	Away	Reading	Won	55-53
4 September	Away	King's Lynn	Lost	34-74
9 September	Away	Ipswich	Lost	41-67
11 September	Away	Coventry	Won	56-52
18 September	Home	Ipswich	Won	57-51
25 September	Away	Cradley Heath	Lost	52-56
26 September	Home	Reading	Won	58-49
10 October	Home	King's Lynn	Won	79-29
15 October	Away	Poole	Lost	45-63
17 October	Home	Cradley Heath	Won	67-41
23 October	Away	Bradford	Lost	40-68
24 October	Home	Bradford	Won	60-47

P40 W23 D1 L16 For 2,189 Against 2,087 Pts 47 BP 14 Position 3rd (out of 11)

Knock-Out Cup

First Round

Date	H/A	Against	W/L	Score
27 June	Home	Bradford	Won	63-45
4 July	Away	Bradford	Lost	42-66

Lost 105-111 on aggregate

1993 – British League and Knock-Out Cup

Rider	Matches	Rides	Points	BP	Total	Average
Martin Dugard	40	213	461	17	468	8.98
Peter Nahlin	36	185	343	28	371	8.02
David Norris	39	198	318	45	363	7.33
Dean Barker	37	195	298	45	343	7.04
Andrew Silver	34	172	257	40	297	6.91
Stefan Danno	37	191	268	44	312	6.53
John Wainwright	11	37	48	5	53	5.73
Darren Grayling	32	122	149	18	167	5.48
Scott Swain	6	18	17	5	22	4.89
Nathan Gaymer	31	102	79	18	97	3.80
Paul Dugard	8	25	18	1	19	3.04
Mark Burton	8	29	7	4	11	1.52

1994

Eastbourne had made huge strides by going back to basics in 1993, with the return of prodigal sons Martin Dugard, Dean Barker and David Norris having affected a wind of change down Arlington way. The club's fortunes had been transformed as the team that had finished just one point above relegated Swindon in 1992 was replaced by the side that had soared into third place twelve months later, just two points short of league champions Belle Vue. This resurgence had a notable effect, not least in terms of attendances on the terraces.

Naturally enough there seemed little reason to change a winning formula, though the club was forced to downsize in order to remain below the points limit. It was with considerable reluctance that they decided that it would be the prolific and popular (both in the pits and on the terraces) Peter Nahlin who would be forced to make way. While the Eastbourne promotion had spent big during the previous winter increasing their asset base, the fact that Nahlin was only on loan to the club proved to be the deciding factor. The Swede's departure allowed the Eagles to retain their 'old boys', an outstanding heat leader trio of Dugard, Norris and Barker, while the inclusion of Stefan Danno and Andrew Silver gave their top five a more-than-potent look. At reserve both Darren Grayling and Nathan Gaymer, who was to tragically lose his life in a road accident in the autumn, were eased out and replaced by Paul Dugard, who had expressed a desire to return to his local club, and Darren Shand, after the Eagles had won the race to sign the talented sixteen-year old.

Before the season the Eastbourne management had signed a further three riders for whom 1994 team places could not be offered. Swede Stefan Andersson had been the man who had most impressed riders and officials alike and he had duly been pencilled in as a starter for the 1995 season. However nobody at Arlington, not least Andersson himself, could have envisaged how quickly the blueprint for the future was about to change. Just three days after their opening league match at Coventry, Andrew Silver suddenly decided he'd had enough of speedway and quit the sport. With Sweden having joined the European community, and no work permit being needed, Andersson was immediately installed as Silver's replacement within hours of arriving in the country on Good Friday. The Swede arrived barely having time to fit a dirt deflector before opening with two second places and then a win in his final ride in the Eagles' curtain-raising challenge match victory over Arena-Essex, 56-40. Though Andersson's arrival proved a breath of fresh air, it was tinged with regret at Silver's departure, particularly as Andrew's father Len subsequently decided that he was unable to continue with his promoting duties. Len's influence was something that the Eagles were sad to lose. In little more than a season he had helped create a legacy that was to stand the team in good stead in the years to come. Silver's co-promoter Jon Cook took over the reins, knowing that he had inherited a side wholly capable of winning trophies.

Unlike 1993, when they had finished in third place in the First Division, there were no home slip-ups, the Eagles ending the year with a 100 per cent record in all matches contested at Arlington. The only blight on that record was due to the weather causing the Eagles' 'B' fixture against eventual champions Poole to be abandoned, as a result of which the SCB awarded the Pirates an 80-0 victory at the end of the season. Away from home the Eagles' form remained patchy, though victories at Arena-Essex, Belle Vue and Reading and draws at both Wolverhampton and Coventry throughout the course of the season helped them improve their final position by one place as they finished runners-up to Poole. The 'old boy' trio had performed well with Dugard and Norris both recording 9-plus averages and Barker 8.98. The H.E.A.T. Four-Team Tournament offered better fortunes than experienced in previous seasons and, having qualified for the final at Peterborough with 130 points from their group over Poole (107), Ipswich (98) and King's Lynn (91), the Eagles finished third in the final on 15 points behind Poole (28) and Cradley Heath (25), but ahead of Coventry on just 9.

But it was in the Knock-Out Cup that Eastbourne were able to celebrate their first-ever silverware in the top flight. Following aggregate victories over both Belle Vue and Wolves, the Eagles survived a tense semi-final, going through in a replay against King's Lynn. There was no mistake in the first leg of the final, however, which was a total triumph for the Eagles as they trounced the Cradley Heath Heathens 59-37 at Arlington. The second leg became a foregone conclusion, especially after the first heat in which Dugard roared away from the gate, defeating home skipper Greg Hancock with Andersson passing Scott Smith to make it a 4-2 for Eastbourne. Heat two, the reserves heat, was even better for the Eagles as Paul Dugard and Scott Swain, riding in only his fourth match for Eastbourne, took a 5-1. Although Cradley did make a comeback later in the meeting and, in fact, eventually went on to win it 49-47, they were never in with any real chance as the Eagles ran out winners by 106 points to 86. It was a triumph not only for the riders but also for the joint team managers, former Eastbourne favourites Steve Weatherley and Trevor Geer.

On the individual front both Dugard and Norris qualified for the Dunlop First Division Riders' Championship, Dugard finishing third on 11 points while Norris totalled 9. Stefan Danno qualified for the World Championship final, scoring 2 points.

Before the 1995 season started, Eastbourne were able to announce yet another big sponsorship deal as they clinched a £30,000 deal with the multi-billion dollar Korean-based conglomerate Hyundai. The deal was secured because of the good relationship that existed between the Dugards' Machine Tools company and the Hyundai Corporation.

1994 – British League

Date	H/A	Against	W/L	Score
26 March	Away	Coventry	Lost	35-61
3 April	Home	Cradley Heath	Won	53-25
9 April	Away	King's Lynn	Lost	35-61
10 April	Home	King's Lynn	Won	46-32
30 April	Home	Reading	Won	51-45
5 May	Away	Ipswich	Lost	46-50
6 May	Away	Arena-Essex	Won	49-47
9 May	Away	Reading	Lost	36-50
25 May	Away	Poole	Lost	42-54
30 May	Away	Wolverhampton	Lost	46-50
11 June	Home	Belle Vue	Won	57-39
13 June	Away	Belle Vue	Won	50-46
19 June	Away	Bradford	Lost	46-50
25 June	Home	Bradford	Won	55-41
2 July	Home	Ipswich	Won	62-34
11 July	Away	Wolverhampton	Lost	46-50
13 July	Away	Poole	Lost	40-56
16 July	Home	Wolverhampton	Won	63-32
23 July	Home	Arena-Essex	Won	50-45
6 August	Home	Coventry	Won	58-38
13 August	Away	Cradley Heath	Lost	41-55
14 August	Home	Cradley Heath	Won	50-46
20 August	Home	Belle Vue	Won	66-30
25 August	Away	Ipswich	Lost	46-50
27 August	Home	Ipswich	Won	59-37
17 September	Home	Reading	Won	63-33
21 September	Away	Cradley Heath	Lost	42-54
24 September	Away	Coventry	Drew	36-36#
25 September	Home	Bradford	Won	57-38
26 September	Away	Belle Vue	Lost	45-51
30 September	Away	Arena-Essex	Lost	40-56
2 October	Home	Coventry	Won	60-36
3 October	Away	Reading	Won	54-42
5 October	Home	King's Lynn	Won	58-38
8 October	Home	Poole	Won	61-35
12 October	Home	Wolverhampton	Won	55-41
15 October	Away	Bradford	Lost	35-61
16 October	Home	Arena-Essex	Won	62-34
26 October	Away	King's Lynn	Won	80-0*
29 October	Home	Poole	Lost	0-80*

#Match abandoned. Result stands
*Matches not ridden; Away team awarded 80-0 victory in both cases

P40 W23 D2 L15 For 1,978 Against 1,767 Pts 48 BP 14 Position 2nd (out of 11)

Knock-Out Cup

First Round
Bye

Second Round

Date	H/A	Against	W/L	Score
16 May	Away	Wolverhampton	Lost	46-50
28 May	Home	Wolverhampton	Won	51-45

Won 97-95 on aggregate

Semi-final

Date	H/A	Against	W/L	Score
30 July	Away	King's Lynn	Lost	41-55
31 July	Home	King's Lynn	Won	62-33

Won 103-88 on aggregate

Final

Date	H/A	Against	W/L	Score
23 October	Home	Cradley Heath	Won	59-37
31 October	Away	Cradley Heath	Lost	47-49

Won 106-86 on aggregate

1994 – British League and Knock-Out Cup

Rider	Matches	Rides	Points	BP	Total	Average
Martin Dugard	48	240	522	38	560	9.33
David Norris	47	233	516	19	535	9.18
Dean Barker	47	237	494	38	532	8.98
Stefan Danno	41	195	314	47	361	7.41
Stefan Andersson	44	207	279	47	326	6.30
Paul Dugard	35	152	145	23	168	4.42
Darren Shand	25	107	66	19	71	3.18
Darren Grayling	33	122	74	17	91	2.98

 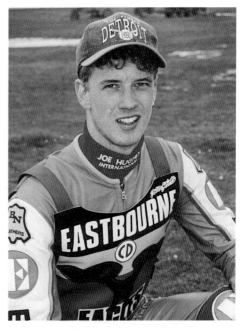

Above left: Darren Shand signed for Eastbourne as a sixteen-year-old in 1994 but left the following season.

Above right: The Swede Stefan Andersson rode for the Eagles for five years, from 1994 to 1998.

1995

A major reorganisation took place over the close season as Divisions One and Two were amalgamated to make one league of twenty-one teams to be known as the Premier League. In an attempt to even up team strengths it was proposed to limit each team to only one rider with an 8-plus average, but this was strongly opposed by Eastbourne, Poole and Bradford and the idea was dropped, though it was obvious that some equalisation would have to take place and the rider to lose out was David Norris, who was transferred to Reading. However, given the big changes that were taking place, Eastbourne did not come off too badly, retaining the services of Dugard, Barker, Andersson, Danno and Swain, while Darren Shand was recalled from a loan spell with Peterborough. Paul Whittaker was signed to complete the team-building jigsaw in the early weeks of the season, but sadly the former Hackney rider failed to settle and a third Swede, remarkably a third Stefan, Ekberg, was duly drafted in as a replacement.

Over the years Arlington had witnessed many winning sequences in the lower-league glory years, but a three-month spell that included fifteen straight league wins raised the stakes and ultimately inspired them to claim, for the first time ever, the title of the best team in Britain.

Eastbourne outlined their intentions for the year ahead with wins, both home and away, against the Pirates in the Premier League, while a draw at King's Lynn kicked off their league campaign in impressive style. Bradford and Cradley Heath were both despatched point-less from Arlington, as were Ipswich in the month of April and a win at Swindon further enhanced Eastbourne's credentials as title chasers. Martin Dugard triumphed in the British Championship semi-final around his home circuit but the perfect month was denied them as Arena-Essex pulled off a shock two-legged victory to end their grip on the Knock-Out Cup. They were to fare little better in the fours and again it was the Hammers who proved the architects of the Eagles' downfall with 119 points to the Sussex side's 109, with both Poole on 87 and Reading on 69 finishing well short of the lead two.

Elsewhere the league campaign was proceeding according to plan. Once again fortress Arlington proved impenetrable to all comers in the league, the only exception to their home dominance being Arena's two-point cup win. Once more Dugard was all but unbeatable around the Sussex venue as he chalked up four 18-point maximums (three full and one paid) on his way to topping the Eagles' averages with 10.22. Glasgow, Sheffield, Hull and Swindon in particular felt the force of Arlington as the Eagles rattled up 60-points-plus scores against them while Exeter pegged them to within a point of that landmark, but that was to prove the day that Eastbourne actually lifted the title. Away from home a profitable Northern tour saw them return with wins from Middlesbrough and Edinburgh while a further draw at Belle Vue two weeks later strengthened their hand.

July and August proved the clincher, however, as the Sussex men remained unbeaten on the road, Oxford, Reading and Arena-Essex all falling victim to them before a win at Sheffield, never previously a happy hunting ground, thanks to a star display from Ekberg really had them believing it was to be their year. A win at Wolverhampton, albeit on a bad-tempered night at Monmore Green, and then another travelling draw, their third of the year, at Poole set the stage nicely with Eastbourne only needing to beat Exeter in their final home match to claim the title. The Falcons' challenge, as expected, was mercilessly swept aside but sadly the day and the celebrations were marred as Dean Barker suffered a serious and complex fracture of his right leg in an horrific crash in the early part of the meeting.

Dugard's brilliant 10-plus average was well supported by Barker's 9.35 and Danno's 8.7 as the Eagles carried all before them to romp home in the league by eight clear points. This was the eighth time that Eastbourne had become league champions, the difference this time being that, for the first time in their history, they were champions of the country's top league and therefore officially the best team in Great Britain.

1995 – Premier League

Date	H/A	Against	W/L	Score
25 March	Away	King's Lynn	Drew	48-48
1 April	Away	Bradford	Lost	43-53
2 April	Home	Bradford	Won	55-41
8 April	Away	Coventry	Lost	46-50
9 April	Home	Cradley Heath	Won	50-43
14 April	Away	Peterborough	Lost	43-53
17 April	Away	Swindon	Won	48-47
29 April	Home	Ipswich	Won	50-46
3 May	Away	Hull	Lost	47-49
4 May	Away	Middlesbrough	Won	51-45
5 May	Away	Edinburgh	Won	49-46
6 May	Home	Long Eaton	Won	54-40
13 May	Home	Wolverhampton	Won	51-45
19 May	Away	Belle Vue	Drew	48-48
20 May	Home	Oxford	Won	53-43
22 May	Away	Exeter	Lost	45-51
27 May	Home	Reading	Won	58-38
7 June	Away	Long Eaton	Lost	41-55
10 June	Home	Middlesbrough	Won	55-40
1 July	Home	Coventry	Won	53-43
7 July	Away	Oxford	Won	53-42
8 July	Home	Hull	Won	60-36
10 July	Away	Reading	Won	50-46
15 July	Home	Arena-Essex	Won	59-36
28 July	Away	Arena-Essex	Won	51-45
29 July	Home	Poole	Won	52-44
5 August	Home	Glasgow	Won	64-32
12 August	Home	Belle Vue	Won	49-46
26 August	Home	Sheffield	Won	63-33
31 August	Away	Sheffield	Won	52-44
3 September	Home	Swindon	Won	60-36
9 September	Home	Peterborough	Won	59-36
16 September	Home	Edinburgh	Won	54-42
24 September	Away	Glasgow	Lost	41-54
25 September	Away	Wolverhampton	Won	53-43
1 October	Home	King's Lynn	Won	51-45
4 October	Away	Poole	Drew	48-48
7 October	Away	Cradley Heath	Lost	39-56
8 October	Home	Exeter	Won	59-37
19 October	Away	Ipswich	Lost	36-60

P40 W28 D3 L9 For 2,041 Against 1,785 Pts 59 BP 18 Position 1st (out of 21)

Knock-Out Cup

First Round

Date	H/A	Against	W/L	Score
21 April	Away	Arena-Essex	Lost	53-56
22 April	Home	Arena-Essex	Lost	52-54

Lost 105-110 on aggregate

1995 – Premier League and Knock-Out Cup

Rider	Matches	Rides	Points	BP	Total	Average
Martin Dugard	42	218	536	21	557	10.22
Dean Barker	32	157	351	16	367	9.35
Stefan Danno	41	220	444	35	479	8.71

Stefan Andersson	39	201	339	53	392	7.80
Darren Shand	39	171	156	44	200	4.68
Stefan Ekberg	28	133	119	28	147	4.42
Scott Swain	39	157	119	28	147	3.75
Paul Whittaker	6	22	15	4	19	3.45
Mark Bruton	6	22	12	3	15	2.73

1996

It is never considered an easy thing to do, defending a league title, with many of the sport's wise heads deeming it a more difficult task than winning it in the first place. Eastbourne were set to learn this lesson first hand in what promoter Jon Cook was to describe as a patchy season at Arlington. No team had won back-to-back championships in the top division since the Coventry Bees had achieved the feat in 1987 and 1988 and, although the Sussex club themselves had accomplished the task at the lower level (1986 and 1987), this was a whole different shooting match.

Keeping below the 46-point limit was the first problem posed but the first name on the team sheet was easy as the Eagles announced that Martin Dugard would lead them into action once more. With Dean Barker ruled out, having broken his leg in the side's title-winning match against Exeter in 1995, some welcome news followed as David Norris, who himself had suffered a badly broken leg while spending a season on loan to Reading, declared himself fit and intent on resuming his Eastbourne career. Though Barker set his sights on a mid-season comeback he never reached his target, meaning that 1997 would surely prove crunch time for the popular Eagle, newly voted the club's 'Rider of the Year'. Swede Stefan Andersson, having added a point-and-a-half to his average in the previous campaign, was handed a team place, as was his compatriot Stefan Danno, who had also played a key role in 1995. The four so far named formed a powerful top end for the Eagles to go forward with, especially if Andersson could fulfil the continued progress expected of him. Darren Shand, who had proved a capable reserve-cum-second string in 1995, was intended to complete the top five by filling the number two berth, but circumstances were set to dictate otherwise, his services being lost to the club just days before their championship defence began. Further down the order there were changes, Scott Swain proving the makeweight in a swap deal that brought thirty-year old Neville Tatum, who had not ridden competitively since the tail end of 1993, in from Peterborough. Tatum's tenure was also to prove short-lived, however, as a further trade with the London Lions in the early weeks of the season saw him depart to north-east London with Alan Mogridge, who was to prove a very popular figure with the fans, coming in the opposite direction. The tail end of the team found room for one further rider with junior Tara O'Callaghan taking his place in the lower order. Team affairs and crowd figures were both subject to some turbulence during 1996. The price of a season ticket increased on the back of Norris's return and the league-winning euphoria surrounding the club, but after starting with healthy attendances, the crowds dropped sharply, although they did begin to rise again late in the season.

The season began with a 12-point victory in the newly formed (and quickly ditched) Euro Cup competition against Rospiggarna and a two-legged Premiership success over reigning champions Bradford. The Eagles' title-defending exploits got off on the right foot with a league double over London Lions, and then Arlington visits from Ipswich and Sheffield were both rewarded with points in the bag. The visit of Cradley Heath, now resident at Stoke's Loomer Road, sparked something of a downfall as they became the first team to take league points from Sussex in a while. Though they remained a force to be reckoned with at Arlington, away from home things were not quite so rosy. With Norris struggling on his return from injury and both he and Danno finding difficulty in coming to terms with the new lay-down engines, their away form took a nosedive from the previous year. The Swindon Robins ejected them from the Knock-Out Cup competition by just five points but their exit from the new-format Fours was more clear cut, the Eagles finishing on 94 points compared to group winners Peterborough's 119 and runners-up Ipswich's 113. The teams below them were Reading with 80 and London 73. They also suffered disappointment on the European stage, finishing bottom of the Euro Cup pile on 18 points in Wroclaw (Poland) while the competition was won by Diedenbergen on 35 points, ahead of hosts Atlas-Polsat, 34, and Rospiggarna, 33.

Former Eagle Dean Standing made a return to the side following a break of some seasons, bursting back into action with a 12-point maximum in a Conference League fixture at Ryde. The popular Standing slotted comfortably into the first team, recording a creditable 5.30 in 15 matches, giving it an element of stability until, sadly, a broken leg sustained against Poole as to bring the curtain down on his speedway career. With silverware almost becoming expected at Arlington, third place might have been regarded as something of a failure but it still marked the strides made by the club since its return to the top flight, especially considering the injuries suffered by Eastbourne during the year. A run of nine straight league victories at Arlington, after Wolverhampton had become the second team to triumph in Sussex, 50-45, in mid-July, and five wins in their final eight travelling fixtures, including memorable successes at both Cradley/Stoke and Bradford underlined just what might have been. Dugard remained the undisputed Eagles number one, turning in yet another 10-plus average, while Andersson emerged as a real star, scoring 8.98 for the season. Norris came good towards the end of the year after finally shaking off the after-effects of the broken leg he had suffered in the 1995 Overseas final.

1996 was also the year in which Eastbourne entered a side in British speedway's third tier, the Conference League. It was felt that the time was right for such a move, with young riders once again being produced on the mini-track in the car park, plus ready-made heat leaders in Bobby Eldridge, Paul Lydes-Uings, Brent Collyer and Tara O'Callaghan. But injuries to the last two and defections by other riders who wanted more regular action than was on offer meant that the Toyota Starlets, as they were known, finished twelfth of thirteen teams. By the end of the season, manager Mick Corby and coach Steve Weatherley were searching here, there and everywhere for riders just to fulfil the team's commitments. Entering a team in the Conference League was thought to be the right thing to do at the time, but it wasn't a success and hasn't been repeated.

1996 – Premier League

Date	H/A	Against	W/L	Score
13 April	Home	London	Won	56-38
18 April	Away	London	Won	51-43
20 April	Home	Ipswich	Won	53-43
27 April	Home	Sheffield	Won	58-38
3 May	Away	Peterborough	Lost	39-57
4 May	Home	Cradley Heath	Lost	46-50
11 May	Home	Reading	Won	52-44
15 May	Away	Hull	Lost	37-59
16 May	Away	Middlesbrough	Won	56-39
17 May	Away	Belle Vue	Lost	38-58
30 May	Away	Ipswich	Lost	41-55
1 June	Home	Middlesbrough	Won	58-38
2 June	Away	Exeter	Drew	48-48
29 June	Home	Long Eaton	Won	58-38
6 July	Home	Coventry	Won	55-41
13 July	Home	Wolverhampton	Lost	45-50
17 July	Away	Scottish Monarchs	Lost	46-49
18 July	Away	Sheffield	Lost	45-51
20 July	Home	Peterborough	Won	51-45
22 July	Away	Wolverhampton	Lost	41-53
7 August	Away	Long Eaton	Won	50-46
10 August	Home	Exeter	Won	62-34

12 August	Away	Reading	Won	49-46
17 August	Home	Scottish Monarchs	Won	52-43
25 August	Home	Hull	Won	57-38
26 August	Away	Swindon	Lost	37-59
28 August	Away	Poole	Lost	43-53
1 September	Home	Poole	Won	55-41
11 September	Away	Cradley Heath	Won	52-44
15 September	Home	Belle Vue	Won	56-40
20 September	Away	Oxford	Won	54-41
21 September	Away	Coventry	Lost	45-51
22 September	Home	Swindon	Won	52-44
5 October	Away	Bradford	Won	50-46
6 October	Home	Bradford	Won	62-33
13 October	Home	Oxford	Won	58-38

P36 W23 D1 L12 For 1,808 Against 1,634 Pts 47 BP 12 Position 3rd (out of 19)

Knock-Out Cup

First Round

Date	H/A	Against	W/L	Score
25 May	Home	Swindon	Won	56-39
27 May	Away	Swindon	Lost	37-59

Lost 93-98 on aggregate

1996 – Premier League and Knock-Out Cup

Rider	Matches	Rides	Points	BP	Total	Average
Martin Dugard	38	198	487	12	499	10.08
Stefan Andersson	35	180	362	42	404	8.98
David Norris	38	187	338	31	369	7.89
Stefan Danno	32	163	270	29	299	7.34
Dean Standing	15	80	93	13	106	5.30
Alan Mogridge	31	154	174	34	208	5.40
Justin Elkins	26	88	55	11	66	3.00
Darren Grayling	13	41	23	3	26	2.54
Tara O'Callaghan	7	17	1	1	2	0.47

1997

The winds of change were set to blow over speedway's top flight once more as the Premier League set-up was replaced by the new Elite League. Some of the leading teams had felt that the Premier League was too big, with too wide a gulf between the top and bottom teams. The new Elite League would have just ten teams. This was a move welcomed by the Eastbourne hierarchy with promoter Jon Cook stressing that the club saw it as a vital step forward in the sport's credibility. Eastbourne had an enviable record of not finishing outside the top three in the previous five seasons and their continuing upward mobility had crafted them as fervent advocates of the newly proposed Elite League structure. Cook therefore opted to take the Eagles into speedway's elite.

He already knew the top five that they wanted to track and that included Dean Barker, who declared himself fit to race again following a long injury lay-off that had seen him miss the 1996 season completely. There was more than a ring of familiarity about the place with Martin Dugard, David Norris and Stefans Danno and Andersson all joining Barker in the line-up. It was the same top five that they had tracked in 1994, in fact. The new Elite League formula meant that teams were reduced in size from seven riders to six, and the final place in the Eastbourne team went to the fans' favourite Alan Mogridge, 'Moggo', who, in the words of Cook, had already been dubbed a legend at the club following his early-season switch from London the previous year. Though a well-worn cliché at Arlington, the set-up typified the family feel at the Sussex venue, a spirit of togetherness that had been rewarded with so much success in the past.

The season kicked off with a new style *Speedway Star* Knock-Out Cup competition, the first round being contested as two mini-leagues. Eastbourne's group consisted of Poole, who the Eagles were destined to beat in the final, Ipswich, Peterborough and King's Lynn as well as themselves. A heavy defeat at Peterborough, 62-27, was soon forgotten as the Eagles rode unbeaten at home in the competition, as well as racing to a 46-44 win at Ipswich to qualify for the semi-finals in second place behind the Pirates in their section. A narrow defeat at King's Lynn, 46-44, was encouraging but a controversial 73-17 reverse at Wimborne Road, which caused Eastbourne to complain about Poole's alleged abuse of the rules regarding tyres, followed. No further action was taken and the score stood but the Eagles provided the perfect answer by going unbeaten against the Pirates in six further matches throughout the year.

As well as the promise of success in the cup, the Eagles made a promising start in the league, a near miss at Brandon Stadium, 48-42, being followed by home wins against Bradford 58-32, Coventry 56-34, Poole 59-31 and Belle Vue 48-42. They first tasted victory on the road on their return to Dorset in the latter part of May, 46-44, but this was countered just three days later as Wolverhampton triumphed 46-42 at Arlington, this proving to be their sole home defeat in 1997. June witnessed the Eagles fending off the challenges of Swindon, Peterborough and Ipswich in Sussex as well as furthering their cause in the cup with a 58-32 first-leg victory over Bradford. That month also saw Danno and Andersson reach the Inter-Continental final, while Barker overcame the hurdle of the Overseas final to join the Swedes in the next round. The joy was to prove short-lived for the young Eagle however as he crashed awkwardly against Wolverhampton, badly breaking an arm, in what was to otherwise prove the match of the season as they gained revenge over the Monmore outfit by a 52-37 margin. Up to the moment of Barker's injury, things seemed to be shaping up well for the run-in to the end of the season. Just days before, the Eagles had won through to the cup final and, despite losing 56-34 at Odsal, they progressed to a date with Poole by an aggregate four-point margin. Both sides were destined to end the season holding silverware. Though Eastbourne's home record proved more impressive than that enjoyed by Bradford, who suffered three home losses to the Eagles' one, they couldn't match the Dukes' away exploits, the Yorkshire outfit winning away nine times compared to just three for their Sussex rivals. Consequently it was Bradford who took the Elite League title by a clear ten points. The Craven Shield looked to offer further success, following wins in each leg of their quarter-final against Wolverhampton. However, King's Lynn were to end their interest in the competition, protecting a 56-39 first-leg lead from Saddlebow Road by restricting Eagles to a 52-37 victory in the return in Sussex.

The cup final win was positive proof of the team's standing as they completely outclassed Poole in both legs. The win at Wimborne Road by six points set the Eagles up for a convincing victory and when they stormed into a sixteen-point lead after just six heats, it was all over. Dugard and Danno both scored maximums while Andersson dropped just one point. There were ten 5-1s to Eastbourne as the Eagles raced to a 50-point aggregate victory.

The Eagles had come close to pulling off the double in the first year of Elite League racing. Being cup winners and runners-up in the league firmly cemented Eastbourne's claim to be one of the top clubs in the country. The sextet of Dugard, Andersson, Barker, Danno, Norris and Mogridge had proved themselves to be a formidable outfit until the moment of Barker's injury. At the end-of-season social, Mogridge announced his retirement.

1997 – Elite League

Date	H/A	Against	W/L	Score
29 March	Away	Coventry	Lost	42-48
13 April	Home	Bradford	Won	48-32

3 May	Home	Coventry	Won	56-34
17 May	Home	Poole	Won	59-31
18 May	Away	Bradford	Lost	35-55
22 May	Away	Ipswich	Lost	30-60
24 May	Home	Belle Vue	Won	48-42
26 May	Away	Swindon	Lost	36-54
28 May	Away	Poole	Won	46-44
30 May	Away	Belle Vue	Lost	36-54
31 May	Home	Wolverhampton	Lost	42-46
8 June	Home	Swindon	Won	48-42
13 June	Away	Peterborough	Lost	44-46
14 June	Home	Peterborough	Won	56-33
28 June	Home	Ipswich	Won	63-27
4 July	Away	Belle Vue	Lost	33-57
5 July	Home	King's Lynn	Won	53-37
6 July	Away	Swindon	Lost	43-47
12 July	Home	Belle Vue	Won	51-39
16 July	Away	Poole	Won	46-44
19 July	Home	Wolverhampton	Won	52-37
27 July	Home	Swindon	Won	55-35
28 July	Away	Wolverhampton	Lost	31-59
2 August	Home	Coventry	Won	54-36
8 August	Away	Peterborough	Lost	36-53
10 August	Home	Poole	Won	55-35
20 August	Away	King's Lynn	Lost	34-56
23 August	Home	Ipswich	Won	49-41
25 August	Away	Coventry	Lost	37-53
28 August	Away	Ipswich	Lost	31-59
30 August	Home	Peterborough	Won	66-24
15 September	Away	Wolverhampton	Won	50-40
17 September	Away	Bradford	Lost	31-59
21 September	Home	King's Lynn	Won	61-29
28 September	Home	Bradford	Won	56-34
30 September	Away	King's Lynn	Lost	42-48

P36 W20 D0 L16 For 1,665 Against 1,570 Pts 40 BP 11 Position 2nd (10)

Speedway Star Cup

First Round (Run on league basis)

Date	H/A	Against	W/L	Score
23 March	Home	Ipswich	Won	53-37
28 March	Away	Peterborough	Lost	27-62
30 March	Home	Poole	Won	54-36
3 April	Away	Ipswich	Won	46-44
6 April	Home	King's Lynn	Won	55-35
9 April	Away	King's Lynn	Lost	44-46
19 April	Home	Peterborough	Won	52-37
23 April	Away	Poole	Lost	17-73

Finished second in group

Semi-final

Date	H/A	Against	W/L	Score
21 June	Home	Bradford	Won	58-32
15 July	Away	Bradford	Lost	34-56

Won 92-88 on aggregate

Final

Date	H/A	Against	W/L	Score
4 September	Away	Poole	Won	49-43
7 September	Home	Poole	Won	67-23

Won 116-66 on aggregate

Craven Shield

First Round

Date	H/A	Against	W/L	Score
4 October	Home	Wolverhampton	Won	52-38
6 October	Away	Wolverhampton	Won	51-38

Won 103-76 on aggregate

Semi-final

Date	H/A	Against	W/L	Score
22 October	Away	King's Lynn	Lost	36-53
25 October	Home	King's Lynn	Won	52-37

Lost 88-90 on aggregate

1997 – Elite League, *Speedway Star* Cup and Craven Shield

Rider	Matches	Rides	Points	BP	Total	Average
Martin Dugard	46	234	468	26	494	8.44
Stefan Andersson	52	271	513	45	558	8.24
Dean Barker	31	153	250	30	280	7.32
Stefan Danno	50	248	371	61	432	6.97
David Norris	52	255	358	61	419	6.57
Alan Mogridge	52	277	251	65	316	4.56

1998

During the winter months both skipper Martin Dugard and Dean Barker were troubled with wrist injuries. Although Dugard took heart that his would clear up naturally, Barker's problems were to prove far more acute. The injury was the legacy of an horrendous fall in mid-season the previous year and, although the bones had knitted together well, it was nerve damage that was to prove the problem. Though he didn't know it yet, the popular Eagle was not to see any action in 1998. Swede Stefan Andersson returned to the fold and he was eventually joined on the team sheet by fellow countryman Stefan Danno, an Eagle since 1992. For a time his place in the team had been under threat, thanks to a possible ban hanging over him having been accused of assaulting an FIM official in the days leading up to the 1997 Grand Prix Challenge, in which he had finished second and therefore qualified to ride in the 1998 Grand Prix Series. In the end, the Swede was cleared to ride and with David Norris also confirmed as a starter, the Eagles had four definite starters. In January, the reality of Barker's plight hit home and he admitted that he wouldn't be fit in time for tapes-up on the forthcoming campaign. In order to plug the gap, co-promoter Jon Cook moved swiftly to engage the services of 1992 World Champion Gary Havelock, a signing heralded as probably the biggest in the history of the club. Indeed, Havvy's impact was immediate as he was handed the captain's armband with Dugard stepping down from the role. Scott Robson became the sixth rider through Arlington's doors and, as the clock ticked towards the start of the new season, Cook remained confident of the successful season that lay ahead.

Certainly they began with a bang, with a home demolition of King's Lynn 65-25, but although the result was all they could have hoped for, other factors dictated something of a false dawn for the Eagles. The non-arrival of their own race suits, the visiting riders indistinguishable from one another with no numbers on theirs, and the absence of King's Lynn's top rider all added up to a pretty sorry affair. They beat Poole comfortably in the cup the following week, the league-type qualifying format having been retained, and then Coventry posed few problems in their first league encounter. It was then that the all-conquering Ipswich Witches hit town and, although the Eagles' first encounter with the Suffolk outfit remained their best performance against them throughout the year, the 46-44 home reverse immediately had a dramatic effect on attendances. Indeed the Witches were to become the proverbial thorn in the Eagles' side that year with eight meetings resulting in eight defeats as Ipswich headed towards the first treble of the modern era of league, Knock-Out Cup and Craven Shield. Eastbourne's inability to beat the Witches had a demoralising effect on all involved with the club, and then to be drawn against them in the cup semi-final, after the two sides had qualified from the same group, proved possibly the straw that broke the camel's back.

A troubled year saw the Sussex side finish outside the top four for the first time in a number of seasons. Although the home form, four defeats against Ipswich apart, remained reasonably solid, Coventry being the only other team to win at Arlington, results just didn't go their way on the road. Two victories, one at Poole 49-41, one at Oxford 51-39, both in the month of June, was all they had to show from a season's toil on their travels, which added up to a finishing position of fifth place.

Dugard continued to dominate proceedings at Arlington, finishing the year with an 8.70 average, while Norris moved up to second place with 7.15. Havelock proved to be an experiment that never quite worked out and he departed to ride for Poole in mid-August. He was soon joined through the exit door by Robson, as the Eagles lined up ready-made replacements Peter Nahlin and Toni Kasper. Both were destined to suffer with injuries, however, and the team finished the year patchedup with guests. In addition, a brief runout in the side for Robban Johansson ended prematurely as the Swede never found his feet and soon returned to his homeland. Ipswich duly bundled the Eagles out of the cup to effectively end their season, though elsewhere individuals within the team were still enjoying varying degrees of success. Dugard, the 'Master of Arlington', held the Golden Helmet for a time with successes against both Steve Johnston at Oxford and Mikael Karlsson at home against Wolves, before losing the honour to Joe Screen at Belle Vue. Danno finished thirteenth in the World Championship Grand Prix standings at the end of the year.

The Craven Shield offered no consolation as an away leathering at Swindon, 68-22, almost negated the need for a home leg. The Wiltshire venue offered no better fortunes for Dugard and Norris as they returned to contest the Elite League Riders' Championship, scoring 5 and 2 respectively.

1998 – Elite League

Date	H/A	Against	W/L	Score
4 April	Home	Coventry	Won	49-41
13 April	Away	Coventry	Lost	39-51
18 April	Home	Wolverhampton	Won	57-33
24 April	Home	Oxford	Won	60-30
2 May	Home	Belle Vue	Won	49-41
4 May	Away	Wolverhampton	Lost	35-54
8 May	Away	Belle Vue	Lost	36-54
9 May	Home	Swindon	Won	52-38
13 May	Away	King's Lynn	Lost	43-47
16 May	Home	King's Lynn	Won	48-42
21 May	Away	Ipswich	Lost	37-53
23 May	Home	Ipswich	Lost	42-48
30 May	Home	Poole	Won	52-38
17 June	Away	Poole	Won	49-41
20 June	Home	Belle Vue	Won	59-31
21 June	Away	Oxford	Won	51-39
27 June	Home	Wolverhampton	Won	55-35
3 July	Away	Belle Vue	Lost	34-56
13 July	Away	Wolverhampton	Lost	28-62
18 July	Home	King's Lynn	Won	56-34
23 July	Away	Swindon	Lost	41-49
25 July	Home	Poole	Won	52-38

8 August	Home	Ipswich	Lost	38-51
9 August	Away	Swindon	Won	26-64
21 August	Away	Oxford	Lost	34-56
22 August	Home	Swindon	Won	55-35
29 August	Home	Oxford	Won	47-43
31 August	Away	Poole	Lost	34-56
5 September	Home	Coventry	Lost	44-46
9 September	Away	King's Lynn	Lost	44-46
10 September	Away	Ipswich	Lost	43-47
17 October	Away	Coventry	Lost	40-50

P32 W15 D0 L17 For 1,430 Against 1,449 Pts 30 BP 7 Position 5th (out of 9)

Speedway Star Cup

First Round

Date	H/A	Against	W/L	Score
22 March	Home	King's Lynn	Won	65-25
29 March	Home	Poole	Won	52-38
1 April	Away	King's Lynn	Lost	31-41
2 April	Away	Ipswich	Lost	41-49
11 April	Home	Ipswich	Lost	44-46
22 April	Away	Poole	Lost	43-47

Finished second in group

Semi-final

Date	H/A	Against	W/L	Score
4 July	Home	Ipswich	Lost	42-48
16 July	Away	Ipswich	Lost	33-57

Lost 75-105 on aggregate

Craven Shield

First Round

Date	H/A	Against	W/L	Score
8 October	Away	Swindon	Lost	22-68
10 October	Home	Swindon	Won	49-41

Lost 71-109 on aggregate

1998 – Elite League, Speedway Star Cup and Craven Shield

Rider	Matches	Rides	Points	BP	Total	Average
Martin Dugard	40	228	468	28	496	8.70
David Norris	41	217	335	53	388	7.15
Stefan Danno	41	217	346	26	372	6.86
Gary Havelock	32	164	228	42	270	6.59
Stefan Andersson	40	191	264	38	302	6.32
Scott Robson	19	68	37	11	48	2.82
Robban Johansson	13	44	19	7	26	2.36

1999

Over the close season, a major change was made to the track by radically widening the exit on turn two. Following a visit there at the beginning of April, Ipswich complained that the track was now the wrong shape as it was no longer formed with two straights joined by smooth curves. Ipswich promoter John Louis complained, 'You could say it was cone, or even pear-shaped.' Jon Cook, on behalf of the Eastbourne management, countered that Arlington was the shape of the future. He said that the Speedway Control Board had inspected the track and were most complimentary about it. He added that his supporters liked the new shape and that they were voting with their feet. 'Our crowd on Saturday night,' [for the Ipswich match] he said, 'was massive, the place was heaving. We are at the forefront of change for speedway.' He felt the new shape gave more room for 'riders who want to race'.

Eastbourne Eagles had finished in fifth place in the 1998 Elite League table, their worst for a number of years, and the time seemed ripe for some team changes at Arlington. A further change in the race format meant having to increase the team from six to seven and all within the confines of the 40-point limit. Of the class of 1998, Swedish trio Peter Nahlin, Stefan Andersson and Stefan Danno, all riders synonymous with the Eastbourne story through the 1990s, were not scheduled to return, though were eventually to play a part, with Andersson becoming the subject of one of speedway's most talked-about incidents for many years. Both Martin Dugard and David Norris were retained and the popular Dean Barker prepared to make his comeback, following a season on the sidelines. The Eagles then startled everyone by signing Russian rider Roman Povazhny, a young man and noted performer on the international stage, though doubts were raised whether he would be able to cut it at Elite League level. The American Josh Larsen, who had previously made his name riding for Arena-Essex, signed on the dotted line but the naming of the Eagles' two reserves did raise eyebrows. Australian Brent Collyer was handed one of the places while Cornishman Seemond Stephens jumped straight from the Conference League into the Elite to complete the line-up.

With yet another new sponsor, the Ballamys Saab Eagles did not start the season well. Around Arlington they numbered no fewer than six home defeats in all competitions, while away from home they had to wait until the tail end of August for their first travelling success of the campaign, a 47-46 victory at Oxford's Sandy Lane. Poole were the first team to triumph in Sussex, winning 49-41 in the Craven Shield. They were followed over the course of the year by Oxford 48-44, also in the Craven Shield, and Poole again 46-44, Belle Vue 53-37, Ipswich 46-44 and Peterborough 47-43, all in the Elite League.

While the 1999 season was seldom one to savour, Eastbourne were plunged into further gloom in front of the Sky Sports cameras as they were involved in one of the greatest controversies to hit the sport in many a year. The night of 2 September saw King's Lynn visit Sussex, complete with former Eagles' asset Stefan Andersson in their ranks. A hotly contested fixture eventually saw the Sussex men run out 47-43 winners but not before an unfortunate coming together between Andersson and Dugard saw the Eagles skipper hit the Arlington shale with alarming ferocity. Anxious moments followed as Dugard rose from the track before walking purposefully back to the pits, clearly seething. With the Sky cameras in attendance, mechanics and officials generally had to make themselves scarce in order that the riders could be filmed and so it was that nobody walked back with the Eagles captain and nobody was able to stop him striding up to Andersson and flooring him with a single punch, putting the Swede out of the meeting. It was pure heat-of-the-moment stuff; on the track Dugard had clearly been wronged by an over-zealous move from his former teammate but, running on adrenalin, his off-track reaction played right into the hands of his critics as it cast him instantly in the role of villain, a mantle it took him some time to shake off.

Ipswich added further to the Eagles' woe by dumping them out of the Knock-Out Cup in the month of June, 94-86 on aggregate. In the meantime the changes going on at Arlington kept the interest high. The first to go was Stephens, whose sudden jump from Conference League to Elite League had proved too much for him. He asked for a move to the Premier League and found happiness plying his trade with Exeter. Mark Lemon, who had proved a worthy guest for Eagles in the past, joined the fold, but with the Australian struggling to return to form following an injury and the Eagles struggling in general, the move never really got off the ground. Danno made a brief return with a three-match spell that included helping the team to wins over Wolverhampton and Coventry. Then, as the season moved towards a conclusion, Nahlin returned to become a popular addition, amassing a 7.56 average in the Eagles' final ten matches. Barker had a successful return to action, his efforts being rewarded with the club's Rider of the Year award. As far as the Eagles collectively were concerned it proved not such a memorable year as they finished ninth, out of ten teams, in both the Elite League and the Craven Shield standings. Individually Dugard still led the way but his average was down to 7.81. Norris and Barker also returned 7-plus averages.

During the season a seventieth anniversary meeting was held with former riders Andrew Silver, Dean Standing, Malcolm Ballard, Paul Woods, Keith Pritchard, Eric Dugard, David Kennett, Barney Kennett and Trevor Geer all taking part in a special parade. The meeting was started by Jimmy Gleed, a member of the 1950s Southern Area League team. Despite suffering disappointments from a results perspective, there were a number of positives to draw on in 1999. It proved a success in terms of racing quality and keeping the fans entertained and Sky's intervention had undoubtedly raised the sport to new levels.

1999 – Elite League

Date	H/A	Against	W/L	Score
2 June	Away	Poole	Lost	36-54
10 June	Home	Poole	Lost	44-46
10 July	Home	Belle Vue	Lost	37-53
12 July	Away	Wolverhampton	Lost	32-58
16 July	Away	Belle Vue	Lost	32-58
17 July	Home	Wolverhampton	Won	50-40
22 July	Home	Coventry	Won	47-44
23 July	Away	Peterborough	Lost	38-52
28 July	Away	King's Lynn	Lost	35-55
4 August	Away	Hull	Lost	37-53
5 August	Away	Ipswich	Lost	32-58
7 August	Home	Ipswich	Lost	44-46
14 August	Home	Hull	Won	48-42
21 August	Home	Oxford	Won	55-35
27 August	Away	Oxford	Won	47-46
30 August	Away	Coventry	Lost	41-49
2 September	Home	King's Lynn	Won	47-43
11 September	Home	Peterborough	Lost	43-47

P18 W6 D0 L12 For 745 Against 879 Pts 12 BP 1 Position 9th (out of 10)

Speedway Star Cup

First Round

Date	H/A	Against	W/L	Score
17 June	Away	Ipswich	Lost	39-51
26 June	Home	Ipswich	Won	47-43

Lost 86-94 on aggregate

Craven Shield

(Run on a League basis)

Date	H/A	Against	W/L	Score
27 March	Home	King's Lynn	Won	50-40
3 April	Home	Ipswich	Won	50-41
7 April	Away	Poole	Lost	34-57
8 April	Away	Ipswich	Lost	40-53
10 April	Home	Poole	Lost	41-49
19 April	Away	Wolverhampton	Lost	35-57
24 April	Home	Oxford	Lost	44-48
28 April	Away	King's Lynn	Lost	34-57
1 May	Home	Coventry	Won	51-39

15 May	Home	Peterborough	Won	47-42
22 May	Home	Hull	Won	49-41
28 May	Away	Peterborough	Lost	25-65
29 May	Home	Belle Vue	Won	49-41
31 May	Away	Coventry	Lost	41-49
19 June	Home	Wolverhampton	Won	47-42
14 July	Away	Hull	Lost	41-49
30 July	Away	Belle Vue	Lost	34-56
13 August	Away	Oxford	Lost	32-52

P18 W7 D0 L11 For 744 Against 878 Pts 14 BP 1 Position 9th (out of 10)

1999 – Elite League, *Speedway Star* Cup, Craven Shield

Rider	Matches	Rides	Points	BP	Total	Average
Martin Dugard	30	147	271	16	287	7.81
Peter Nahlin	10	45	78	7	85	7.56
David Norris	37	172	274	31	305	7.09
Dean Barker	38	178	278	35	313	7.03
Josh Larsen	35	158	224	29	253	6.41
Mark Lemon	14	58	81	7	88	6.07
Roman Povazhny	27	120	138	30	168	5.60
Brent Colyer	38	124	56	20	76	2.45
Seemond Stephens	6	20	6	1	7	1.40

THE 2000s

As co-promoter Jon Cook put the final pieces of the Eastbourne jigsaw in place to face the rigours of the Millennium campaign, he announced to the world that 'We are in for a season to remember.' But even he couldn't have anticipated what was to follow, as there ensued one of the most exhilarating championship campaigns in the history of the sport, boiling down to a single climactic meeting at Arlington in the presence of the Sky Sports cameras at which his beloved Eagles emerged triumphant from a cauldron-type atmosphere in front of a reported modern record Sussex crowd. It couldn't get more memorable than that.

The first seeds of their 2000 title success had been sewn at the tail end of the 1999 season, one that hadn't proved the best for the Sussex outfit with ninth place out of ten teams in both the Elite League and the Craven Shield competitions and an early exit from the *Speedway Star* Knock-Out Cup. Cook was anxious that there would be no repeat, and it was during a late-season challenge match at Arena-Essex that he set the wheels in motion. His priority was to land an out-and-out number one, and when Hull announced that one of Britain's leading riders, Joe Screen, a rider more readily associated with the Northern scene, was available, he quickly became an Eastbourne target. Preliminary discussions took place at Arena that night with Screen's main sponsor Martin Hagon, with the possibility of Joe moving south definitely on the cards. It proved something of a miracle that the deal was kept under wraps until December when it was finally made public, the club admitting that it had smashed its own transfer record to land the rider concerned. Though no figures were revealed, the previous highest had been the £20,000 paid to Oxford in 1993 to bring favourite son Martin Dugard back to Arlington, which gives some idea of the amount of money involved.

Dugard himself was guaranteed a place of course, only first he had to face a Speedway Control Board hearing to receive any punishment meted out following the previous season's infamous punch. In the event he was cleared on a technicality. Having been fined £250 on the night, it was decided that he couldn't be punished twice for the same offence. There was relief throughout the Sussex contingent at the hearing and Dugard, having sold all his equipment anticipating a ban, was finally able to prepare for the season ahead. David Norris had already agreed terms and the comeback man of 1999, Dean Barker, was also a must and was quickly added to the list. Australian Brent Collyer was rewarded for his earlier efforts with another stint in an Eagles race suit, and the line-up was completed with two new faces, those of Petri Kokko from Reading and Paul Hurry, who signed following a spell with Oxford.

Their opening two matches both ended in defeat, 49-41 at King's Lynn and 47-43 at Ipswich, but it was then that the Eagles truly clicked, the next ten passing without defeat, four of them away from home. It was King's Lynn who set the pace in the early days and with the Knights cantering through their fixtures with continuing success at an alarming rate, it led a number of the sport's senior figures to declare that they had all but won the league already. That in turn served to lessen the pressure on the chasing Sussex side and, when they did rise to the top of the table, it proved almost perfect timing as they carried the momentum through right until the end of the season. It was true that the Eagles did not have the distraction of the Knock-Out Cup to contend with, Wolverhampton seemingly coming from nowhere to end their interest in the competition with a first-round double success, winning 46-44 at Arlington before wrapping things up 51-39 at Monmore Green in June. That disappointment apart, their encounters brought success after success. Despite a blip as they lost at both Coventry 50-40 and at King's Lynn 58-32, the Eagles' next six matches all ended in wins, including a second at Peterborough (without the injured Paul Hurry) and a revenge victory at Brandon 52-38, in which Screen recorded a delightful 18-point maximum. They remained unbeaten in the league at Arlington but it was their away form that brought them to within touching distance of the title, with wins at Wolverhampton 49-41 and a brace of successes at Belle Vue, 53-37 and 52-37, proving decisive.

At one point in the season, King's Lynn were twelve points clear of the Eagles in the league but, bit by bit, the Eagles pulled back the deficit and reeled the Knights in. As fate would have it, Eastbourne's last home match of the season was against their rivals, King's Lynn, and the situation couldn't have been more exciting as it came down to the fact that whoever won the match would win the league. As this winner-takes-all match approached, however, the Eagles hit the sort of problems they could well have done without and found themselves in some difficulty just being able to field a team. Home star Martin Dugard was injured, while Stefan Danno, who had returned as cover for the injured Dean Barker, was sidelined after being banned for an off-track misdemeanour. Two guests, Scott Nicholls and Savalas Clouting, were brought in to cover for the absent pair.

The atmosphere at Arlington on 30 September was absolutely electric. It was estimated that a crowd of between 6,500 and 7,000 turned up, including many from King's Lynn. What they witnessed was one of the most exciting matches of this or any other season, with fifteen pulsating heats of speedway. Eastbourne took the lead in heat two thanks to their reserves Kokko and Clouting taking a well-deserved 5-1. To add to the tension there was a dispute over whether the result should be allowed to stand as the flag marshal had shown the yellow-and-black flag

Petri Kokko rode for Eastbourne in 2000, but unfortunately had to leave just as he was showing promise.

instead of the chequered flag at the end of the four laps. Much to the Eagles' team manager, former rider Olli Tyrvainen's, relief, the referee ruled that the result would stand. Gradually, thanks to some excellent riding, particularly by Norris and Screen, the Eagles pulled ahead. At the end of heat twelve the scores stood at Eastbourne 42 King's Lynn 32. The Knights had one last trick up their sleeve as they gambled on sending in Jason Crump as a golden double tactical substitute. From the start it was Boyce for King's Lynn who took the lead in front of Clouting, Norris and Crump. Norris and Crump both moved past Clouting and then Norris went after Boyce, taking him on the last lap. Boyce slowed up to allow Crump to take the four points for coming second, making the heat a 5-3 to King's Lynn. They'd won the heat but it was not what they had wanted. On his return to the pits, Norris was greeted as a hero. King's Lynn now needed two 5-1s and a 4-2 to take the title. Heat thirteen saw Screen and Nicholls up against Crump and Leigh Adams, who was so far unbeaten. As the race got underway, Nicholls went down on the third bend and was excluded. Screen was left to face the two Australians alone. He just managed to get to the first bend in front of Crump, but it was Adams who chased him all the way. It was a photo finish but it was Screen who had held on by a whisker to give the Eagles the match and the Elite League title. The victory had been won thanks to an all-round team effort by Eastbourne, something that was indicative of the season as a whole.

After his comparatively poor form in 1999, Dugard had returned to the top of the pile, recording a 9.67 average, with Joe Screen on 8.82. Norris, Hurry and Barker all scored at more than 7 points per match. Individually, Danno finished twelfth in the Grand Prix series, while Screen came sixteenth. But perhaps the best performance of all was reserved for Martin Dugard, who appeared in the British Grand Prix as a wild card entry. Not only did he win it but, in doing so, became the first and so far only British rider to win his own country's Grand Prix.

As Jon Cook had prophesied at the start of the year, it had certainly been 'a season to remember'.

2000 – Elite League

Date	H/A	Against	W/L	Score
29 March	Away	King's Lynn	Lost	41-49
6 April	Away	Ipswich	Lost	43-47
8 April	Home	Ipswich	Won	48-42
10 April	Away	Wolverhampton	Drew	45-45
14 April	Away	Oxford	Won	50-43
22 April	Home	Belle Vue	Won	55-35
29 April	Home	Oxford	Won	55-35
30 April	Away	Poole	Won	48-42
12 May	Away	Peterborough	Won	49-41
13 May	Home	Poole	Won	56-34
18 May	Home	Coventry	Won	48-43
27 May	Home	Wolverhampton	Won	43-29
29 May	Away	Coventry	Lost	40-50
7 June	Away	King's Lynn	Lost	32-58
10 June	Home	King's Lynn	Won	50-39
17 June	Home	Poole	Won	53-37
8 July	Home	Belle Vue	Won	60-30
14 July	Away	Peterborough	Won	46-44
15 July	Home	Peterborough	Won	54-37
19 July	Away	Coventry	Won	52-38
20 July	Away	Ipswich	Lost	32-58
22 July	Home	Oxford	Won	54-36
24 July	Away	Wolverhampton	Won	49-41
30 July	Home	Coventry	Won	49-40
4 August	Away	Oxford	Lost	44-46
11 August	Away	Belle Vue	Won	53-37
19 August	Home	Ipswich	Won	51-39
26 August	Home	Wolverhampton	Won	50-40

30 August	Away	Poole	Lost	44-46
9 September	Home	Peterborough	Won	48-42
20 September	Away	Belle Vue	Won	52-37
30 September	Home	King's Lynn	Won	50-42

P32 W24 D1 L7 For 1,544 Against 1,322 pts. 49 BP 13 Position 1st (out of 9)

Knock-Out Cup

First Round
Date	H/A	Against	W/L	Score
24 June	Home	Wolverhampton	Lost	44-46
26 June	Away	Wolverhampton	Lost	39-51

Lost 83-97 on aggregate

Craven Shield

First Round (Run on league basis)
Date	H/A	Against	W/L	Score
4 October	Away	Poole	Lost	38-52
6 October	Away	Oxford	Lost	41-49
14 October	Home	Poole	Drew	45-45
22 October	Home	Oxford	Won	50-40

Finished third in group

2000 – Elite League, Knock-Out Cup, Craven Shield

Rider	Matches	Rides	Points	BP	Total	Average
Martin Dugard	33	151	352	13	365	9.67
Joe Screen	36	176	363	25	388	8.82
David Norris	38	164	278	39	317	7.73
Paul Hurry	31	139	226	29	255	7.34
Dean Barker	33	139	200	44	244	7.02
Petri Kokko	37	176	220	32	252	5.73
Brent Colyer	19	65	34	13	47	2.89

2001

Though 2000 had proved a glorious year for the Eastbourne Eagles, Elite League champions in the tightest finish to a season in recent memory, the Sussex side were now the possessors of speedway's poisoned chalice, namely the defenders of the title. However, with Dugard, Screen, Barker and Norris all lining up for the 2001 Eagles, there were high hopes that Eastbourne could become the first team to retain the Elite League title, but a dreadful injury to Joe Screen at King's Lynn on 25 April, in which he broke his thigh, put a real dampener on the season. As Jon Cook put it, 'It takes a lot for everyone in the club to pick themselves up from that. To lose Joe was a blow we were just not to recover from.'

Eastbourne had already had to say goodbye to two of their title-winning team thanks to the points limit rule. The two to go were the two riders on loan, Paul Hurry and Petri Kokko. It was a big blow for Kokko in particular as his good work the year before had given him an average of 5.73, rendering him virtually untouchable for any other team building for the season ahead. Sadly it effectively forced the likeable Finn's premature retirement from the sport. Joonas Kylmakorpi, labelled a prodigious talent, and who had been on the club's books for a number of years, was brought in to contest his first season, as was Brent Werner, who was the subject of some interest from two other Elite League promotions before the Eagles finally won the race to land his signature from Workington. Marcus Andersson, a

Swede who had previously dabbled in British speedway without too much success but had the convenience of an average that fitted, was also engaged to complete the Eastbourne starting line-up.

The season began with the Premiership, the traditional showdown between the league champions and cup winners, one that was to end in disappointment for the Sussex club. Even though they had won the first leg 48-42, despite holding a sixteen-point lead after heat ten, Nigel Wagstaff's King's Lynn recovered sufficiently to take the title and gain revenge for their league defeat courtesy of a 55-37 victory in the return. The league campaign was to fare little better as successive defeats at Ipswich 49-29, Oxford 47-43 and Poole 54-36, combined with a home draw with Oxford, the team who were eventually to relieve them of their title, hardly started their defence off on the right foot. An encouraging 47-43 win at Coventry in mid-April, in which Werner rode in seven races scoring 19 paid 20, was nullified by a home reverse at the hands of the Pirates the following night, but the Eagles were further boosted with a draw at Peterborough's East of England Showground and a follow-up home win, 49-41, the first of the season in the league, to take the 'A' points from the Panthers. It was at that point in the year that disaster struck as Screen was involved in the horrific accident at King's Lynn's Norfolk Arena that robbed the Sussex club of his talents for the remainder of the season. This was followed by the memorable occasion on 28 April when Eastbourne recorded the highest score ever in the Elite League with a 75-0 victory over King's Lynn. The reason for this was that the King's Lynn management had withdrawn its team in protest following Eastbourne's objection to King's Lynn using Danny Bird to ride at number seven in place of the injured Lee Redmond. Although the King's Lynn riders had gone home, the Eagles still had to ride every race to earn the points. Bob Dugard called King's Lynn's

The third generation of Dugards to ride for Eastbourne, Martin, winner of the 2000 British Grand Prix.

decision 'unbelievable' and said, 'I can see no possible way they [the King's Lynn promoters] can keep their licences.'

A more satisfying victory followed at Monmore Green just over a week later as Eagles triumphed 47-43 against Wolverhampton, but more disappointment was in store as Oxford put an end to their cup hopes, 103-77 on aggregate, at the first hurdle. Stefan Andersson returned to the fold for a four-week period following Screen's injury but, although the Eagles' management harboured hopes of him staying for the remainder of the season, it soon became apparent that he wasn't set up for the rigours of a UK campaign and he went home. Toni Svab and Roman Povazhny were the next two through the entry door. By this time the Eagles had put together a run of four successive home victories at the expense of Wolverhampton twice, 49-41 and 51-39, Belle Vue 51-39 and Peterborough 47-42, but the run wasn't to last, as Coventry arrived to inflict a stinging 51-39 defeat in Sussex at the beginning of August. The Aces were to feel the backlash as the Eagles won out 64-26 and then came an amazing travelling victory at league leaders Oxford, 46-44, which temporarily put the Cheetahs' title charge on hold. Although this cheered the Eastbourne collective, the topsy-turvy season continued as Poole secured their second Arlington victory of the campaign, 46-44, and then Oxford all but wrapped up the championship, winning 51-41 in Sussex on 1 September, the Eagles' seventh home defeat of the year. The season-ending Craven Shield offered little consolation as the Pirates triumphed from the qualifying group containing the Eagles and Oxford.

Dugard finished the season as top man once again with an 8.16 average, followed by Barker on just 6.80, though he had suffered from yet another injury that had put him out of action for ten matches. All in all it was a season to forget for the Eagles.

Eastbourne Eaglets ran again in 2001, entering the Southern Junior League with a team that included Daniel Giffard, Barrie Geer, Jason King, Chris Geer, Matt Fearn and a name very familiar to longstanding Arlington patrons, Edward Kennett. This time the Eaglets had a far more successful time than their big brothers as they won the league, winning six out of their eight matches.

2001 – Elite League

Date	H/A	Against	W/L	Score
29 March	Away	Ipswich	Lost	29-49
31 March	Home	Oxford	Drew	45-45
6 April	Away	Oxford	Lost	43-47
13 April	Away	Poole	Lost	36-54
14 April	Away	Coventry	Won	47-43
15 April	Home	Poole	Lost	44-46
20 April	Away	Peterborough	Drew	45-45
21 April	Home	Peterborough	Won	49-41
28 April	Home	King's Lynn	Won	75-0*
7 May	Away	Wolverhampton	Won	47-43
19 May	Home	Ipswich	Lost	40-50
27 May	Home	Coventry	Drew	45-45
2 June	Home	Ipswich	Lost	40-50
7 June	Away	Ipswich	Lost	34-56
10 June	Home	Wolverhampton	Won	49-41
20 June	Away	Poole	Lost	34-56
23 June	Home	Belle Vue	Won	51-39
27 June	Away	King's Lynn	Lost	31-59
29 June	Away	Peterborough	Lost	28-62
12 July	Home	Wolverhampton	Won	51-39
21 July	Home	Peterborough	Won	47-42
23 July	Away	Wolverhampton	Lost	43-47
4 August	Home	Coventry	Lost	39-51
11 August	Home	Belle Vue	Won	64-26
24 August	Away	Oxford	Won	46-44

25 August	Home	Poole	Lost	44-46
27 August	Away	Coventry	Lost	25-65
1 September	Home	Oxford	Lost	41-51
10 September	Away	Belle Vue	Lost	41-49
15 September	Home	King's Lynn	Won	51-39
26 September	Away	Belle Vue	Lost	30-42
24 October	Away	King's Lynn	Lost	39-51

*King's Lynn withdrew from match in protest

P 14 W11 L18 D3 For 1373 Against 1463 Pts 25 BP Position 7th (out of 9)

Knock-Out Cup

First Round

Date	H/A	Against	W/L	Score
11 May	Away	Oxford	Lost	37-53
12 May	Home	Oxford	Won	50-40

Lost 87-93 on aggregate

Craven Shield

First Round

Date	H/A	Against	W/L	Score
22 September	Home	Oxford	Won	51-39
3 October	Away	Poole	Lost	33-57
5 October	Away	Oxford	Lost	43-47
6 October	Home	Poole	Lost	36-54

2001 – Elite League, Knock-Out Cup and Craven Shield

Rider	Matches	Rides	Points	BP	Total	Average
Martin Dugard	36	176	343	16	359	8.16
Joe Screen	10	50	88	7	95	7.60
Dean Barker	29	123	181	28	209	6.80
David Norris	39	184	281	27	308	6.70
Toni Svab	11	52	72	12	84	6.46
Stefan Andersson	7	72	72	19	91	6.07
Roman Povazhny	16	72	93	15	108	6.00
Brent Werner	40	177	205	35	240	5.42
Joonas Kylmakorpi	38	158	185	28	213	5.39
Marcus Andersson	21	72	72	19	91	5.06

2002

2002 proved to be the year that Eastbourne were saddled with a piece of unwanted history when they became the first team to attain the dubious distinction of topping the league table at the end of the year and yet not be crowned champions, as it was the year that the Elite League Play-offs were introduced. Unfortunately they were to run into an 'in-form' Wolverhampton side in the two matches that ultimately decided the destination of the league title. Even so, it proved to be a good year for the Sussex side as they had the consolation of winning the Knock-Out Cup, some reward for what had proved a season of impressive performances both home and away.

It was a year of considerable change at Arlington as 2002 saw Eastbourne legend Martin Dugard hang up his Kevlars, prematurely in the eyes of many of his supporters, but nobody could argue that he had not gone out at the very top of his game and that in itself was poetry. In his wake came a new hero in the guise of the 2000 World Champion Mark Loram, a rider who to this day remains one of the most popular to sport the Eagles' blue and yellow. It was a season that also witnessed a change of promoter as Terry Russell, who had already done much to foster the sport's relationship with Sky television, picked up the reins from stadium owner Bob Dugard, who continued to concentrate on stadium matters while Dugard Machine Tools continued to sponsor the club. Russell arrived, having struck a deal in early March, to inherit a team put in place by the previous regime, but one he could see was rich in promise and one that he was happy to run with. Loram's arrival came at the eleventh hour, Eastbourne having already signed the Polish Grand Prix star Krzysztof Cegielski in the run-up to Christmas after he found himself surplus to requirements at Poole following a glittering debut season. However, as time moved on, an ongoing dispute between Cegielski and his Polish club saw the Polish authorities withdraw his licence, leaving him unable to ride in official fixtures anywhere in the world. With just days to go before the start of the season, Eastbourne were left with just one top-class rider in Joe Screen, who was raring to go after his long lay-off. Fortunately for the Eagles, the Elite League promoters, concerned that Grand Prix riders were missing too many league matches, had brought in a new rule for 2002 banning Elite League teams from having more than one Grand Prix rider unless they'd had three the year before, in which case they could retain two of them. This left a number of Grand Prix riders without British clubs. One of those was England's last world champion, Mark Loram. Within twenty-four hours of Cegielski's enforced lay-off, Jon Cook learnt of Loram's situation through a chance telephone call with the rider himself when speaking to him about Martin Dugard's testimonial meeting. The Eagles' co-promoter jumped at the chance of bringing him to replace the Pole and signed him up immediately. The remainder of the side slotted nicely into place. Dean Barker and David Norris returned from the previous season, while Savalas Clouting, who had been a target in 1993 and 2001, finally made the move to Sussex. Stefan Andersson made a welcome return, having last ridden for the Eagles in 1998, while Toni Svab was also included following some superb displays the previous year.

The new-look Eagles certainly hit the ground running, Barker and Andersson both riding unbeaten by an opponent as they crushed Peterborough 64-26 at Arlington, then Loram was paid for the lot as Eagles triumphed in their first away match at King's Lynn 53-37. Indeed their first four matches on the road resulted in wins as Peterborough 46-44, Oxford 47-43 and Ipswich 51-39 in a cup match were also put to the sword. Remarkably, their only defeat in their opening eight fixtures came at home, to the Coventry Bees by a single point, 45-44.

Wolverhampton's 47-43 victory finally saw them beaten on their travels, but it was to be another five matches before the Sussex men tasted defeat again, going down on consecutive nights to Peterborough 50-40 and Ipswich 45-44 in mid-May. A 46-44 win at King's Lynn, in front of the Sky cameras with Loram and Screen sharing a final heat 4-2, proved particularly pleasing, and then further successes were to follow at Belle Vue 45-45, with a revenge win coming at Coventry 47-43. Wolves went the same way in the Knock-Out Cup, the Eagles winning both legs in a 101-78 aggregate victory to qualify for a final appearance against the Peterborough Panthers. Consecutive defeats away to Poole 47-44 and Wolves 47-43, with a shock home loss to bottom-of-the-table Ipswich 46-44, failed to knock the Eagles out of their stride as they embarked on another six-match unbeaten run. Sadly, during that period they were to lose the services of the free-scoring Svab, who badly broke a leg in a World Cup practice session.

By now Wolves were on a roll, and looked set to provide Eastbourne's chief opposition for league honours. However, a home draw and the bonus point against Coventry, thanks to Loram coming from the back to defeat Coventry guest Nicki Pedersen, ensured that the Sussex club finished top of the pile. Eastbourne then put themselves in the driving seat for cup glory with a 55-35 home success over the Panthers but then followed those historic play-off matches against Wolverhampton. The Eagles had to dig deep at Monmore Green and with Wolves threatening to kill off the tie at the very outset by taking a substantial lead, the visitors produced a late-meeting rally to eventually go down by just eight points, 49-41, after the first leg. Confidence remained high, but the Eagles hit problems in the run-up to the return. Both Norris and Andersson carried injuries into the second leg and Clouting was ruled out, having been struck down with illness and rushed into hospital. Eastbourne were forced to blood teenager Edward Kennett at reserve where he partnered guest Billy Janniro from Coventry. Both Loram and Janniro fought valiantly and Kennett did as much as could reasonably have been expected of him, but the injuries affecting both Norris and Andersson and a veritable nightmare machinery-wise for Screen ensured that the league title remained just out of the Eagles' grasp as they failed to make up the eight-point deficit on Wolverhampton.

Winning the cup at Peterborough, 94-86 on aggregate after something of a struggle, provided a measure of consolation and some deserved silverware, but the Craven Shield was not to offer any further reward as the Eagles again missed out to Poole at the group stage. Under the old rules and in any other year, the Sussex club would have been celebrating the league and cup double, however the innovative play-offs had put paid to that as the Eagles were prevented from being labelled champions thanks to an aggregate defeat by Wolverhampton in what effectively proved the only two important matches of the season. Nevertheless, Eastbourne's place as one of the country's leading clubs was reaffirmed and great things were hoped for from the 2003 season. The individual members of the team had all ridden exceptionally well, no fewer than six of them recording averages of 6.8 or over. As expected, Loram took over the number one spot from Dugard with 9.56, while Screen proved to be the perfect number two.

2002 – Elite League

Date	H/A	Against	W/L	Score
23 March	Home	Peterborough	Won	64-26
27 March	Away	King's Lynn	Won	53-37
5 April	Away	Peterborough	Won	46-44
6 April	Home	Coventry	Lost	44-45
12 April	Away	Oxford	Won	47-43
13 April	Home	King's Lynn	Won	58-32
22 April	Away	Wolverhampton	Lost	43-47
25 April	Home	Belle Vue	Won	60-30
4 May	Home	Oxford	Won	48-42
6 May	Away	Belle Vue	Won	48-42
9 May	Home	Wolverhampton	Won	56-34
18 May	Home	Ipswich	Won	55-35
22 May	Away	Peterborough	Lost	40-50
23 May	Away	Ipswich	Lost	44-45
29 May	Away	King's Lynn	Won	46-44
1 June	Home	Belle Vue	Won	50-40
15 June	Home	King's Lynn	Won	58-32
17 June	Away	Belle Vue	Drew	45-45
19 June	Away	Coventry	Won	47-43
28 June	Away	Oxford	Lost	39-51
13 July	Home	Wolverhampton	Won	51-39
17 July	Away	Poole	Lost	44-47
27 July	Home	Ipswich	Lost	44-46
29 July	Away	Wolverhampton	Lost	43-47
11 August	Home	Poole	Won	60-30
15 August	Away	Ipswich	Won	47-43
17 August	Home	Peterborough	Won	54-36
22 August	Home	Poole	Won	49-41
24 August	Home	Oxford	Won	51-38
26 August	Away	Coventry	Drew	45-45
28 August	Away	Poole	Lost	38-52
7 September	Home	Coventry	Drew	45-45

P32 W20 D3 L9 For 1,562 Against 1,316 Pts 43 BP 15 Position 1st (out of 9)

Play-off Final

Date	H/A	Against	W/L	Score
25 September	Away	Wolverhampton	Lost	41-49
2 October	Home	Wolverhampton	Won	46-44

Lost 87-93 on aggregate

Knock-Out Cup

First Round

Date	H/A	Against	W/L	Score
18 April	Away	Ipswich	Won	51-39
20 April	Home	Ipswich	Won	54-36

Won 105-75 on aggregate

Semi-final

Date	H/A	Against	W/L	Score
29 June	Home	Wolverhampton	Won	52-38
1 July	Away	Wolverhampton	Won	49-40

Won 101-78 on aggregate

Final

Date	H/A	Against	W/L	Score
21 September	Home	Peterborough	Won	55-35
9 October	Away	Peterborough	Lost	39-51

Won 94-86 on aggregate

Craven Shield

Date	H/A	Against	W/L	Score
18 September	Away	Poole	Lost	41-49
30 September	Away	Oxford	Lost	44-46
5 October	Home	Poole	Won	49-41
11 October	Home	Oxford	Won	52-38

Finished second in group

2002 – Elite League, Knock-Out Cup and Craven Shield

Rider	Matches	Rides	Points	BP	Total	Average
Mark Loram	44	216	489	27	516	9.56
Joe Screen	43	208	405	35	440	8.46
David Norris	40	188	313	54	367	7.81
Antonin Svab	22	107	168	25	193	7.21
Dean Barker	36	154	238	38	276	7.17
Stefan Andersson	35	142	194	38	232	6.54
Savalas Clouting	39	148	123	30	153	4.14

The 2000 World
Champion Mark
Loram rode for the
club in 2002.

2003

The success that the Eastbourne Eagles enjoyed in 2002, the topping of the Elite League table and the winning of the Knock-Out Cup, was brought sharply into perspective as they were forced to endure another injury-affected campaign in season 2003. The plan was to build upon the foundations laid and learn from any mistakes made, in order to go one better the following year. The top four of Mark Loram, Joe Screen, David Norris and Dean Barker were all retained. Stefan Andersson was not totally committed to returning while neither Toni Svab or Savalas Clouting was owned by the club and subsequently all three left. In their wake, Joonas Kylmakorpi was recalled following a successful season on loan to Ipswich, while hot property Adam Shields was engaged to double-up between the Elite and Premier Leagues with the Eagles and the Isle of Wight. Hull's Garry Stead was signed to share duties with Shields, leaving Eastbourne with just one berth to fill. Swede Peter Ljung arrived on Andersson's recommendation but although he was highly regarded in his homeland he failed to settle at Arlington and proved only to be a bit-part player during 2003.

The bones were all in place for another successful season ahead and that was how things looked set to pan out as the Eagles kicked off their campaign in style, riding to four successive wins, at home to Wolverhampton, 47-42, Ipswich 50-40 and title contenders Coventry 47-43, as well as away to Reading 51-42 in the British League Cup. The Bees gained their revenge, narrowly claiming the aggregate bonus thanks to a 48-42 success in the return at Brandon, but another home win against Oxford, 47-43, then a travelling victory at Belle Vue 49-41, ensured everything was still rosy in the Eagles' garden.

It was on Good Friday that their fortunes were to turn in dramatic, not to mention disastrous, fashion. It was maybe bad enough for the Eastbourne faithful that the Poole Pirates were the ones responsible for the Eagles' grip on the Knock-Out Cup being relinquished following an aggregate victory, both legs being contested on the same day. However, that disappointment paled into insignificance following a heat-thirteen crash at Arlington that resulted in a broken arm for number one and kingpin Loram. It was an injury that was to sideline him for the most important weeks of the campaign. Loram proved to be irreplaceable. Clearly his points potency was much missed, but it was his supportive and unflappable behind-the-scenes influence in the pits that the management found hard to recreate and it wasn't long before the cracks started to appear. Although their home form remained reasonably solid with both Poole (46-43) and Coventry (46-44) finding themselves wanting at Arlington, it was the Eagles' away prowess that was to drop off alarmingly, a draw at Belle Vue providing the only

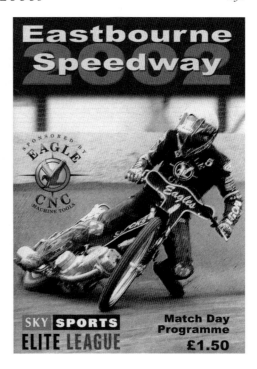

A programme cover from 2002, the year Eastbourne topped the league but did not become champions.

other point Eastbourne were to score all season from their remaining travelling engagements in the league.

The promotion cast their net far and wide in a bid to replace Loram, Greg Hancock being briefly courted as his successor. But then the news filtered through that Nicki Pedersen had fallen out with the Oxford management and been sacked. Jon Cook moved swiftly to engage the services of the World Champion in waiting, but inevitably Pedersen's arrival meant that changes needed to be made. Joe Screen found himself the unlucky one who had to make way, although hindsight has shown that the move back to Belle Vue has ultimately worked in his favour. Loram made an ambitious return against Poole at Wimborne Road, the night of Pedersen's debut, but was clearly ring rusty with just a 5 paid 7-point return in the Eagles' 47-43 defeat to show for his efforts. However it was a cruel blow when a mere six days – and four matches – later he was ruled out again, sustaining a broken collarbone in the Eagles' 46-44 defeat in front of the Sky Sports cameras at Oxford. Thanks to Loram's injury problems he only rode with Pedersen a handful of times, and one of those resulted in Eastbourne's second home reverse at the hands of Poole, 47-43, in their final league match of the campaign, a campaign that saw them finish in a lowly sixth place out of eight teams in the table.

The British League Cup did at least furnish the Eagles with a final appearance to show for their efforts. They qualified for the latter stages from a group that included Reading, Isle of Wight and Swindon as well as Elite League rivals Oxford. A quarter-final against Sheffield witnessed a 47-43 first leg victory in an excellent match at Owlerton, and the semi-final against Wolves provided more succour as they triumphed both away, 46-43, and home, 51-42, to close the season with another two-legged showdown against Poole. With the Pirates on course for the treble, the Eagles were unable to stand in their way and although they triumphed 48-42 in the Arlington-staged first-leg, the Dorset outfit took the trophy thanks to a 56-34 win in the return.

With Loram's injuries, Pedersen had taken over as number one, with an average of 8.48 in nine matches. Loram had dropped to 8.23 with Dean Barker just behind on 8.17. There was one individual success for the Eagles however, as Nicki Pedersen took the biggest prize of all, becoming World Champion on 4 October with a total Grand Prix tally of 152 points, eight ahead of his nearest rival Jason Crump. It was the first time that an Eastbourne rider had won the World Championship.

2003 – Elite League

Date	H/A	Against	W/L	Score
25 March	Home	Wolverhampton	Won	47-42
29 March	Home	Ipswich	Won	50-40
5 April	Home	Coventry	Won	47-43
9 April	Away	Coventry	Lost	42-48
12 April	Home	Oxford	Won	47-43
14 April	Away	Belle Vue	Won	49-41
26 April	Home	Belle Vue	Won	47-43
3 May	Home	Peterborough	Won	55-35
5 May	Away	Poole	Lost	30-60
8 May	Away	Peterborough	Lost	38-52
10 May	Home	Poole	Lost	43-46
24 May	Home	Ipswich	Won	54-36
29 May	Away	Ipswich	Lost	41-49
2 June	Away	Wolverhampton	Lost	42-48
9 June	Home	Coventry	Lost	44-46
16 June	Away	Belle Vue	Drew	45-45
21 June	Home	Oxford	Won	52-38
23 June	Away	Ipswich	Lost	43-47
16 July	Away	Poole	Lost	43-47
18 July	Away	Peterborough	Lost	34-56
19 July	Home	Wolverhampton	Won	46-38*
21 July	Away	Oxford	Lost	43-47
11 August	Away	Wolverhampton	Lost	37-53
15 August	Away	Oxford	Lost	44-46
16 August	Home	Belle Vue	Won	56-34
25 August	Away	Coventry	Lost	38-51
8 September	Home	Peterborough	Won	61-29
13 September	Home	Poole	Lost	43-47

*Meeting abandoned after fourteen heats. Result stands

P28 W12 D1 L15 For 1,261 Against 1,250 Pts 25 BP 8 Position 5th (out of 7)

Knock-Out Cup

First Round

Date	H/A	Against	W/L	Score
18 April	Away	Poole	Lost	34-56
18 April	Home	Poole	Won	40-32*

*Meeting abandoned after twelve heats. Result stands
Lost 74-88 on aggregate

British League Cup

First Round (Run on league basis)

Date	H/A	Against	W/L	Score
31 March	Away	Reading	Won	51-42
20 April	Home	Isle of Wight	Won	55-34
22 April	Away	Isle of Wight	Drew	45-45
18 May	Home	Swindon	Won	52-37
2 August	Home	Oxford	Won	46-38
22 August	Away	Oxford	Drew	45-45
24 August	Home	Reading	Won	60-30
7 September	Away	Swindon	Lost	39-51

P8 W5 D2 L1 For 393 Against 322 Pts 12 BP 4 Position 1st (out of 5)

Second Round

Date	H/A	Against	W/L	Score
25 September	Away	Sheffield	Won	47-43
27 September	Home	Sheffield	Won	59-31

Won 106-74 on aggregate

Semi-final

Date	H/A	Against	W/L	Score
1 October	Away	Wolverhampton	Won	46-43
12 October	Home	Wolverhampton	Won	51-42

Won 97-85 on aggregate

Final

Date	H/A	Against	W/L	Score
19 October	Home	Poole	Won	48-42
29 October	Away	Poole	Lost	34-56

Lost 82-98 on aggregate

2003 – Elite League, British League Cup and Craven Shield

Rider	Matches	Rides	Points	BP	Total	Average
Nicki Pedersen	9	50	102	4	106	8.48
Mark Loram	15	69	129	13	142	8.23
Dean Barker	42	187	331	51	382	8.17
Joe Screen	21	98	183	11	194	7.92
David Norris	39	183	332	25	357	7.80
Adam Shields	29	129	213	31	244	7.57
Joonas Kylmakorpi	38	176	295	30	325	7.39
Gary Stead	8	30	39	9	48	6.40
Ulrich Ostergaard	9	40	44	13	57	5.70
Matt Read	12	52	53	13	64	4.92
Joel Parsons	8	29	24	5	29	4.00
Glenn Cunningham	8	28	20	8	28	4.00
Peter Ljung	7	24	11	5	16	2.67

2004

2004, Eastbourne's seventy-fifth anniversary season, proved to be another of rollercoaster fortunes and emotions for the Eagles and their army of adoring supporters. Having finished in sixth place out of eight teams in the previous campaign, one troubled by injury and continual change, 2003 had proved a season that would hardly have been considered successful down on the Sussex coast. However the team that they finished the season with, Pedersen, Loram, Norris, Barker, Kylmakorpi, Shields and Kennett, would surely have proved one capable of sweeping all before them in 2004. Not that we can know for sure, but that could so easily have been the outcome had the Eagles been allowed to keep such a powerhouse-looking outfit together. Sadly for Eastbourne, it was not to be. With both Arena-Essex and Swindon making the step up to bolster the Elite League, and the ongoing problem of keeping teams viable within tight cost limits, the BSPA imposed new rider gradings as a blueprint for clubs to refer to in order to assemble their septets for the season ahead. As a consequence, the Eagles were forced to restructure their team strength accordingly. With Nicki Pedersen having already agreed a contract before the 2003 season had ended, and Eastbourne having to lose two riders from their top three, there was to be no place available for either the immensely popular Mark Loram or longstanding Arlington servant Dean Barker, both of whom were seconded to form the front end of the new Arena-Essex offensive. Adam Shields signed to contest his first full season with the Eagles and David Norris was also retained, which, given the season that he was set to enjoy, was to prove, though maybe unwittingly, a masterstroke of selection by co-promoter Jon Cook.

Adam Shields leads Dean Barker. Shields, originally signed as a 'double-up' rider in 2003, became a heat leader in 2004.

Joonas Kylmakorpi was another returnee, and things looked to be going in the right direction as Edward Kennett agreed terms to move up full time to the senior league. This left two slots to fill and the time felt right to hand another opportunity to Peter Ljung, a World Cup winner with Sweden the previous year, while it was felt that Dane Ulrich Ostergaard had impressed sufficiently in his British League Cup outings to warrant a full-time recall.

The Eagles began with a one-point challenge match defeat at the home of the Arena-Essex Hammers, one that witnessed superb performances from both Norris and Shields. That result served to encourage the team but they weren't to enjoy such good fortunes at Ipswich, although they recovered from a twenty-point deficit after heat six to lose by just eleven points, 51-42, in the Knock-Out Cup first leg at Foxhall Heath. Arena then gatecrashed the party in the Arlington curtain raiser, Barker starring in Hammers' 46-44 win to complete an Air-Tek Challenge double. Rain called a halt to both their matches away and at home against Swindon and then their spirits spiralled further downhill as Poole inflicted a double defeat, 52-44 at Wimborne Road and 50-40 at Arlington on Good Friday, getting the Eagles' Elite League campaign off to the worst possible start. They were bottom of the table at that point without a win to their name, but the mood lightened as Pedersen and Shields secured a rostrum place in the League Pairs at Swindon behind the host club and Belle Vue. Coventry were dispatched with a degree of comfort, 62-29, but then Wolverhampton piled on the agony as they triumphed 46-45 in late April, the Eagles' third defeat in four matches in Sussex. The home form, along with confidence levels, started to lift, however, as Eastbourne put a run of seven successive victories together at Arlington. They continued to rise up the table, tasting success at Wolverhampton 45-44 and claiming a draw at Swindon, but undoubtedly the highlight of the year had to be the Eagles' three-point victory, 46-43, at Wimborne Road to complete a 'B' fixture double in what was to prove Poole's second successive treble-winning season.

Wolves again triumphed at Fortress Arlington, 49-43, to complete a double of their own, but this was to prove the only other time that the Eagles lost at home, except when Ipswich won 48-46 to progress to the Knock-Out Cup semi-final, incredibly a full five months after the first leg had been ridden, in the last Arlington match of the season. Travelling victories at Belle Vue and Coventry helped Eastbourne rise to the giddy heights of fourth place and into a play-off slot, but their season was effectively wrecked as Norris, who had enjoyed an outstanding season, finishing with a near 10-point average and deservedly winning the Elite League Rider of the Year award, suffered a badly broken leg in the Eagles' final home League match with Swindon after being involved in an alarming crash following a brush with former teammate Ljung who, by this time, had defected to the Robins. The closing weeks of the season were not kind to the Eagles as Andrew Moore, who had been recruited as a 'double-up' rider from

Eastbourne's only world champion, Nicki
Pedersen.

Sheffield after Kennett had decided to take a break from the Elite League scene, also suffered a
broken leg in their home match against Arena-Essex to end what had been a run of impressive
appearances from the youngster. Despite the best efforts of Pedersen and Davey Watt, who by
now had also signed on loan from Poole, the Sussex men couldn't live with their first round
play-off opponents, Ipswich, around their own circuit and duly lost 55-39 thus bringing to an
end a very middle-of-the-road season.

The major success had been David Norris, with 2004 proving to be the 'Year of the Norris', as
the local-born hero defied all his critics and delighted his many followers by turning his speedway
career around through sheer hard work and endeavour. Norris produced top-scoring performances
up and down the country. From an average to fairly good rider he now became one of Britain's
best and an automatic choice for Team GB. Tracks that he had previously found difficult to master
suddenly held no fears and his performances both for Eastbourne and Team GB as well as his
appearances as a guest presenter for Sky Sports won him a whole new army of fans.

At the end of Eastbourne's seventy-fifth-anniversary year, Eastbourne was able to boast that,
apart from 1931, the Second World War years, three years in the late 1940s and early 1950s and
four years in the 1960s, Arlington had seen speedway every year since those pioneers had first
ridden round a dirt track in a field on their stripped-down road machines back in 1929. In
all it was a total of sixty-one years. There is no other track in the country that can match this
record and for practically the whole of that period the Dugard family have been involved in
one capacity or another. On a number of occasions they have saved the track from extinction
by digging deep into their own pockets.

Eastbourne's contribution to British speedway is incalculable, not only because of its
longevity, not only because of its impressive league and cup record (nine league titles; nine
cup wins), but also because of its commitment to training youngsters, the future lifeblood of
the sport, which has continued from pre-war days up to the present and has turned out many
of the country's leading riders.

2004 – Elite League

Date	H/A	Against	W/L	Score
9 April	Away	Poole	Lost	44-52
9 April	Home	Poole	Lost	40-50

Andrew Moore, signed up as a 'double-up' rider in 2004.

17 April	Home	Coventry	Won	62-29
24 April	Home	Wolverhampton	Lost	45-46
8 May	Home	Peterborough	Won	47-43
12 May	Away	Peterborough	Lost	46-50
17 May	Home	Ipswich	Won	50-40
20 May	Away	Ipswich	Lost	46-47
21 May	Away	Oxford	Lost	43-53
22 May	Home	Belle Vue	Won	57-38
24 May	Away	Belle Vue	Lost	45-48
27 May	Away	Swindon	Lost	42-48
5 June	Home	Poole	Won	51-44
7 June	Away	Wolverhampton	Won	45-44
10 June	Away	Swindon	Drew	45-45
14 June	Home	Oxford	Won	47-46
16 June	Away	Arena-Essex	Lost	43-47
19 June	Home	Arena-Essex	Won	53-40
25 June	Away	Peterborough	Drew	48-48
30 June	Away	Poole	Won	49-46
3 July	Home	Peterborough	Won	50-40
5 July	Away	Oxford	Lost	43-51
10 July	Home	Wolverhampton	Lost	43-49
12 July	Away	Wolverhampton	Lost	42-54
17 July	Home	Coventry	Won	55-39
21 July	Away	Belle Vue	Won	45-44
24 July	Home	Belle Vue	Won	51-39
9 August	Home	Ipswich	Won	52-45
11 August	Away	Arena-Essex	Lost	46-47
12 August	Away	Ipswich	Lost	31-63
14 August	Home	Arena-Essex	Won	50-43
19 August	Away	Coventry	Won	50-45
21 August	Home	Swindon	Won	60-32
28 August	Home	Oxford	Won	47-43
6 September	Home	Swindon	Drew	45-45
9 September	Away	Coventry	Lost	41-49

P36 W18 D3 L15 For 1,699 Against 1,632 Pts 39 BP 11 Position 4th (out of 10)

Play-Off First Round

Date	H/A	Against	W/L	Score
20 September	Away	Ipswich	Lost	39-55

Knock-Out Cup

First Round

Date	H/A	Against	W/L	Score
25 March	Away	Ipswich	Lost	42-51
11 September	Home	Ipswich	Lost	41-49

Lost 83-100 on aggregate

2004 – Elite League, Knock-Out Cup and Craven Shield

Rider	Matches	Rides	Points	BP	Total	Average
David Norris	34	166	387	26	413	9.95
Nicki Pedersen	33	160	367	12	379	9.48
Adam Shields	38	174	333	23	356	8.18
Joonas Kylmakorpi	30	127	187	36	223	7.02
Peter Ljung	17	80	87	13	100	5.00
Andrew Moore	14	69	67	11	78	4.52
Edward Kennett	24	100	95	10	105	4.20
Davey Watt	6	28	22	3	25	3.57
Ulrich Ostergaard	20	74	42	12	54	2.92
Adrian Miedzinski	8	33	15	5	20	2.42
Steen Jensen	7	27	13	1	14	2.07

APPENDICES

Appendix One

Eastbourne Eagles*

Address: Arlington Stadium, near Hailsham, Sussex.
Years of operation: 1929-1930: Open licence
1931: Not open
1932-1937: Open licence
1938: Sunday Amateur Dirt Track League
1939: Open licence
1940-1945: Not open
1946: Open licence
1947: National League Third Division
1948: Open licence
1949: Not open
1950: Open licence
1951-1952: Not open
1953: Open licence
1954-1957: Southern Area League
1958: Open licence
1959: Southern Area League
1960-1963: Open licence
1964: Metropolitan League
1965-1968: Not open
1969-1974: British League Second Division
1975: New National League
1976-1978: National League
1979-1984: British League
1985-1990: National League
1991-1994: British League
1995-1996: Premier League
1997-present: Elite League

Track Length: 1929-1954: 352 yards
1955-1978: 342 yards
1979-1997: 302 yards
1998-present: 275 metres
Current track record holder: Tony Rickardsson: 55.01 seconds, set 10 May 2003
Promoters: Charlie Dugard, Bob Dugard, Danny Dunton, Dave Lanning, Don Scarf, Gareth Rogers,

Chris Galvin, Jon Cook, Terry Russell
League Champions: 1938, 1947, 1959, 1971, 1977, 1986, 1987, 1995, 2000
Cup winners: 1975, 1977, 1978, 1985, 1986, 1987, 1994, 1997, 2002
*The team operated as Eastbourne Dons in 1991

Hastings Saxons

Address: The Pilot Field, Elphinstone Road, Hastings, Sussex
Years of operation: 1948-1949 National League Third Division
Track Length: 388 yards
Track Record Holder: Ken Middleditch 70.8 seconds
Highest League Position: 6th (1948)
Promoter: Charlie Dugard

Appendix Two

The Championship of Sussex

The Championship of Sussex was first staged in 1932 and ran until 1993. The first winner was Rube Wilson, a great favourite at Arlington in the days before team events were introduced to the public. Other local favourites to win this prestige title have been Phil 'Tiger' Hart, wee Georgie Newton, then riding under the name of Bill Bennett, Wally Green, Malcolm Ballard, former world number two Gordon Kennett and Martin Dugard.

Until 1964 the championship was run over a sixteen-heat formula with the four top-scoring riders meeting in a grand sudden-death finale. When speedway restarted at Arlington in 1969 the championship switched to the more well-known twenty-heat formula used in World Championship events. In 1983 the championship was raced as the Argus Trophy and won by Paul Woods.

Champion of Sussex

1932: Rube Wilson
1933: Stan Lemon
1934: Jack Riddle
1935: Jack Riddle
1936: Bill Bennett (George Newton)
1937: Jack Riddle
1938: Phil 'Tiger' Hart
1939-1946: Not staged
1947: Peter Robinson (Southampton)
1948: Wally Green (Hastings)
1949: Not staged
1950: Ron Burnett (Eastbourne)
1951-1952: Not staged
1953: Ron Barrett (Eastbourne)
1954: Maurice McDermott (Rayleigh)
1955: Bert Little (Eastbourne)
1956: Merv Hannam (Eastbourne)
1957: Ray Cresp (Eastbourne)
1958: Frank Bettis (Eastbourne)
1959: Colin Goody (Eastbourne)
1960: Eric Hockaday (Eastbourne)
1961: Ross Gilbertson (Eastbourne)

1962: Bob Dugard (Eastbourne)
1963: Postponed, never restaged
1964: Abandoned after heat nine, never restaged
1965-1968: Not staged
1969: Martyn Piddock (Canterbury)
1970: Richard May (Reading)
1971: Malcolm Ballard (Eastbourne)
1972: Allen Emmett (Rayleigh)
1973: Roger Johns (Eastbourne)
1974: Phil Herne (Birmingham)
1975: Not staged
1976: Steve Weatherly (Eastbourne)
1977: Mike Sampson (Eastbourne)
1978: Not staged
1979: Gordon Kennett (Eastbourne)
1980: Bo Petersen (Hackney)
1981-1982: Not staged
1983: Paul Woods (Eastbourne)
1984: Not staged
1985: Jamie Luckhurst (Wimbledon)
1986: Neil Middleditch (Arena-Essex)
1987: Nigel Crabtree (Stoke)
1988: Not staged
1989: Dean Standing (Ipswich)
1990: Alan Mogridge (Ipswich)
1991: Martin Dugard (Oxford)
1992: Andrew Silver (Eastbourne)
1993: Martin Dugard (Eastbourne)
1994-present: Not staged

Appendix Three

British League Top Ten Eastbourne Calculated Match Averages

1. Colin Richardson	10.63	1977
2. Gordon Kennett	10.47	1985
3. Martin Dugard	10.40	1987
4. Steve Weatherley	10.35	1976
5. Martin Dugard	10.22	1995
6. Mike Sampson	10.09	1977
7. Martin Dugard	10.08	1996
8. Gordon Kennett	9.97	1988
9. David Norris	9.95	2004
10. Malcolm Ballard	9.94	1972

If you are interested in purchasing other books published by Tempus, or in case you have difficulty finding any Tempus books in your local bookshop, you can also place orders directly through our website

www.tempus-publishing.com